Presumed Superior

❖❖❖❖❖❖❖❖❖❖❖❖❖❖❖❖❖❖❖❖❖❖❖❖❖❖❖❖❖❖❖❖❖❖❖❖❖❖

Presumed Superior

Individualism
and
American Business

❖❖❖❖❖

John D. Aram

Weatherhead School of Management
Case Western Reserve University

Prentice Hall, Englewood Cliffs, New Jersey 07632

Aram, John D.,
    Presumed superior : individualism and American business / John D.
Aram.
        p.   cm.
    Includes index.
    ISBN 0-13-720699-2 (pbk.)
    1. Free enterprise--United States.   2. Individualism--United
States.   3. Business enterprises--United States.   I. Title.
HB95.A73 1992
330.973--dc20   92-18797
                                                                 CIP

Acquisitions editor: Alison Reeves
Production editor: Elaine Lynch
Copy editor: Mary Louise Byrd
Editorial assistant: Diane Peirano
Cover design: Anne Ricigliano
Pre-press buyer: Trudy Pisciotti
Manufacturing buyer: Bob Anderson
Page layout: Joh Lisa

© 1993 by Prentice-Hall, Inc.
A Simon & Schuster Company
Englewood Cliffs, New Jersey 07632

Cover: Joyce Kozloff, "New England Decorative Arts," hand-painted glazed ceramic tiles,
    1985, 8'x83' - Harvard Square Subway Station, Cambridge, MA. Commissioned by
    Massachusetts Bay Transportation Authority through the Cambridge Arts
    Council's Arts on the Line Program. Photo © 1985 Cymie Payne.

Printed in the United States of America

10 9 8 7 6 5 4 3 2 1

ISBN 0-13-720699-2

Prentice-Hall International (UK) Limited, *London*
Prentice-Hall of Australia Pty. Limited, *Sydney*
Prentice-Hall Canada Inc., *Toronto*
Prentice-Hall Hispanoamericana, S.A., *Mexico*
Prentice-Hall of India Private Limited, *New Delhi*
Prentice-Hall of Japan, Inc., *Tokyo*
Simon & Schuster Asia Pte. Ltd., *Singapore*
Editora Prentice-Hall do Brasil, Ltda., *Rio de Janeiro*

Contents

Preface

Advances in technology and the global scope of business competition are making traditional management concepts and values obsolete. Few companies that manage themselves according to yesterday's specialized, hierarchical management systems will survive. In the future, success will belong to firms that are able to focus on processes, such as quality improvement, continuous innovation, and employee involvement, that transcend distinct functions and that cross the boundaries of organization units.

The old management perspective calls for organizing and coordinating specialized functions; the new thinking calls for understanding how activities and functions are interdependent. In the traditional approach, managers control tangible assets and direct organizational units. In the new context, they manage processes and values. The new approach is integrative and holistic; it also recognizes the value of looking at problems and priorities from a number of different perspectives. This new approach is causing managers to redefine activities such as manufacturing, distribution, and product development.

Contemporary managerial tasks are often expressed in terms of specific techniques, such as manufacturing automation, worker participation, or activity-based accounting. Managers will not be effective, however, simply by learning the latest technique. Effectiveness will come from understanding the assumptions of a particular technique and its reasons for success. Much more is at stake in the issue of American competitiveness than the learning of techniques. The competitive challenge to American business is fundamentally a question of how widely and how readily managers adopt a new general perspective.

Specialization, independence, and autonomy are deeply ingrained in social behavior in the United States. These values reflect our strengths as a nation; they also help to explain why American managers often struggle to adapt to the new realities of competition. An understanding of the issues involved in American competitiveness begins with an examination and reappraisal of American values.

For this reason, I have taken the most basic of American values, *individualism*, as a basis for examining the American business environment. The notion of individualism captures the spirit of autonomy and independence in the United States and it explains Americans' inclination toward specialized activities and functions. Most important for the analysis that follows, the philosophy of individualism underlies the economic and political systems Americans depend upon to generate a high standard of living and a satisfying quality of life.

As a general and multifaceted concept, individualism will lead us to evaluate a number of social, political, and institutional processes outside the traditional purview of business. Since the business system is shaped by large-scale social, cultural, and institutional factors, examining how individualism is defined and expressed in the United States will contribute to a clearer understanding of the challenges that face American business.

This book has its origins in my experience teaching courses in Business and Society to undergraduate management and M.B.A. students. This experience has encouraged me to develop an integrating theme for the diverse concerns and issues that arise in the areas of public policy, ethics, and social and technological change. Decision situations and policy problems facing managers are more than a collection of unique, idiosyncratic, and isolated phenomena.

I also want my students to understand current issues in a general historical and intellectual context. I encourage them to see how the present opportunities and problems of business constitute issues for American society as a whole. Contemporary concerns in the business environment inevitably express social aspirations and conflicts, and coping successfully with these problems requires that we understand issues in general social and political terms. The social sciences, and the humanities in particular, contribute to a clearer understanding of effective management.

Finally, I have always expected students to explicate their own analyses and to communicate their views effectively. I have been greatly rewarded by the thoughtfulness, precision, and forcefulness of their thinking. This book has been inspired by them, and in many respects it represents my attempt to fulfill a reciprocal obligation by committing my own perpective to writing. My hope for the future of American business is, to a great degree, based on the breadth of understanding and the visions for society that these managers and future managers have shared with me.

It is my hope that the issues and ideas that my students and I have found so relevant to the future of business will also be useful to other people's consideration. I intend this book primarily for use as a supplementary reading for upper level undergraduate and M.B.A. courses in Business and Society, Business Ethics, The Managerial Environment, or Business and Public Policy. If it is read late in a course, I hope that it will serve to further stimulate students' thinking, as well as to provide a context for many issues considered in the students' courses. Alternatively, the book can be used early in a course to suggest general themes for the wide range of issues to be considered in detail.

I also hope that practicing managers can gain something of value from this book. The subject matter addresses issues of interest to policy makers who are concerned about the future of American social, political, and economic institutions. I hope that these ideas receive some consideration by leaders in this country's businesses, government institutions, and foundations, as well as the wide range of nonprofit service organizations.

A number of people have helped enormously with this effort. In the process of working directly on the manuscript, my daughter Bethany provided invaluable assistance both early in the project and in its final stage. Reading and reacting to some of the early chapters, Beth gave me encouragement for the concept as a whole, critical comments on a number of ideas, and excellent editorial recommendations. Later, she provided helpful editorial suggestions on the final manuscript. Her interest and her responses validated my goals for the project and gave me great personal satisfaction. Although they have been less directly involved in the material, my wife Dorothy and my son Jon have also been important sources of personal support throughout my work on this book.

I am also grateful to Katherine Soltis, who provided two detailed and thorough editorial reviews of the entire manuscript. Kathy's work salvaged many an unclear or awkward thought or ill-chosen word. I counted heavily on her and admire her ability to enhance the clarity and effectiveness of written communication.

Donna Pack worked as my research assistant for virtually the whole period of manuscript preparation. I thank Donna for her reliable, careful, and tireless work and the many frustrating hours she spent chasing down elusive materials.

Many friends and colleagues have given their time and interest to this project. Mohan Reddy, Tom Bier, Jean Kilgore, Ernesto Poza, Jagdip Singh, and Sayan Chatterjee commented on various chapter drafts, often indicating important omissions or suggesting valuable references. Other faculty of the Department of Marketing and Policy Studies at the Weatherhead School of Management—Vasu Ramanujam, Leonard Lynn, Rob Widing, Jan Heide, Ted Alfred, Jill Teplensky—have given support and encouragement. My departmental assistant at the Weatherhead School, Dolores Kale, consistently ensured a high-performance support system; I thank Tami Ward and Karen Glowacki in particular for their secretarial assistance. In this book and many other activities, I have greatly benefited from the supportive environment made possible by the personal efforts and leadership of the School's Dean, Scott S. Cowen.

Finally, I thank the outside reviewers for their encouragement, constructive criticism, and specific suggestions. Feedback provided by Kristin Aronson, Central Connecticut University, John Mahon, Boston University, Patricia Kelley, Western Washington University, Amitai Etzioni, The George Washington University, Alan Westin, Columbia

University, Robert Stern, Cornell University, Bruce Paternoster, Glassboro State College, William Griffith, The George Washington University, Philip Cochran, Penn State University, and Michael Howard, attorney at law, greatly assisted my work. I have also benefited from the excellent editorial support and advice of Alison Reeves, the expert and timely production work of Elaine Lynch, and the marketing efforts of Sandy Steiner, all of Prentice-Hall.

With all this help, I should have been able to produce something of value. Any shortcomings that the reader may experience belong, of course, entirely with me.

Presumed Superior

The Idea of Individualism in the American Business Environment

❖❖❖❖❖

As the end of the twentieth century approaches, discomforting events in American society cause us to reflect on the future of this country. For example, expressions of cynicism and apathy toward politics and public service appear inconsistent with a democratic political system. Increasing separation of one American from another on the basis of class and race, and a growing tendency to politicize race, seem incompatible with an open society. The apparent inability of American businesses, relative to international competitors, to cultivate employees' loyalty, attain superior manufacturing efficiency, or successfully commercialize technology generates widespread concern for our economic future. A growing tendency to express our interests as legal rights speaks poorly for the give-and-take, the norm of reciprocity, upon which civil society depends. One might be hard-pressed to prove that indifference and alienation among Americans are greater today than at other times in this country's history. Nevertheless, we would be unwise to ignore the apparent evidence of polarization in Americans' views and behavior.

Concern for the future of American society leads our attention directly to our central social value, *individualism*. Defined as "a mode of life in which the individual pursues his own ends or follows his own ideas,"[1] individualism characterizes many Americans' aspirations, explains our political philosophies, and reveals a number of expectations for the country's institutions. As much as any other social value, the way individualism is understood and realized will determine the future of the society. If our core value permits, or encourages, increasing degrees of apathy and polarization, then surely there is reason for concern about the future.

In addition to internal social patterns, recent changes in the world's political and economic landscape compel attention anew to the American value of individualism. The achievement of economic integration in Europe, for example, demonstrates that the distinct interests of individual countries *and* the benefits of collective action can be obtained simultaneously, although the way may be arduous, slow, and uncertain. The ability of many Japanese corporations to build employee cooperation and reduce resistance to technological change shows the value of noneconomic and nonindividualistic motives to economic organizations. The necessity of standing united against the totalitarian ideology and military threat of the former Soviet Union has dissolved, opening the possibility of a healthy self-appraisal by America. Contemporary developments outside the United States create important opportunities for reexamining the nature, successes, and limitations of traditional American individualism.

The way individualism is defined and realized in society at large will determine the future of the private economic sector. An ethic of pure self-advantage undermines the firm as a cooperative system. Employers depend on norms of cooperation and reciprocity as much as on motives for personal gain and self-advancement. In the context of society as a whole, pure self-advantage impedes the development of national goals, undermines the integrity of political institutions, fragments community life, and generates debilitating social conflict. Social and political polarization jeopardizes the long-run viability of the corporation. Managers must be able to integrate people's many and varied interests in today's diverse society.

Twentieth-century philosopher Alfred North Whitehead, in discussing business education, once wrote that the world needs people with both imagination and the knowledge of experience: "Fools act on imagination without knowledge; pedants act on knowledge without imagination."[2] The task of the university is to develop managers who, according to Whitehead, combine imagination and experience in building a vital society. The concept of individualism reveals a wide spectrum of worrisome issues that will present major challenges to the imagination and experience of the next generation of managers in the United States.

THE TWO SIDES OF INDIVIDUALISM

❖ A Proven American Value

The personal opportunities and comforts provided by American society to its members serve to justify Americans' belief in individualism. Individualism shapes business ideology and behavior, and it is considered a superior value by which to organize economic and social relationships.

American individualism grants the right to possess property, and it makes economic rewards for most people contingent mainly on individual initiative and performance. This is an eminently successful method of orienting action. The opportunity to enjoy the material benefits of one's own intellectual, artistic, or commercial efforts is a powerful source of ingenuity. Globally and historically, economic liberty has proven to be the only effective formula for overcoming economic deprivation and for enhancing standards of living.

American individualism has grown, in part, out of Puritan values of honesty, hard work, and personal responsibility. Protestantism linked goodness with commercial activity; one could fulfill a duty to God by engaging in business and trade. These beliefs produced a culture that valued initiative, hard work, and competence over birthright. Ben Franklin's aphorisms, written in the late eighteenth century, captured the nuances of individualism, and many of his sayings remain familiar cultural guides. Franklin's couplet, "No man e'er was glorious / Who was not laborious,"[3] for example, suggests a close connection between morality and commerce.

Today, immediate and direct personal interest ranks highly in American society. Policies that explicitly enhance personal rights and protect immediate interests typically persuade people more strongly than actions proposed to gain more indefinite and diffuse social benefits. For instance, nonsmokers' claims that cigarette smoke infringes on their personal rights gave far greater impetus to the antismoking movement than would have incremental general appeals to public health and personal safety.

Americans are deeply skeptical of policies that may reduce their choices and opportunities. Those who would limit individual liberty or diminish personal advantage in the service of a "public interest" carry a heavy burden of proof. Love of personal freedom defines and distinguishes the society, and the country's economic and political institutions serve as models to other nations that aspire to organize themselves according to principles of liberty.

Values of self-reliance and autonomy in the United States generate socially beneficial and personally gratifying quests for individual success. The economic and cultural accomplishments of American society result, in great part, from these values. The preference for autonomy also underlies an insistence on personal privacy, and it encourages the enjoyment of material conveniences, mobility, and the most up-to-date product, technique, or idea.

❖ The Other Side of the Coin

Like most values, individualism can be a double-edged sword. External independence and autonomy can conceal inner loneliness and insecurity. An ethic of personal advantage can lead to neglect of the well-being of the community, and self-preoccupation can mean indifference to others' opportunities and living conditions. The experience of worldly success can result in a heady perception of invincibility and can lead to disregard, even disrespect, for the contributions of others that have made one's own success possible.

In this country social traditions and obligations fetter individuals only mildly; compared with the influence of family, community, and religion in many other countries, social institutions bind individuals less strongly in the United States. The influence of traditional social restraints, such as parental surveillance, seems ever more diffuse as American society becomes larger, more technologically sophisticated, and more mobile. In the 1940s, Erich Fromm recognized the psychic pressure that American autonomy and independence place on the person. In *Escape from Freedom*, Fromm questioned whether Americans would flee from freedom rather than face the need for responsible behavior that freedom demands.[4]

Hesitant to impose prior restraints on individual freedom, society at large copes with, but does not prevent, antisocial behavior. The United States has the dubious distinction of per capita rates of homicide, robbery, and rape four to nine times higher than in Europe.[5] But rather than trying to alter the social conditions that breed violence, public policy debate focuses on managing the consequences of violence. For example, the question of whether to administer the death sentence to drug dealers gains more attention than do the effects of poverty on family structure; whether to require registration of handguns occupies more political debate than do the sources of urban gang warfare. Personal restrictions and strong punishment invariably threaten some people's civil liberties. As a result, even policies attempting to cope with antisocial behavior generate controversy about the loss of freedom.

The culture of individualism has also allowed differences in race, ethnicity, and gender to create unequal access to educational and employment opportunities. Historical judgment confirms that some individuals and groups have defined their self-interest in prejudicial and discriminatory ways. Individualism that creates obstacles to others' opportunities erodes society's ability to fulfill the overall promise of individual liberty.

Although personal initiative and freedom of choice retain high standing in the public mind, there exists great skepticism about how others' choices will be exercised. Americans create checks and balances, inspectors general, watchdog agencies, and auditors, and their government generates numerous regulations in order to check perceived private excesses. Americans are wary of business collusion, insider trading, hazardous dumping of toxic wastes, dangerous products, and other ways in which industry might put the public at risk. There also appears to be little confidence that public officials will balance their natural political self-interest with a good dose of public-spiritedness. Americans esteem individualism but are also wary of self-seeking behavior.

PATTERNS OF INDIVIDUALISM IN AMERICAN SOCIETY

Individualism constitutes an ideology in American society—a set of concepts or ideas about proper and desired relations among persons. Political, economic, and social components of the ideology of individualism, often reinforcing each other and occasionally conflicting, have deeply influenced U.S. institutions. To a great degree, these components define American beliefs.

❖ Political Individualism

To many American citizens, freedom from arbitrary and oppressive state action is the centerpiece of individualism. The Declaration of Independence, the U.S. Constitution, and the Bill of Rights assert that political freedom cannot legitimately be separated from the person. The political liberty on which the American system of government is based appears ever more appealing as the peoples of Poland, Hungary, Czechoslovakia, the states of the former Soviet Union, and other countries attempt to reconstruct their own governmental systems. The liberal ideal of personal independence depends on the creation and preservation of free political institutions.

The institution of private property also plays a key role in ensuring political freedom. Private property establishes a sphere of personal action beyond the reach of the state. Economic and political institutions are intimately linked; the ability to own property constrains the state and protects political autonomy. Property rights create a necessary defense of human dignity.

❖ Economic Individualism

To other Americans, individualism primarily means economic freedom. In addition to its role in circumscribing the state, economic liberty allocates resources efficiently and increases the general level of prosperity. Adam Smith's "invisible hand" says that people do best for society in doing well for themselves. Smith's concept of how economic self-interest can be harnessed in the service of the general welfare provides a vital intellectual foundation for economic individualism and industrialization.

In recent decades, more and more countries have accepted the notion that economic growth and social well-being depend on unleashing the ambitions and energies of their people. In the eyes of those who see individualism as economic freedom, the superior ability of the world's free economies to achieve prosperity justifies the importance of economic liberty. The central importance of economic freedom to national prosperity imparts a strong moral justification to economic individualism as well.

Economic freedom is also fundamentally humanistic. Capitalism gives personal choice, encourages individuals to utilize their abilities fully, and rewards people in rough proportion to their contributions. Under precepts of economic freedom, society organizes itself according to human strengths rather than weaknesses. By challenging individuals to develop and employ their talents to the fullest, economic freedom makes the most of human nature.

❖ Social Individualism

To still other Americans, individualism means caring about the quality of individual persons' social experience. The mid-nineteenth-century French writer Alexis de Tocqueville feared that American individualism would regress into isolated self-satisfaction.[6] He thought that loss of social commitment and voluntary civic involvement would ultimately undermine democracy. American individualism had to be grounded in social participation and behavior that he called "enlightened self-interest."

The Progressive movement at the beginning of the twentieth century sought to counteract the apparent excesses of economic individualism. Reformers drew attention to the impact of industrialization on human health and living conditions and advocated greater public control over industry. In a way reminiscent of the earlier transcendentalists' revulsion toward empiricism, Progressives aimed to put a human face on the impersonal forces of technology and industrialization. They sought to graft community values onto the country's affinity for economic freedom. The vast array of social programs developed in the United States since the 1930s reflects a public commitment to social individualism. Social security, unemployment assistance, public health insurance, Aid to Dependent Children, and civil rights and environmental-quality legislation represent but a few of the many programs for remedying perceived shortcomings of the marketplace.

Social individualism places no less value on the person than does economic individualism; it simply places concern for the social by-products of industrialization ahead of its economic accomplishments. Social individualism holds that communities, in addition to markets, must be strong in order to ensure a vital society.

Political, economic, and social individualism are the three major aspects of individualism in American society. There are numerous additional nuances. One author criticizes Western "possessive individualism";[7] another explores America's "popular individualism";[8] and still a third calls for "ethical expressions of individualism."[9] A recent study of middle-class Americans identifies "biblical individualism," "civic individualism," "utilitarian individualism," and "expressive individualism."[10] The term *individualism* seems as large and as diverse as American society itself.

Having one straightforward, specific meaning to work with may seem appealing but, still, the breadth and complexity of the concept of individualism are important. The United States is a large and diverse society that requires considerable space for different points of view. Central concepts must be sufficiently complex to allow people to express contrasting experiences and aspirations. The need to interpret ambiguous values, such as individualism, allows society to argue within itself and to shape its future.

ADDRESSING DIFFERING FEELINGS
TOWARD INDIVIDUALISM

The range of conflicting feelings about the value of individualism poses a significant challenge to writing on this topic. For some people, individualism symbolizes the worst that they see in America—greed, insensitivity to social justice, hostility toward public purpose. For others, individualism represents the best of America—economic opportunity, political freedom, and unprecedented choices in lifestyle and personal expression. Feelings about individualism run sufficiently deep that one person or another may interpret an attempt to develop a balanced view as a major affront. The path to dialogue is fraught with obstacles. Yet the highly political nature of the topic, people's uncompromising feelings about this core value, and the significance of the consequences of the ways individualism is expressed—all make the task of critical review ever more necessary.

In this book I ask readers to consider the opportunities and challenges of American social values for business. My goal is to seek a perspective from which American business leaders and professionals can more clearly understand and manage an increasingly complex, and potentially ominous, environment. My intention is not to discard the past or to endorse a communitarian ideal; nor is it to defend that which *is* simply *because* it exists. Rather, the aim is to argue the merits of a concept of individualism capable of reaching beyond its immediate setting. I seek an orientation, based solidly in historical experience and tied to contemporary events, that offers potential for optimizing the well-being of both the individual and the community.

INDIVIDUALISM AS AN ORIENTATION FOR ACTION

A series of events during the summer of 1991 in the United States provide windows through which to view some of the action implications of individualism. Explosive social conflicts; exemplified in Wichita, Kansas, and in Crown Heights, a section of Brooklyn, New York, consistently appeared in the national news. By late August, still another major scandal in the financial services industry renewed questions about personal ethics on Wall Street. These events move discussion of values out of the realm of abstractions and ideologies and place it squarely in the everyday world of personal actions and concrete reality. Each of these incidents illuminates an aspect of the polarization of American society, polarization either between individual and institution or between groups. In each case, the central question is: "Who takes responsibility for the well-being of the community in the long run?"

❖ Personal Behavior in Institutional Roles

Trouble on Wall Street in the Government Bond Market. The U.S. Treasury bond market is a $2.3 trillion behemoth. More than $100 billion in U.S. government bonds is traded daily in the world's largest securities market. The economic stability of the United States and, to a great extent, of the world rests on perceptions of order, fairness, and efficiency in the buying and selling of bonds.

The Treasury Department and the Securities and Exchange Commission have set rules for trading that attempt to preserve a competitive market. For example, in order to prevent one bidder from controlling a particular auction of new issue bonds, the Treasury has established that no firm can bid for more than 35 percent of the bonds issued at a particular auction. In commodity markets, firms compete solely on the basis of price. Bids reflect expectations about changes in interest rates, and methods of risk management and speculation must be complex, sophisticated, and aggressive to succeed. The U.S. government bond market regularly involves huge, multibillion-dollar transactions. Traders generate enormous gains and losses by the accuracy of their bets on minute differences in price.

The private market for government bonds provides great opportunities for those who seek to realize the positive side of economic individualism. Long-term success depends purely on one's competence—one's intelligence, mental discipline, and informed judgment. The system rewards winners handsomely; at times, the annual salary and bonuses for a particularly successful individual can reach several million dollars.[11]

Facts that came to light in the second half of 1991 about the bidding tactics of Salomon Brothers, Inc., damaged the firm's reputation. In mid-August, Salomon officials revealed that several times in the previous six months the firm had violated the Treasury rule limiting bidders to 35 percent of an auction. In addition, Salomon had not reported violations to appropriate government agencies when they were discovered, as is also required by law. These revelations resulted in the departure of Paul Mozer, managing director of government bond trading, and a number of lesser employees; in addition, the firm's chairman, vice chairman, president, and internal counsel resigned in the glare of negative publicity and intense criticism.

The scandal focused most attention on the actions of Mozer.[12] A dedicated, talented, and energetic executive in his mid-thirties, Mozer had seen rapid early career advancement with Salomon through aggressive and successful bidding tactics. Bids in government auctions are filled from the highest to the lowest. Where low bids outstrip the remaining supply of bonds, bids are filled in proportion to the size of the bids remaining. In order to capture a high volume of bonds at low prices, Mozer submitted huge orders. In 1989, for example, he submitted an order for $15 billion in an auction in which only $5 billion worth of bonds were being offered.[13] This tactic allowed Mozer to capture a large share of the bonds available by dominating the bids of other trading firms.

The Treasury's rule of limiting the bid of any one firm to 35 percent of the total offering had been implemented specifically in response to Mozer's earlier aggressive bidding, which, if adopted by all traders, would have escalated bids to absurd levels.

Specific troubles developed at Salomon in 1990 and 1991, when Mozer began to circumvent the Treasury's 35 percent rule. By falsely submitting bids in the names of customers, Mozer disguised the amount of bidding Salomon controlled. Between December 1990 and the end of May 1991, Salomon controlled 46, 57, 63, and 85 percent of the offerings at four different auctions.[14] In September 1991, Salomon disclosed that it had controlled 94 percent of the bids at an auction the previous May.[15]

Other problems arose when the firm's chairman, vice chairman, president, internal counsel, and external counsel failed to disclose their knowledge of at least one trading violation to the Treasury Department. By late April 1991, these officials apparently had specific knowledge of a violation of trading rules that had occurred in February. They failed to take action until August, when the Securities and Exchange Commission and the Justice Department had already subpoenaed Salomon records and were clearly investigating its trading practices. Top officials resigned amid a number of lawsuits, client defections, and full investigations of the industry by the SEC and the Justice Department.

Observers within the firm reported that Mozer was incensed by the Treasury's attempt to restrict his bidding. He resented being fettered by the Treasury, and he resisted being influenced by the rules designed to constrain him. It seemed clear that a passion for unfettered freedom of action guided his actions as much as a desire for higher profits. Exceeding the 35 percent rule did not always ensure success; associates claimed Salomon had lost money in several of the auctions in which Mozer pursued this tactic. Referring to Mozer's disregard for the rules of the game, one press report termed Mozer an "errant cowboy."[16] Some Salomon executives were quoted as having observed that "his tactics were more about ego and getting the best of the Treasury than they were about earning bonuses or career enhancement at Salomon."[17]

To a certain degree, the behavior of high Salomon officials parallels that of Mozer. The chairman and others claimed that, on learning about the February violation, they had agreed to disclose it to the regulatory agencies. Yet no action was taken until the men apparently felt the heat of the government investigation. Those involved seem to have lacked the will to deal with the embarrassing circumstances in a forthright manner. A report in the *Wall Street Journal* termed their behavior "hubris."[18] The arrogant, defiant attitude of the firm's chairman, John Gutfreund, is captured in his reported statement to top executives at a closed-door meeting: "I'm not apologizing for anything to anybody. Apologies don't mean [expletive]. What happened, happened."[19] Gutfreund, a dominant figure on Wall Street, gave the sense that he, too, was angry and resentful at having his personal actions fettered by public expectations.

Observations on the Salomon Incident. Most people would probably agree that the orderly, efficient operation of a multitrillion-dollar financial market is a virtual miracle of the modern age. Private property, economic freedom, private and decentralized decision making, and high rewards for excellent performance create and sustain this miracle. The Salomon incident draws attention to the enormous public service that the private market for government bonds does perform.

One can also conclude that this impressive market does not function by means of economic interest alone. A variety of public policy choices support the market's reliability and efficiency. Capitalization requirements for large trading firms protect the market from wrong bets and large losses by individual companies. Restraints on the size of one firm's bid in a single auction maintain competition. Disclosure requirements reinforce market efficiency by providing full information and keeping the playing field level. Although public policy can also be misguided and impede market efficiency, the miracle of the market depends on more than individual motives and the competitive instincts of traders.

The supportive role of public policy often seems to be lost in the ideology of economic individualism. The Salomon incident points out how individual actions can undermine the normal, taken-for-granted aspects of the market, and it draws attention to the interconnection of private markets and public policy.

The Salomon incident teaches us that bond traders (in this case, Mozer and Gutfreund) have an institutional role in addition to an economic role. Bond traders live in an exhilarating world, putting their wits, judgment, and emotional capacity on the line every day. The pace of action, the worldwide scope of influence, and the enormous potential rewards can lead successful bond traders to experience themselves as "masters of the universe," like the young bond trader in *Bonfire of the Vanities,* Tom Wolfe's novel set on Wall Street.[20] Salomon Brothers was the dominant firm in a huge, fast-moving, and vital securities market; John Gutfreund had been dubbed the "king of Wall Street."[21]

But such inflated titles only create deception and self-delusion in modern, complex social systems. Gutfreund, Mozer, and others may have wanted to circumvent the normal expectations of society. They may have been deceived by their own sense of invincibility, allowing themselves to neglect, or at least to underplay, their roles as public figures and institution leaders. But society as a whole would not agree to release them from their social roles, identities, and responsibilities. The heady sensation of unfettered success may have distorted their understanding of themselves as members of organizations and of the broader society.

❖ Social Protest and Individualism

Value Conflicts in Wichita.   In mid-July 1991, militant antiabortion protesters began what was to be a prolonged effort to close three clinics performing abortions in Wichita, Kansas. Members of the protest organization, Operation Rescue, attempted to block physical access to the clinics. Protesters defied court orders that protected access to two of the clinics, knocking down barricades and scaling iron fences to block a driveway entrance. By the end of August, nearly 2,600 persons had been arrested. Three protest leaders from other cities had refused to post a peace bond, a requirement that can be imposed when a group's activities might lead to disorder or property damage.[22] Failing to post a bond, the three leaders were jailed and fined $10,000 each. In addition, each of the three was fined $500 a day for the next ten days or until they agreed to comply with the judge's order to leave the city. The protests continued.

Six weeks into the protests, pro-choice forces mounted a rally of their own, drawing roughly 5,000 supporters.[23] No one was physically harmed in this conflict, although the atmosphere remained tense throughout. Wichita's 300,000 residents were strongly divided over the intentions and tactics of the antiabortion protesters and regretted the negative national publicity the conflict had received.

Observations on the Wichita Protests. The abortion issue in the United States demonstrates the powerful role of social ideals and values in motivating Americans to action. Personal, material interest appears unimportant to either pro-life or pro-choice forces. Opponents pursue different visions of society: for pro-life activists, the sanctity of the life of the unborn, and for pro-choice activists, the sanctity of a woman's bodily integrity. The abortion debate represents a conflict between high moral values. Advocates on each side are highly individualistic, acting to realize principles, regardless of public opinion, public authority, or personal consequences. Antiabortion and abortion rights activists may often be acting in group settings, but the groups themselves receive no benefit. The goal is simply to remake society according to one's values. The power of individualism expresses itself in pursuit of social ideals as well as material gain.

The Wichita incident shows that American individualism can be impatient and inflexible. The aggressive, defiant antiabortion forces in Wichita demanded that the clinics stop performing abortions immediately. America has a long and important history of social protest. Civil disobedience may be justified when avenues of political influence are closed; but the U.S. Supreme Court had assigned aspects of social policy on abortion to the state legislatures not long before the Wichita protests. Reasons to engage in political action rather than in militancy had been enhanced for persons opposing abortion especially, but impatience seems to have won the upper hand.

Divisions generated by contemporary conflicts put stress on traditional social institutions. The *New York Times* reported that "residents [of Wichita] say they can not recall a time of such discontent on their streets, a time of divided families and congregations, of splintered friendships and shaken love."[24] It has often been observed that the ingredients and by-products of industrialization—occupational and job specialization, mobility, affluence—are socially centrifugal forces; they often depersonalize relationships and fragment communities. The abortion debate shows a parallel tendency for value-driven social conflicts to strain the cohesiveness of traditional social communities.

❖ Identity and Social Conflict

Confrontations Involving Race and Religion in Crown Heights. Social conflict expressed itself differently in the Crown Heights section of Brooklyn, New York, in August 1991. In this community, where 85 percent of the population is black or Hispanic and the rest are mainly Hasidic Jews, a car driven by a Hasidic man jumped the sidewalk and killed a seven-year-old black child named Gavin Cato. A crowd of angry black persons, mostly teenagers, arose immediately. Marches were organized and clashes occurred between groups of blacks and groups of Hasidic Jews; police efforts to quell the disturbances had limited success. A few days later, Yankel Rosenbaum, a Hasidic scholar from Australia who lived in this neighborhood, was fatally stabbed, apparently a victim of group hostilities.

Open hostility, charges, and countercharges broke out between the two groups in the weeks following these incidents. Crown Heights blacks challenged the way police and rescue squads had handled the Cato incident and spoke out against high levels of poverty, violence, and discrimination against blacks. Large protests were held in the black community. The Hasidic community defended itself in the press. A grand jury issued an indictment against the person believed to have murdered Rosenbaum. A second grand jury decided not to issue charges against the Hasidic driver of the car that had killed Cato. The situation in Crown Heights recalled other recent instances of racial conflict in New York: inflammatory, racially charged speeches against Jews by a professor at City College; an attack by white teenagers on three black men at Howard Beach; the murder of Yusuf Hawkins by whites in Bensonhurst; Tawana Brawley's claim of racially based rape, which was later discredited; and an attack on a Central Park jogger by a group of young black men and the ensuing trial.[25] The Crown Heights incident fits into a larger pattern of racial and religious conflict in New York City.

Observations on the Crown Heights Incident. What exploded into national awareness in Crown Heights may, as in the case of Witchita, represent emotions lying slightly below the surface in many communities. These events provide insight into American individualism in the early 1990s.

What sets a person apart from others often includes identification with a group. In Crown Heights, being black or being Hasidic appears to be a defining characteristic to many people's sense of themselves. A group may express its identity by claiming that another group is perpetrating injustice or inequity against it. American individualism includes ethnic, racial, gender, religious, and other cultural differences, and group identities are essential to people's sense of individuality.

Also, the concept of a social community transcends subgroup identities. Traditionally, the United States (and especially New York City) has prided itself on being a "melting pot," where "the world's wretched refuse emerge as middle-class, non-hyphenated Americans."[26] David Dinkins, mayor of New York at the time of the Crown Heights crisis, expressed his vision of this community of difference as a "gorgeous mosaic," a live-and-let-live society in which "pieces of different sizes and colors help to form a larger whole more attractive than its components."[27]

Bigotry and racial or religious conflict challenge this vision of American society. It may be that the melting pot has become an antiquated notion, no longer symbolic of people's social perceptions and desires. The wider community may find itself undermined by a lack of tolerance of differences, by competition for resources, and by mutual antagonism between groups. The mosaic may be unable to cohere; groups may be less and less capable of allowing for differences without feeling a threat to their own separate identities.

❖ Choices in Defining and Expressing Individualism

Each of these incidents may be an exception. On the whole, bond traders internalize the rules of the game and allow their institutional roles to balance their competitive economic instincts. Where forums for social policy are open, people feeling strongly about one or another side of a value-laden issue generally organize politically and lobby, campaign, and attempt to persuade. For the most part, people of different races, religions, ethnic groups, genders, and sexual preferences act with civility toward members of other groups.

These cases illustrate, however, the fine line between the positive and the negative sides of individualism. Mozer and Gutfreund pushed the productive instinct for personal success and economic gain to a point that threatens, rather than creates, economic value. The value-based individualism of opposing groups in the abortion controversy is anchored in each side's constructive desire to "improve" society, even at substantial personal cost. People holding these values can be impatient and demanding, however, in ways that increase enmity and weaken communities. The individualism of group identity in Crown Heights gives people satisfying social support and personal security. Group conflicts, however, can fuel the passion for separatism and cast doubt on the possibility of multicultural communities.

If we were to extrapolate from these few cases to wider incidence, we would perceive a distinct threat to the social fabric. Financial markets could not sustain the universal application of Mozer's ethics. Society would be an armed camp if all social issues were decided physically in the streets and relations among social groups became radically polarized. Taken together, these cases demonstrate that an unfettered, impatient, inflexible, exclusive, and unaccepting individualism undermines the norm of reciprocity upon which each person depends.

These incidents are not unfamiliar events in American society. In the last 20 years we have witnessed numerous instances in which public and private sector leaders acted without being accountable to the wider society, as if they were indeed "masters of the universe"—activities that included the illegal financial manipulations of Dennis Levine, Ivan Boesky, Michael Milken, and others; the deception of the public in the Iran-Contra affair; and fraud and embezzlement in the savings and loan crisis.

In addition, social conflict based either on values or on racial and religious identities often lies at or just below the surface in American society. Verbal and physical violence in Wichita or Crown Heights fits into a larger pattern of American social experience.

Will such incidents be more the rule or the exception in the future? Will members of this society express their interests and identities broadly or narrowly? Answers to these questions have serious consequences for the future of business because they will determine the course of society as a whole. If as members of society we fail to balance individual wishes with community values in the way we live our lives, society as a whole will lack the stability and freedom that a private economic system needs in order to function effectively and efficiently.

❖ Liberty and Restraint

We can explore ways of balancing individual interests and community interests through the relationship between liberty and restraint. Unlimited freedom may create a path toward anarchy, and unrestrained individualism may degenerate into debilitating social conflict, even chaos. As threats of anarchy and conflict may induce strong social control, extreme liberty risks totalitarianism. Columnist James Reston spoke to these relationships between individual and collectivity when he wrote, "Liberty without restraint is like a river without banks . . . it must be limited to be possessed."[28] In discussing the relationship between liberty and equality, professor and diplomat Jeane Kirkpatrick makes a similar point; "Extremism in the pursuit of justice (or any other political value) *is* a vice; and moderation in the defense of liberty (or any other political value) *is* a virtue."[29]

The question for American society, then, is how limits or restraints can be applied without doing violence to personal freedom. Most restraints in American society are self-imposed, as opposed to social, restraints. Bond dealers generally conform to the expectations of their institutional roles and constrain impulses toward arrogance. Most people address and settle conflicts in social and political forums. Most cultural groups successfully retain their distinct identities while also seeing themselves as part of a larger social mosaic or community. Generally, people do perceive that they have a stake in membership in broad social entities.

self-oriented behavior and civic participation in American society. In his book *Democracy in America*,[1] written between 1835 and 1840, Tocqueville expressed his admiration for the dynamic energy generated by American egalitarianism, but he worried that individualism could have the effect of isolating people from one another. He believed that America might either decline into social conformity or retreat into social indifference; if America were to take either course, citizens risked losing their political liberties to despotism.

Other social analysts have worried about the isolating tendency of modern American society. At midcentury, David Riesman, in *The Lonely Crowd*,[2] perceived the evolution of the "other-directed" person and argued that conformity was rising to a new level in the United States. In a study of middle-class America in the 1980s,[3] Robert Bellah and his colleagues found that Americans express an unfulfilled longing for community to balance the loneliness of acting autonomously.

Sociological perspectives on American society have been formulated mainly apart from the nation's business creed, which holds that material success and social welfare result purely from personal initiative, hard work, and strong economic incentives. By and large, American businesspersons have allied themselves with the claim that the unfettered pursuit of economic self-interest leads to public well-being. Beyond allowing for personal philanthropy, the business creed has rarely acknowledged the role of communities or the quality of social relationships. Instead, business values emphasize freedom, or, as stated by business philosopher Gerald F. Cavanagh, in his *American Business Values*, the business creed consists of "free markets, free competition, free movement of people and capital, and most especially freedom of the individual."[4]

British sociologist Herbert Spencer, in his 1850 book *Social Statics*,[5] made an aggressive effort to subordinate social relationships to the process of economic competition. Drawing from Charles Darwin's observations on the differential adaptability of species to environmental circumstances, Spencer concluded that natural selection works in the social realm just as it does in the biological world. According to this view, which established a following in the United States in the late nineteenth century, those who do not adapt to the conditions of modern industrial life will, properly, become extinct. Spencer and others justified indifference to the lives of those at lower economic levels with the belief that class differences are natural and inevitable. The slogan "survival of the fittest" sums up one view, now generally discredited, of the interaction between business and society.

A diametrically opposed concept of business and society was articulated by a source that may be surprising to many: economic theorist Adam Smith. Smith's classic insight that the "invisible hand" translates private interest into social welfare is a fundamental premise of economic individualism. However, as a moral philosopher, Smith took a different tack. He argued that individual behavior must be shaped by sympathy, by the ability to enter into the feelings of others, and by conscience, which involves evaluating one's actions from others' perspective.[6] In *The Theory of Moral Sentiments*, for example, Smith had a kind word for altruism: "How selfish soever man may be supposed, there are evidently some principles in his nature, which interest him in the fate of others, and render their happiness necessary to him, though he derives nothing from it, except the pleasure of seeing it."[7] This aspect of Smith's thinking that deals with the human and social side of behavior has not been so widely recognized as his notion of the virtues of the "invisible hand." The relationship between the two perspectives is unclear in Smith's writings and generally remains unclear today.

Debate over corporate social responsibility in management literature parallels the general conflict between the economic and social perspectives. For some, interaction between business and society necessitates a "social policy process" for deciding issues of social and moral significance.[8] Others propose that managers should subscribe to the concept of corporate social responsibility and strive for a high level of corporate social performance.[9] In *The New American Ideology*,[10] Harvard Business School Professor George C. Lodge argues that the traditional American ideology of individualism is actually giving way to social concerns and community values. Lodge believes that the complexity of contemporary American society and its tendencies toward large-scale and highly organized systems are forcing an ideological transition to a new ideology, which he calls communitarianism. Others believe that such change in American values is both unlikely and highly inadvisable; many agree with Milton Friedman's bold assertion that "the social responsibility of business is to increase its profits."[11]

Current prescriptions for business and social relationships polarize mainly over differences between an economic perspective and a social or communitarian perspective. This chapter follows the efforts of people seeking to bridge this gap.[12] The maximization of wealth by strongly self-oriented individuals is a valid and socially beneficial form of behavior. At the same time, the wider social context influences opportunities for economic individualism in ways not generally acknowledged by those holding the economic perspective.

Everyday examples show the close association between the economic and the social aspects of behavior. Managers see themselves as autonomous decision makers, although the nature of the problems they solve is heavily influenced by others inside and outside the organization. Managers' assumptions, perceptions, and values also are influenced by the expectations of people in their work groups and organizations. In one sense, the firm is an independent economic entity. In another sense, the firm is inseparable from the wider society's cultural assumptions; it is influenced by the constraints and opportunities created by other organizations, such as unions, government agencies, trade associations, and consumer groups. Similarly, the prosperity of the business sector of an entire country depends on macroeconomic factors, such as currency stability and openness of trade policy, that are subject to larger social and political forces.

Though we idealize economic actors as autonomous maximizers of self-interest, the experience of autonomy remains relative to one's perspective. Individuals and firms are participants in a number of "societies" that strongly influence economic actions. Firms are embedded in institutional relationships, and each country's business sector participates in a global economic system that depends on the noneconomic processes of international cooperation. An economic *and* social perspective encourages managers to broaden the traditional business creed in order to incorporate the observation that behavior is a function of broad, as well as narrow, social identification. Understanding individuals and firms as economic entities ought not to lessen our appreciation of their roles as social participants.

Effective managers understand the individualism of collective action as well as the individualism of autonomous behavior. Recognition of individuals as members of communities, as persons with broad social identifications, and as entities that can and do act collectively, should direct managers' attention to the wider social and institutional relationships in which autonomous action occurs.

The sociological insights of Tocqueville, Riesman, and Bellah illustrate the basic fact of interdependence between individual and society. Their social analyses also offer ways to understand the social roles of economic institutions. Far from attacking the validity of economic individualism, an interdependence perspective combines social realities with assumptions based on self-interest.

The first half of this chapter reviews, in detail, the three sociological perspectives already mentioned: Alexis de Tocqueville's commentary on American society written nearly 160 years ago; David Riesman's view of the "other-directed" America of the 1950s; and Robert Bellah et al.'s much more recent study of individualism and commitment in modern American society. Other studies and theories from the social sciences complement these perspectives. This discussion demonstrates the significance of social participation and community membership to a person's sense of individualism. This perspective illustrates the observation that autonomy and freedom can be maintained only through social commitments.

The second half of the chapter draws upon these social analyses to make a case for supplementing the notion of autonomy with the concept of interdependence in management thinking. Relationships of interdependence recognize that people are *both* independent and dependent. The interdependence perspective requires managers to play both economic and social roles and to depolarize thinking about the relationship between business and society. I argue the validity of economic and social interdependence in three contexts: policy making groups, the diffusion of industrial innovation, and the institutional setting of world trade.

THE ROLE OF COMMUNITY

❖ A Perspective on Nineteenth-Century Individualism

In the mid-nineteenth century the United States was mainly an agrarian country with abundant natural resources, a vast frontier, and an energetic people. Alexis de Tocqueville wrote an enduring account of social life in this country at midcentury.[13] Historian, anthropologist, sociologist, he observed the young and ambitious country against the backdrop of French society, which was redefining itself in an age of democratic liberalism. Tocqueville sought to understand the social implications of American democracy.

Recalling the extent to which revolutionary fervor had torn apart the fabric of French society a half-century earlier, Tocqueville is intensely interested in the stability of the young American democracy. "Aristocracy links everybody, from peasant to king, in one long chain," he writes, referring to fixed social positions that encourage people to give and receive help from others, creating stable social relationships. "Democracy," however, "breaks the chain and frees each link."[14] Equality, states Tocqueville, allows people to think of themselves in isolation and encourages individuals to believe, incorrectly, that their destinies are independent of those of other people. Tocqueville is concerned about whether democracy would provide sufficient "common links" to hold people and society together. He writes:

> not only does democracy make men forget their ancestors, but also clouds their view of their descendants and isolates them from their contemporaries. Each man is forever thrown back on himself alone, and there is danger that he may be shut up in the solitude of his own heart.[15]

Tocqueville uses the term *individualism* to suggest this potentially isolating tendency of an egalitarian society. In his view, individualism, a troublesome human tendency, arises when a society is released from the strictures of aristocracy. Individualism, for Tocqueville, is a step away from egoism, and egoism is only another step away from despotism.

From his vantage point, Tocqueville has seen Napoleonic despotism grow out of the French Revolution. He fears that America's abandonment of social tradition and the subsequent growth of egoism run the risk of inducing an insidious conformity. Self-reliance could, paradoxically, make individuals more dependent on public opinion. Self-absorption could lead people to be callous toward anything that did not affect them directly. Lacking the security of social relationships, they might become overly dependent on public opinion and the views of others. The road toward totalitarianism could begin with the weakening of social institutions resulting from a retreat into self-preoccupation.[16]

Tocqueville also sees redeeming features in American society that could counteract pressures toward isolation and social conformity. The remarkable characteristic of American life, in his view, was the citizens' inclination to engage in commercial, religious, moral, intellectual, and civic associations. Acting together in the affairs of daily life is the saving grace for members of the society. Self-help and voluntary social action substitute for aristocracy and counteract excessive individualism: "Feelings and ideas are renewed, the heart enlarged, and the understanding developed only by the reciprocal action of men one upon another."[17]

Thus, he concludes, participation in political, civic, and religious life moderates the destabilizing aspects of individualism. Private interests must be set aside; individuals must participate in public affairs and be willing to look at "something other than themselves" in order to sustain democracy. People recognize their interdependencies by working on common problems; participation in public affairs fosters reciprocity. Tocqueville writes, "Those frigid passions that keep hearts asunder must then retreat and hide at the back of consciousness."[18]

Tocqueville marvels at Americans' benevolence, their habits of acting together in the affairs of daily life, and their willingness to sacrifice some of their own interest in order to save the rest. He labels these positive attitudes "habits of the heart" and he calls the saving American virtue "self-interest properly understood."[19] Tocqueville concludes that voluntarism and civic participation in the United States are sufficiently strong to realize the promise of democracy and to protect against its isolating tendencies. The American spirit of voluntarism creates the social fabric, a sense of mutual commitment, necessary for individualism to thrive.

Tocqueville observed the United States before its rapid expansion to the Pacific, the advent of modern science, the arrival of an industrial and technological society, the Great Depression, and the nation's assumption of world power with its attendant responsibilities. Tocqueville wrote before the Civil War and before America's long and difficult encounter with questions of racial justice. The geographic convergence of opportunities and problems that we call urbanization occurred long after Tocqueville's time. The next section of this chapter moves ahead to an interpretation of the increasing challenge of social conformity in American societal values in a period closer to the present.

❖ An "Other-Directed" Society

Tocqueville's concerns about conformity in American society are echoed by David Riesman.[20] Riesman characterizes cultural and personal behavior in the United States as "traditional," "inner-directed," or "other-directed."[21]

The *traditional* personality is socialized into rituals, routines, and social relationships that change very slowly. In the traditional framework, obedience to minute social prescriptions guides individual action, and age-old problems, such as threats of disease and famine, are simply accepted as the givens of life. Riesman notes that the tightly structured traditional society provides appreciation and respect for individuals, perhaps to a greater degree than industrialized society, whose members often hold callous attitudes toward one another. Each individual has a social niche in a traditional community; even a misfit may have a designated role as shaman or sorcerer. Riesman finds the traditional model to be only marginally applicable in the United States, mostly in rural areas or in enclaves of first-generation immigrants who have brought their social values from less industrially advanced societies.

Inner-directed persons receive life direction and goals from family and other institutions, rather than from rituals and traditional routines. They have "psychological gyroscopes"[22] that help them cope with changing circumstances and new opportunities. America's rapid economic development was spurred by individuals whose internal direction, innovative abilities, and self-reliance helped them master a challenging physical environment and create a new industrial world. Rational, individualistic attitudes toward self, which sociologist Max Weber first referred to as the "Protestant ethic,"[23] mark the inner-directed person. The world of the inner-directed person is harsh in its competition, and survival may be in doubt. There is a premium on the ability to subdue the competition, to be among the most energetic and ingenious.

Riesman perceives America at mid-twentieth century to be in the midst of a movement away from the inner-directed person of the 1700s and 1800s and toward the *other-directed* personality. Other people, rather than the competitive environment, dominate the world of the other-directed person. Social sensitivity and personal adaptability have become critical survival skills. Other-directed persons give up internal gyroscopes for social "radar."[24] The peer group supplants parental discipline; an insatiable need for approval determines a person's goals, and direction comes from social relationships and the mass media. One observer summarizes Riesman's analysis thus:

> The mechanism for enforcing right behavior became the other-directed social character's diffuse anxiety and its relentless concern over the judgment of the group. The inner-directed regime was harsh, rigid, and cruel; the new order was conformist.[25]

Freeing people from traditional social structure, in Tocqueville's framework, coincides with the move away from traditional culture to inner-directed culture. Riesman's perception of the willingness of Americans to submit themselves to the opinions of others recalls Tocqueville's fear that individuals, after losing the security of the aristocratic order, would fall susceptible to conformist pressures. Riesman joins Tocqueville in warning against conformity as an outgrowth of American individualism. Both observers look for a balance between autonomy and social commitment.

Riesman laments the rise of other-directed culture and seeks a means by which a more autonomous social character might develop within an industrialized and urbanized American society. Riesman wants to retain the autonomy of the inner-directed person while dispensing with the crueler aspects of inner-directedness. Riesman hopes people can rediscover their individualities and exert personal control in mass society; he seeks a new individualism within an industrialized and economically advancing America. In the final analysis, Riesman expresses hope:

> While political curiosity and interest have been largely driven out of the accepted sphere of the political in recent years . . . people may, in what is left of their private lives, be nurturing newly critical and creative standards. If these people are not strait-jacketed before they get started—by the elaboration and forced feeding of a set of official doctrines—people may some day learn to buy not only packages of groceries or books but the "larger package" of a neighborhood, a society, and a way of life.[26]

❖ Individualism and Community in Late-Twentieth-Century America

In the mid-1980s, a team of social scientists headed by Robert Bellah conducted interviews with several hundred middle-class Americans. Entitling their study *Habits of the Heart*, in direct reference to Tocqueville, these researchers examined American lives in terms of the analysis of individualism, social commitment, and community set out by Tocqueville.[27]

The authors find individualism in two dominant forms, which they term utilitarian and expressive. *Utilitarian* individualism seeks satisfaction in career, love, marriage, or family, treating these relationships solely as opportunities for private fulfillment. This restless and ultimately unsatisfactory individualism is primarily oriented toward self-satisfaction and does not represent social commitment beyond personal gains. In the *Habits* study, a southern California businessman, financially successful and living comfortably in a suburb of San Jose, is the prototype of the utilitarian individualist. His social commitments go no further than the kindness he shows toward his second wife and his involvement in the lives of his children. Like many others, this man has no words to describe, and perhaps little concept of, commitment to social values outside his immediate family relationships.

The beliefs and choices of people who orient their lives for maximum independence from social constraints characterize *expressive* individualism. This individualism holds people responsible only for their own self-fulfillment; social obligations, duties, and expectations outside one's own interests receive little recognition. The expressive individualist thrives on a fierce sense of independence and self-determination. A woman therapist in Atlanta exemplifies this type of individualism. She values personal responsibility and self-reliance, but only within the limits of her needs. There is no "common good"; relationships represent a freely expressed and negotiated convergence of interests. Though pleasantly unconstrained, this woman is unable to connect her sense of self-fulfillment with that of others.

The authors observe that expressive individualism, like utilitarian individualism, lacks a way for people to engage in social commitment. People assume society will satisfy their needs; they do not acknowledge that maintaining a viable community and a stable society is essential to their own well-being. The authors of *Habits* find that these contemporary forms of individualism lack a social or moral perspective. Their study gives cause for concern that America is realizing Tocqueville's fear of "privatized anxiety and public apathy."[28] These authors' observations resonate with the loneliness of Riesman's other-directed society.

Forms of individualism that allow for more community orientation have lost value and importance in contemporary American culture, according to Bellah et al. Neither utilitarian nor expressive individualism has the language or capacity to create enduring commitments outside the private self. Despite the apparent longings of those involved, the individuals in this study who value public commitment more than private interest and are involved in either civic activities or social action organizations are buffeted by social forces larger than themselves. A civic leader in Suffolk, Massachusetts, for example, finds that the strongest display of solidarity in his community has been the successful effort of residents to reject public housing in order to exclude Boston's African-American and Cuban populations.

The authors see individuals with meaningful commitments to religious and social action organizations and local politics as exceptions to the dominant American experience. *Radical* individualism—individualism in which people's choices are inadequate to sustain society—is found to overpower religious and civic individualism. "The ideal of freedom makes Americans nostalgic for their past," Bellah et al. comment, "but provides few resources for talking about their collective future."[29]

Habits of the Heart portrays a search for consensus on such issues as justice, fairness, and respect for the person in American society—in essence, a search for moral purpose. The authors see America threatened by a radical individualism that subordinates common interests: "we have put our own good, as individuals, as groups, as a nation, ahead of the common good."[30] Following Tocqueville, the authors of *Habits* believe that free institutions will survive only if normative standards of behavior are recovered and private interest is blended and balanced with public purpose. They articulate a need for an individualism whose social commitments allow the person to avoid conformity. These authors call for a social transformation in which individuals recommit themselves to something outside themselves in order to provide needed integration with others and to preserve their independence and freedom. This study presents a provocative critique of contemporary American values.

EXAMINING CONTEMPORARY SOCIETY

The conclusions of *Habits of the Heart* were formed by systematic interviewing. But is this view complete? Does it represent a balanced appraisal of individualism and social commitment in American society? Critics such as Bellah dissect virtually every aspect of American life, often finding the society wanting one or another virtue. In spite of its shortcomings, however, the society has a number of redeeming features, such as political freedom, personal opportunity in nearly all fields of human endeavor, and an enviable prosperity. Nonconforming, and yet cooperative, social behavior may be so deeply ingrained a social value that it is hard to see directly. People rarely articulate to researchers those taken-for-granted assumptions that may be quite influential in guiding their behavior.

❖ A Social Accounting of American Society

An accounting of modern American society according to Tocqueville's criteria of civic association and participation would provide reasons for both hope and concern. For example, the spirit of voluntarism is strong; private, voluntary associations are evident in every aspect of American society. A representative sample of Americans in 1991 revealed that 70 percent were members of voluntary associations, with nearly 63 percent of those people belonging to two or more organizations.[31]

Charitable organizations raise vast sums each year for social service, educational, religious, social action, and cultural activities. Volunteer work is both formal, involving specific time commitments to organizations, and informal, entailing assistance on an ad hoc basis. The amount of formal volunteering in the United States in 1989 was 15.7 billion hours, the equivalent of 9.2 million full-time employees, or $170 billion.[32] Aggregate charitable giving in 1990 totaled more than $122 billion.[33] In 1990, both volunteer work and charitable giving increased from the level of the late 1980s. In contributions of both time and money, voluntarism would be valued at nearly $300 billion annually. This number does not include numerous other social activities that provide social identity and stability, such as fraternal organizations and private clubs, hobby or recreational groups, political activities, and a wide variety of informal social activities.

Weighing against such socially constructive behavior are antisocial actions of various kinds. The cost of street crime—theft, human injury, and property damage—runs into the billions of dollars annually. Revenues from illegal businesses run by organized crime in 1986 were estimated to total $50 billion; by diverting capital, organized crime costs the economy 400,000 jobs per year.[34] It also has been estimated to increase consumer prices by three-tenths of 1 percent and to reduce total economic output by $18 billion per year.[35]

Many organizations experience 5 to 15 percent revenue loss due to fraud and embezzlement. For example, experts estimate that 10 to 15 percent of auto insurance claims in the United States, between $5.4 billion and $8.1 billion a year, are fraudulent.[36] The Health Insurance Association of America claims that between 30 and 40 percent of physicians engage in occasional fraudulent billing practices. Estimates of the cost of these practices run as high as $50 billion per year, more than 8 percent of the national health budget.[37] In 1990, the Internal Revenue Service estimated that the difference between taxes paid and taxes owed in the United States in 1992 would be over $225 billion annually.[38]

No institution or group in society seems immune from the willingness of individuals to gain at the expense of others. Economist David Laband calculates that the public sector in the United States spends more than $10 billion a year in combating organized crime, white-collar crime, theft, street crime, and fraud.[39] He further estimates that the private sector spends over $167 billion per year to protect and insure against theft. These expenses are presented simply as the cost of property in the United States.

The situation in which people or organizations maximize short-run gains while disregarding long-run social costs has been termed an "ethic of personal advantage."[40] The ethic of personal advantage involves imposing costs on others without being accountable to them. In some cases, people may generate these costs unknowingly, without awareness of the consequences. In other cases, cost transfers seem to involve indifference, selfishness, or even outright dishonesty.

Individual patterns of social behavior are complex and contradictory. Some people give their time and money to increase society's well-being; other people defy the norms of mutual benefit and respect and seek personal gain at others' expense. The social cost of the latter may be the price of freedom. Perhaps a 10 percent "loss" rate is simply the cost of freedom of choice and action. Maybe, on the other hand, there is a threshold level of fraud and cheating that causes socially constructive people to lose confidence in the stability and integrity of institutions. At some point, selfish proclivities may well contribute to the irreversible deterioration of the social fabric.

❖ Insights from Group Experiments

Charitable behavior and selfish behavior, and their interplay, have naturally interested social scientists. Numerous studies have examined individuals' tendencies to cooperate or to defect and exploit others' cooperation for personal gain. This line of research sheds light on the nature of human motives and identifies conditions that induce greater selfishness or greater cooperation.

In a typical experiment[41] four subjects each are given five dollars. They are told that they can keep some or all of the money or can "invest" some or all of it in a "public good." The amount of money invested in the public good will be doubled and returned to each participant on an equal basis, regardless whether that person invested in the public good. If all four persons cooperate anu each invests five dollars in the public good, each receives ten dollars at the end of the game.

If only one person invests in the public good, that person's five dollars becomes ten dollars and is distributed to all on an equal basis. Thus, the person who contributed to the public good finishes the game with only $2.50, while each of those who did not contribute to the public good finishes the game with the original five dollars and an additional $2.50 from the public-good distribution, or $7.50. The latter type of person is variously called a defector or a free rider.

Experiments along these lines result in a consistent tendency for cooperation 40 to 60 percent of the time, regardless of the size of the group, subjects' previous experience with the experiment, or the value of the monetary stakes. These results parallel the earlier cited figures on charity and cheating in American society. Actual social behavior is always a mixture of cooperative and noncooperative motives. Summarizing their research in this area, Dawes and Thaler draw the following conclusions about these aspects of human nature:

> Not all people can be expected to contribute voluntarily to a good cause, and any voluntary system is likely to produce too little of the public good (or too much of the public bad in the case of externalities). On the other hand, the strong free rider prediction is clearly wrong—not everyone free rides all of the time.[42]

Other factors tend to raise the average contribution rate in these experiments. First, participants are allowed to discuss whether to contribute or to keep the five dollars. Second, under some conditions participants are told that the public-good investment will be distributed to members of other groups involved in the experiment. People develop strong identification with their own group after only ten minutes of discussion. Contribution rates rise to 70 percent where discussion occurs and the public-good investment will be distributed to the same group. Where no discussion occurs or where others receive the public-good investment, contribution rates drop to 30 percent. Group identification develops after very limited interaction and can exert a powerful influence on people's willingness to contribute to a common good. Personal interaction and group identification appear to be strong factors in the balance struck between cooperative behavior and free-rider behavior.

These experiments permit several observations. First, the experiments confirm people's general willingness to cooperate in creating a public good in situations where they are free to act without regard to the common interest. In this sense, the studies affirm the presence of a strong social basis of behavior and may give comfort to those, such as Tocqueville and Bellah, who see community-oriented behavior as a requisite for a stable and humane society. Second, cooperative behavior is influenced by special, and perhaps limiting, circumstances. For example, interpersonal discussion fosters identification with the group and promotes cooperation. Also, assurance that rewards generated by cooperative behavior remain with one's own group encourages cooperation. Conditions that increase cooperative behavior constitute useful knowledge for managers; they also raise a question about how well cooperation can be induced in large groups. These studies may suggest the limits, as well as the potentials, of cooperation.

Finally, we should recognize that these experiments are designed to test the relationship between cooperation and the creation of public goods. Not all public goods may result from cooperation, however; other experiences show how public goods result from competitive behavior. Both self-orientation and community-orientation, competition as well as cooperation, contribute to social and personal well-being. The manager's task, illustrated in the next section, is to capitalize on the potential of each of these motives and to organize their productive integration.

MANAGING INTERDEPENDENCE AMONG AUTONOMOUS AGENTS

Following are three examples of situations in which a supportive social context enhances the values of autonomous individual behavior. These cases make the point that managers ought to pay attention to the context in which individuals and firms take action, as advocating autonomy for the individual or for the firm has little meaning independent of this context. These studies do not take the social context as an end in itself. They recognize that individuals are the only source of human energy and creative work. At the same time, the cases reaffirm the value of defining individualism broadly, and they demonstrate the community's contribution to the individual.

❖ Decision Making in High Office

In his book *Groupthink*,[43] social psychologist Irving Janis analyzes the nature of effective and ineffective decision making in groups under stress. He reconstructs interaction between individual and group in two successful policy situations, the development of the Marshall Plan and the resolution of the Cuban missile crisis, drawing information for these analyses from historical documents, participants' memoirs, and press reports.

Janis contrasts the instances of successful policy development with five fiascoes in American policy: the invasion of the Bay of Pigs, MacArthur's crossing of the thirty-eighth parallel into North Korea, the lack of American preparation for Japan's attack on Pearl Harbor, the escalation of the Vietnam War, and the coverup of the Watergate burglary beginning in June 1972. In each of these situations, the information needed for successful policymaking was available to key participants, but the prevailing norms of decision making interfered with individuals' critical thinking. Janis relates failure in each of these cases to a process he calls "groupthink"—the suppression of independent judgment and the persistence of unchallenged, faulty perceptions.[44]

Under the anxiety and pressure of high-risk decisions, people are often willing to suppress their personal insecurities to create the appearance of group harmony and to subordinate their better judgment to gain a superficial consensus. The Janis studies make the reader pause and recall Tocqueville's and Riesman's concerns about people's willingness to subordinate their views to the perceived majority opinion. These studies also provide insight into the paradox that social conformity may increase in proportion to the strength of self-reliant individualism and into the conclusion that social participation is the best guarantor of personal independence.

For all of its virtues, pure self-reliance understates the role of social support in maintaining self-esteem. Determining one's own attitude in decision situations may be difficult; stressful or high-stakes situations particularly challenge participants' emotional fortitude. The prospect of failure, the chance of public disapproval, and the possibility of falling short of personal standards pose heavy emotional challenges, and it is natural to seek emotional support from others. Janis finds that the desire for emotional comfort encourages social conformity among individualists. He writes: "Concurrence-seeking and the various symptoms of groupthink to which it gives rise might be best understood as a mutual effort among the members of a group to maintain emotional equanimity in the face of external and internal sources of stress."[45]

In contrast to the policy fiascoes he analyzes, Janis describes the development of two policy decisions with favorable results: the American response in the Cuban missile crisis and the Marshall Plan. As with the policy fiascoes, these two situations were characterized by uncertainty, high stakes, and differing opinions about policy alternatives. But in these instances, policy groups were able to bring out the resources of each member in analyzing the policy problems and finding solutions. Each group combined cohesive relationships with encouragement of open-mindedness and inquiry. In spite of the emotional turmoil and tension that participants experienced in their desire for the emotional security of unanimity, they were able to resist the suppression of individuality and dissent.

Effective decision making calls for integrating, not subordinating, personal differences in thinking, values, and perspectives. Group members cannot be so individualistic as to fragment and divide the group, but they must not be so cohesive as to suppress their opinions in the interest of group harmony. Effective decision making requires collaboration that overcomes the dichotomy of independence and submission. It involves the ability to manage the interdependence of autonomy and community.

❖ Adaptation and Change in Industry

The maritime shipping industry was the subject of an extensive inquiry by Richard Walton of the Harvard Business School.[46] By the early 1980s, the major maritime nations of the world had adapted to a series of common economic pressures that had faced the industry since the 1960s. Walton sought to understand the reasons for the responses of individual countries, as well as the reasons why some countries made a more successful adjustment than others.

After a period of rapid growth averaging 8 percent per year in worldwide maritime shipping between 1965 and 1973, tonnage shipped in the industry declined substantially to about 3.3 percent per year from 1973 to 1979. Then the industry experienced a further reduction in demand and an oversupply of shipping vessels; industry tonnage actually declined an average of 4 percent per year between 1979 and 1983. Escalating costs and technological advancements forced reductions in crew size. In the mid-1960s, an oceangoing ship needed a crew of 45 to 50 persons. By 1973, this had been reduced to about 25. Crew sizes in 1983 were running between 17 and 20, and a few experimental ships were sailing with crews as small as 10 persons.

Economic, technological, and staffing pressures introduced the need for changes in the internal organization of ships, systems that historically had had the look and structure of military organizations. Shipping companies needed greater flexibility in utilizing crew members in more than one job, continuous employment rather than labor contracting for specific voyages, greater participation in work planning and in decision making, and fewer social distinctions between officers and crew.

Walton studied eight countries' maritime industries and their various responses to such changes and looked for factors that would explain why some countries adapted more successfully than others. The Netherlands, Norway, and Japan were found to be highly successful innovators; the United Kingdom, Sweden, and West Germany had moderate success with the innovations; and Denmark and the United States were unsuccessful.

Walton's study draws important conclusions about the ways in which institutional factors in the various countries either facilitated or impeded innovation in the maritime industry. Employers in each country, often speaking through employer associations, had an obvious interest in promoting the changes needed for economic competitiveness. Change also depended on labor unions and on the government agencies that regulated the various aspects of the maritime industry. In some countries, relatively few unions and government agencies were involved; in others, many more nonbusiness organizations were involved. In the United States, for example, eleven different unions and trade groups, at least two different and somewhat isolated employer associations, and two distinct regulatory agencies were involved.

The study examines the extent to which each country was able to form a consensus among interest groups about the need for change and the extent to which each country was able to manage change effectively. These tasks were inherently more difficult where interest groups were fragmented or internally divided. Change was slower in countries where institutions were less strongly oriented toward cooperation or where societal beliefs and customs were resistant to particular innovations. In the United States, the policies of subsidizing inefficient shippers and confining certain shipments to American-flagged vessels regardless of cost both worked against the incentives to innovate.

Walton concludes that public and private leaders in some nations were better able than leaders in other nations to develop a comprehensive understanding of the need for change in the maritime industry and to adjust institutional incentives and public policy in order to facilitate adaptation. The more successful innovating countries were able to create general mechanisms for problem solving, such as union-industry-government forums and third-party facilitators, that provided frequent contact among the parties involved and encouraged them to view problems on the basis of their common interests. In some cases this more comprehensive perspective led to changes in existing regulations and subsidies that facilitated adaptation.

Walton uses the term *metacompetence* to refer to the ability of a country's leaders to achieve a transcendent view of relevant interests. This view recognizes interdependence between one's own institutional interest and the separate interests of other institutions. Metacompetence is the ability to recognize the importance of the wider context to the realization of particularistic goals and to act on this recognition.

High-innovation countries demonstrate the importance of looking at both economic and social factors. The strength of companies in these countries as autonomous agents is supported by each society's ability to create a broader institutional context favorable to economic action. In these situations, the achievement of metacompetence—the ability of a society's institutions to manage their interdependencies—enhances the prospects for success of economic individualism.

Walton identifies and advocates the importance of mutual relationships among institutions to the successful functioning of the business system. Similarly, Richard Wokutch, in *Cooperation and Conflict in Occupational Safety and Health*,[47] finds that national legal, political, and structural arrangements, as well as organizational efforts, have influenced the success with which six different countries have implemented occupational safety and health programs. Here, again, the challenge was to capture the benefits of cooperative, as well as competitive, processes. Barbara Gray, in *Collaborating*,[48] argues that society is increasingly faced with conflicts between and among institutional groups, usually involving businesses, community at large, environmental groups, government, and consumers. The way in which these conflicts are resolved, she states, has a considerable influence on opportunities for business success. Gray advocates a process of collaboration—the constructive management of differences—to create a positive business climate. Walton, Wokutch, and

Gray all point to the fact that business both shapes and benefits from effective institutional arrangements.

❖ Creating a Context of International Cooperation

The General Agreement on Tariffs and Trade. In a few notable economic success stories, beginning in the late 1940s, some countries have found individual benefits in collective action. The success of trading countries belonging to the General Agreement on Tariffs and Trade (GATT) in reducing tariffs on goods by approximately 75 percent since 1947 is an outstanding achievement and has been a major force in post–World War II global economic growth. GATT, a collective organization with 107 member states as of 1991, has worked for reductions in the protection of favored, and often politically influential, domestic industries.

Each country committed to GATT acts with the understanding that the long-term and general benefits of free trade result only from broad collective action. Each understands that an attempt to maximize individual gain at others' expense will result in losses for all, and that successful international cooperation occurs when each country sees its own interests as connected to joint action.

Agreement is far from assured in international negotiations. The Uruguay Round of GATT negotiations begun in 1986, for example, was designed to open the world trading system even further. Key trade issues, such as agricultural subsidies and the protection of intellectual property, required countries to make politically difficult concessions for the sake of free trade. The Uruguay Round had made little progress in early 1992, raising doubt about the future of GATT for liberalizing world trade. Whether or not through GATT, some mechanism of collective action will be necessary for individual countries to give expression to their common interest in free trade.

The European Community. European economic integration is a remarkable achievement, given the member countries' history of religious, ethnic, cultural, and economic differences; extreme nationalism; expedient political coalitions; and territorial aggression. The road to the goals of a unified trade policy and unrestricted movement of people, capital, goods, and services across national boundaries has not been free of impediments. It has taken a half-century of painstaking negotiation (involving numerous regressions and delays), as well as courageous leadership, to institutionalize this vision of peace and prosperity through common effort.

French statesman Jean Monnet was a major driving force and intellectual inspiration for the development of European economic integration. In his *Memoirs*,[49] Monnet describes the development of the European Steel and Coal Community project in the late 1940s, which was the first practical demonstration of the possibility of European economic integration. This was an organization given authority by member countries to open up trade and rationalize production in steel and coal. At the founding of this organization after World War II, Monnet stated the rationale and importance of economic integration:

> We want to turn what divided France from Germany—that is, the industries of war—into a common asset, which will also be European. In this way, Europe will rediscover the leading role which she used to play in the world and which she lost because she was divided. Europe's unity will not put an end to her diversity—quite the reverse. That rich diversity will benefit civilization and influence the evolution of powers like America itself.[50]

European economic integration has been the crowning achievement of Monnet's tireless work. His long-term efforts began as early as World War I with an attempt to coordinate Allied supplies to the Continent. They continued throughout World War II in the facilitation of a united effort by the Allies. Monnet also played a key role in overcoming sectoral differences in the postwar economic recovery in France. In his *Memoirs*, Monnet reflects on the central aim of his efforts: "My sole preoccupation is to unite men, to solve problems that divide them, and to persuade them to see their common interest. . . . I have always been drawn towards union, towards collective action."[51]

In late 1991, another step toward economic integration in Europe was taken as the 12 countries of the European Community agreed to extend their post-1992 single market to the 7 countries of the European Free Trade Association (EFTA). The 19-member free trade market will encompass 380 million citizens.[52] Even more significantly, in December 1991, leaders of the 12 countries of the Community agreed to move toward even greater economic and political union. While leaving a degree of freedom for British autonomy, the countries agreed to pursue a single currency, common foreign policies, a common defense policy, and a stronger European Parliament.[53]

The ongoing, long-term experiment of European economic integration reveals a great deal about the management of interdependence. The essence of economic interdependence, writes economist Paul Taylor, another observer of the European integration system, is "a tension between pressures towards further integration, on the one hand, and pressures towards autonomy, on the other. . . ."[54] Based on his analysis of negotiations on the European monetary system in the late 1970s, Taylor specifies conditions and processes of cooperation. He concludes that economic interdependence will be most easily managed when differences in wealth between countries are small and a sense of "we-feeling," or community, exists.[55] Under these conditions, the European countries have generally been able to progress to higher levels of integration through side payments by the community to the poorer countries. Rich countries such as Germany, for example, pay into a common fund from which payments are make to poor countries, such as Ireland, in exchange for Ireland's acceptance of the Community's monetary policies, industrial policies, and industry laws.

The greatest challenge to integration occurs where there are large differences in wealth between countries and where feelings of community are weak, making it difficult for rationally calculated cooperation to override the desire for national autonomy. In such cases the side payments needed to overcome the reluctance to cooperate become substantial and differences are likely to arise over the amount of control the Community expects to exercise over the use of their payments to the poor countries. The history of the development of European economic integration is a story of the interplay among forces of cooperation and forces of national autonomy.

We can find other instances of rational cooperation through international organizations, especially in response to global environmental problems. John Negroponte's analysis of the resolution of land claims in the last real geographic frontier, Antarctica, is a case in point.[56] By the late 1950s, seven countries, including the United States and the Soviet Union, had made a variety of conflicting land claims to portions of the continent. But, by 1962, the original 12 nations, plus an eventual 23 others, were able to sign a 30-year treaty that suspended land rights claims, demilitarized the continent, and opened the area to scientific inquiry and cooperation. In 1991, 24 nations drafted an extension agreement to ban mineral and oil exploration in the Antarctica for 50 years.[57]

Similarly, 93 countries signed an agreement in the late 1980s to limit and ultimately terminate the production and use of ozone-depleting chlorofluorocarbons. In the spring of 1991, a group of countries began meeting to address the threat of global warming through agreements to reduce the presence of carbon dioxide on an international scale.

The important point about these examples is the attitude of the participating countries toward their individual interests and identities. Individual countries are naturally concerned with their sovereignty and their particular interests of security and prosperity. Each treaty represents a balance struck between countries' immediate, visible interests and their collective interests. Demonstrating Tocqueville's insight in a different context and in a different era, successful international order requires each country to put aside some aspect of its own interest in order to save the rest. Successful experiences of collective organization demonstrate how individual countries can create supportive multinational contexts for their individual aspirations.

❖ The Paradigm of the "Prisoner's Dilemma"

The problem of decision making among interdependent entities is illustrated in the simulation game known as the "prisoner's dilemma."[58] Widely studied in the managerial and social sciences, the prisoner's dilemma situation is based on a scenario in which two persons who have committed a crime are apprehended as suspects; the police have only circumstantial evidence, however, and a conviction would require confessions from one or both suspects. Each suspect is interrogated separately. If neither confesses, both will be released on misdemeanor charges. Each is told that if he or she confesses and the other suspect does not confess, the one who confesses will go free and the one who maintains silence will receive the maximum penalty. If both confess, the police can prosecute both, with a minor mitigation for their confessions.

Each suspect would prefer to confess and have the other not confess, but each also realizes that the other has the same preference. The question is whether they trust each other and neither confesses, or whether trust (collective action) breaks down, they both confess, and both go to jail. The challenge is to act collectively when the payoffs give each an incentive to act autonomously.

The prisoner's dilemma game confronts individualists with their interdependence, placing them in a situation in which they are stripped of status and power differences, asymmetrical payoffs, and opportunities for interaction. The game also exemplifies, in the simplest, purest terms, the situation of sovereign countries facing global interdependence, and, of course, that of interest groups within the maritime industry dealing with innovation and change. The game also portrays the group member who considers whether to "defect" by censoring his or her own views or whether to "cooperate" and trust the others to accept a dissenting opinion. Finding solutions becomes even more complex as one adds differences in social levels, power, and the ability to use communication as a tactic.

Experiments with the prisoner's dilemma and other such games illustrate dynamics between the short-term and long-term interests of individuals. The game and its real-life analogs show that an individualism of pure autonomy and personal advantage may not effectively represent self-interest. Self-interest in many situations involves an awareness of the interdependence among parties and the ability to act collectively in order to structure a context generally favorable to one's own interests. Participants in the prisoner's dilemma game and in many life situations are more likely to succeed when their attitudes take into account other players' need to succeed. In no case is one player responsible for the other's success; each needs simply to consider others' parallel interests. In short, each player must be able to view his or her individualism from a common perspective.

Tocqueville can be said to view American society as a large-scale prisoner's dilemma in which self-indulgent individualism represents a "defect" decision. To cooperate would be to join with others in the spirit of civic participation and sacrifice some of one's self-interest in order to ensure the survival of the rest of one's self-interest. Tocqueville fears egalitarianism will generate an isolating individualism that will undermine personal liberty. He sees salvation in individuals' ability to incorporate the interests of others into their personal choices.

Rightly understood, individualism calls for a "metaview" of oneself as a single player *and* as a participant in a larger structure of social relationships. Resolving problems from this perspective is consistent with this statement attributed to Albert Einstein: "The world that we have made as a result of the level of thinking we have done thus far creates problems that we cannot solve at the same level as the level we created them at."[59] The perspective of interdependence does not abandon autonomous individualism; it just requires a more comprehensive way of thinking about one's own interests.

America's achievements and aspirations depend on each person's autonomy in the defining and pursuit of self-interest. But the effectiveness of Smith's "invisible hand" also depends on sustaining private interest by awareness of and participation in a wider context. The question for this society is whether, and how, American culture can endorse a broad sense of individualism without undermining the essence of autonomy. I have suggested that a perspective of interdependence allows autonomy and community to be kept in equilibrium.

CONCLUSION: THE LIABILITIES OF FIXED THINKING

Experiences discussed in this chapter indicate that there is no small need to overcome the isolating effects of individualism. American society is neither narrowly individualistic nor strongly cooperative, but a complex combination of differing and often conflicting values. Most important, the future will be decided by competition between attitudes, social values, and beliefs that can provide either effective or misleading guidance.

A view of society based on the personal and social benefits of autonomous individual action is incomplete. A distinguished series of observers of American society has consistently drawn attention to the need to balance autonomy with social commitment. These analyses suggest, in fact, that autonomy can be maintained *only* through social commitment. Solutions to the problems faced by firms and countries described in this chapter—making effective policy decisions, adapting to technological and economic change, and ensuring an open environment for trade—defy standard responses of autonomous individualism. Interdependent relationships are simply too visible and too important to be discounted.

Conventional wisdom in the United States emphasizes the virtues of autonomy and self-reliance. Exceptions to this view are just that—exceptions. On the other hand, experience shows that considerations of interdependence are equally valid. Perhaps the assumption of interdependence should be the accepted view and exceptions should be made where assumptions about autonomous behavior can be justified. For the time being, it is wise for managers to have the flexibility to look at problems and opportunities from either standpoint, not prejudging either set of assumptions as being inherently superior. Mental flexibility should stimulate inquiry and dialogue, leading to insights and policies for leaders in both the public and private sectors. A dual approach may best achieve the concept of metacompetence for managers.

[1]Alexis de Tocqueville, *Democracy in America*, ed. J. P. Mayer (Garden City, N.Y.: Anchor Books, 1969).

[2]David Riesman, in collaboration with Reuel Denney and Nathan Glazer, *The Lonely Crowd: A Study of the Changing American Character*, (New Haven, Conn.: Yale University Press, 1950).

[3]Robert N. Bellah, Richard Mudsen, William M. Sullivan, Ann Swidler, and Steven M. Tipton, *Habits of the Heart: Individualism and Commitment in American Life* (New York: Harper & Row, 1985).

[4]Gerald F. Cavanagh, *American Business Values*, 3rd ed. (Englewood Cliffs, N.J.: Prentice Hall, 1990), p. 252.

[5]Herbert Spencer, *Social Statics; or, The Conditions Essential to Human Happiness Specified, and the First of Them Developed* (New York: D. Appleton and Company, 1865).

[6]James Q. Wilson, "Adam Smith on Business Ethics," *California Management Review*, 32, 1 (Fall 1989), 59–72.

[7]Ibid., pp. 64–65. Original quotation from Adam Smith, *The Theory of Moral Sentiments*, ed. D. D. Raphael and A. L. Macfie (Oxford: Clarendon Press, 1976), p. 9.

[8]Edwin M. Epstein, "The Corporate Social Policy Process," *California Management Review*, 29, 3 (Spring 1987), 99–114. This article identifies a number of important statements within the social responsibility/business ethics field. A notable effort to bring together corporate strategy, social responsiveness, and business ethics is R. Edward Freeman and Daniel R. Gilbert, Jr., *Corporate Strategy and the Search for Ethics* (Englewood Cliffs, N.J.: Prentice Hall, 1988).

[9]See, for example, Donna J. Wood, "Corporate Social Performance Revisited," *Academy of Management Review*, 16, 4 (1991), 691–718.

[10]George C. Lodge, *The New American Ideology* (New York: New York University Press, 1986).

[11]Milton Friedman, "The Social Responsibility of Business Is to Increase Its Profits," *New York Times Magazine*, September 13, 1970, pp. 32–33, 122–124, 126.

[12]Several books developing an integrative perspective between economic and social behavior are Amitai Etzioni, *The Moral Dimension: Toward a New Economics* (New York: Free Press, 1988); Roger Friedland and A. F. Robertson, eds., *Beyond the Marketplace: Rethinking Economy and Society* (New York: Aldine de Gruyter, 1990); Albert O. Hirschman, *Rival Views of Market Society* (New York: Viking, 1986); and Kenneth J. Koford and Jeffery B. Miller, *Social Norms and Economic Institutions* (Ann Arbor: University of Michigan Press, 1991).

[13]Tocqueville, *Democracy in America*.

[14]Ibid., p. 508.

[15]Ibid.

[16]Richard Sennet, "What Tocqueville Feared," in *On the Making of Americans*: *Essays in Honor of David Riesman*, ed. Herbert J. Gans, Nathan Glazer, Joseph R. Gusfield, and Christopher Jencks (Philadelphia: University of Pennsylvania Press, Inc., 1979), pp. 105–126.

[17]Tocqueville, *Democracy in America*, p. 515.

[18]Ibid., p. 510.

[19]Ibid., p. 526.

[20]Riesman, *The Lonely Crowd*. Used with permission of Yale University Press.

[21]Ibid., pp. 3–31.

[22]Ibid., p. 16.

[23]Ibid., p. 18.

[24]Ibid., p. 26.

[25]Joseph Featherstone, "John Dewey and David Riesman: From the Lost Individual to the Lonely Crowd," in *On the Making of Americans*, p. 18.

[26]Riesman, *The Lonely Crowd*, pp. 372–373.

[27]Bellah et al., *Habits of the Heart*. Copyright© 1985 The Regents of the University of California. Used with permission.

[28]Sennet, "What Tocqueville Feared," p. 124.

[29]Bellah et al., *Habits of the Heart*, p. 25.

[30]Ibid., p. 285.

[31]James A. Davis and Tom W. Smith, *General Social Surveys 1972–1991: Cumulative Codebook* (Storrs, Conn.: Roper Center for Public Opinion Research, University of Connecticut, July 1991), p. 365.

[32]Independent Sector, *Giving and Volunteering in the United States: Findings from a National Survey* (Washington, D.C.: Independent Sector, 1990), p. 16.

[33]*Giving USA Update*, issue 3, 1991, p. 1.

[34]"The 50 Biggest Mafia Bosses," *Fortune*, November 10, 1986, p. 24.

[35]Ibid.

[36]"More Car Owners Are Scheming to Cheat Insurance Companies as Economy Falters," *Wall Street Journal*, October 10, 1990, pp. B1, B6.

[37]Health Insurance Association of America, "An HIAA Survey of Health Insurers' Anti-Fraud Programs," July 24, 1990, p. 1.

[38]U.S. House of Representatives, Subcommittee on Oversight, Committee on Ways and Means, Announcement of Hearings to Examine the "Tax Gap" and Taxpayer Noncompliance, Press Release 27, April 6, 1990, p. 2.

[39]David N. Laband, "The Cost of Property," *Wall Street Journal*, September 18, 1991, p. A14.

[40]Terence R. Mitchell and William G. Scott, "America's Problems and Needed Reforms: Confronting the Ethic of Personal Advantage," *Academy of Management Executive*, 4, 3 (1990), 23–35.

[41]Robyn M. Dawes and Richard H. Thaler, "Anomalies: Cooperation," *Journal of Economic Perspectives*, 2, 3 (Summer 1988), 187–197.

[42]Ibid., p. 196.

[43]Irving L. Janis, *Groupthink: Psychological Studies of Policy Decisions and Fiascoes*, 2nd ed. (Boston: Houghton Mifflin, 1982).

[44]A behavioral phenomenon similar to groupthink has been termed the "Abilene Paradox," described as the inability to manage agreement. The paradox is the apparent willingness of members of a group to undertake an action that none of the other members prefers. See Jerry B. Harvey, *The Abilene Paradox and Other Meditations on Management* (Lexington, Mass.: Lexington Books, 1988).

[45]Janis, *Groupthink*, p. 256.

[46]Richard E. Walton, *Innovating to Compete: Lessons for Diffusing and Managing Change in the Workplace* (San Francisco: Jossey-Bass, 1987).

[47]Richard E. Wokutch, *Cooperation and Conflict in Occupational Safety and Health: A Multinational Study of the Automotive Industry* (New York: Praeger, 1990).

[48]Barbara Gray, *Collaborating: Finding Common Ground for Multiparty Problems* (San Francisco: Jossey-Bass, 1989).

[49]Jean Monnet, *Memoirs* (Garden City, N.Y.: Doubleday, 1978).

[50]Ibid., p. 310.

[51]Ibid., p. 221.

[52]"European Economic Area: A Short Shelf-Life," *The Economist*, October 26, 1991, pp. 60–61.

[53]"The Deal Is Done," *The Economist*, December 14, 1991, pp. 51–54.

[54]Paul Taylor, "Interdependence and Autonomy in the European Communities: The Case of the European Monetary System," *Journal of Common Market Studies*, 18, 4 (June 1980), 374.

[55]Ibid., pp. 370–387.

[56]John D. Negroponte, "The Success of the Antarctic Treaty," *Department of State Bulletin* (June 1987), 29–30.

[57]"Accord Bans Oil Exploration in the Antarctic for 50 Years," *New York Times*, October 5, 1991, p. 1.

[58]An excellent review of the applicability of the prisoner's dilemma paradigm and description of research on successful choice strategies are presented in Robert Axelrod, *The Evolution of Cooperation* (New York: Basic Books, 1984).

[59]Ram Dass, *The Only Dance There Is* (Garden City, N.Y.: Anchor Books, 1974), p. 38.

Individualism and Community in a Multicultural Society

❖❖❖❖❖

The racial and ethnic composition of the United States is changing at an unprecedented rate. European-Americans now make up only slightly more than three fourths of the nation's population; and immigration patterns and birth rates among racial and ethnic minorities suggest that America is an increasingly heterogeneous society. The rate of population increase among African-Americans, Asians, Hispanics and American Indians doubled in the 1980s compared to the 1970s.[1] By the year 2000, minorities will be the majority in California, which is to say that there will likely be no majority by race or ethnic heritage in that state.[2] These demographic changes will present a significant challenge to maintaining the idea of a common culture in the United States. They will test our past ideas about individuality, justice, and community, and they will present unprecedented policy questions to leaders and members of our institutions.

Growth in minority populations in the United States is due both to the liberalization of immigration policy since the mid-1960s and to higher birth rates among minority groups than among the majority population.[3] Whereas 891,000 Asians immigrated to the United States in 1960, for example, the figure rose to 1.4 million in 1970, 3.8 million in 1980, and approximately 7 million in 1990.[4] The increase in Asian immigration has been seven times as great as growth in the general population since 1980.

The distribution of minority populations varies considerably by state and region. For example, public schools in four states and the District of Columbia will have more than 50 percent nonwhite and Hispanic graduating students by 1995, and another 11 states will have more than 29 percent minority public school graduates by mid-decade.[5] On the other hand, enrollment of minorities in the public schools of 19 states will be less than 18 percent.[6] In addition to disparities between states, segregation by race exists within individual cities and sub-state regions.

Racial, ethnic, and religious differences invariably provide fertile ground for social conflict. In many countries the political landscape is characterized by contentious relations, if not outright hostility and armed conflict, between minority and majority populations. The powerful centrifugal forces of cultural conflict can threaten progress toward universal liberty. The United States faces a long-term challenge to build unity out of diversity, to forge effective relationships for working and living in a multicultural society, and to harmonize, or at least promote respect between, the culture held in common and the cultures of distinct minority groups. The way in which this challenge is met has important direct implications for the human resource needs of business. It also has important indirect implications for the maintenance of the social stability that the American economic system needs in order to prosper.

Alexis de Tocqueville observed the easy part of the challenge of combining individual values with community in American society. He saw that American egalitarianism had abandoned the strictures of royalty, birthright, social title, and inherited privilege. However, he did not witness this country's struggles to abandon slavery and racial, religious, ethnic, and gender prejudice. Tocqueville was optimistic that the spirit of cooperation, voluntary association, and civic participation would counterbalance the potentially isolating consequences of individualism.

In this chapter we examine whether American instincts of association and mutual concern extend across the boundaries of race, ethnicity, and gender—an issue of considerable urgency in a nation that is becoming a society of minority populations. We discuss two ways of thinking about the challenge of integration among different cultural groups in American society. The first model, or paradigm, places great importance on the moral commitment to social equality. From this perspective, society as a whole receives the full benefits of individualism only to the degree that people are freed from unjust and limiting social distinctions. Tocqueville, for example, recognized the importance of equality to freedom in stating the hope that "men will be perfectly free because they are entirely equal, and they will be perfectly equal because they are entirely free."[7] Tocqueville's contemporary, John Stuart Mill, also was a strong advocate of personal liberty. Mill detested oppressive social conventions, such as slavery and the subordination of women in marriage. Mill reinforced the belief that individualism requires a moral commitment to equality and to toleration.

Egalitarian assumptions have been implemented in U.S. public policy toward minorities, especially African-American citizens, since World War II. In this chapter we trace the broad contours of this development. The discussion includes analyses of American society as it was before the dramatic impact of the civil rights movement of the 1960s and a discussion of policy dilemmas associated with the regulatory focus of the civil rights movement, affirmative action.

The second framework for thinking about current multicultural relations in the United States utilizes the notion of the "tragedy of the commons"[8]—a term referring to situations in which rational personal decisions by separate members of a large group combine into an undesirable social outcome for everyone. This model can lend insight into such issues as the widening income disparities between residents of the cities, who are predominantly members of minority groups, and residents of the suburbs, who are primarily white. The issue of multicultural education can also be placed in the framework of a common intangible asset, the ability to achieve cultural unity in settings of diversity.

Each of these two approaches represents a distinct way of viewing America as a multicultural society. Each defines the challenge of combining individualism and community, and each has its own set of policy dilemmas and moral quandaries.

THE MORAL COMMITMENT TO SOCIAL EQUALITY

❖ Justifying Social Equality from the Standpoint of Individualism

The American commitment to the moral basis of individuality can be traced, in part, to the influential British utilitarian philosopher John Stuart Mill. A socially unconventional person, Mill passionately opposed social customs and religious beliefs that even hinted at diminishing the individuality that is essential to human progress. In his essay *On Liberty*, Mill writes:

> Originality is a valuable element in human affairs. There is always need of persons not only to discover new truths, and point out when what were once truths are true no longer, but also to commence new practices, and set the example of more enlightened conduct, and better taste and sense in human life.... [T]he only unfailing and permanent source of improvement is liberty, since by it there are as many possible independent centres of improvement as there are individuals.... A people, it appears, may be progressive for a certain length of time, and then stop; when does it stop? When it ceases to possess individuality.[9]

Mill is aware of Tocqueville's analysis of American society and his concern that an egalitarian society might tend toward conformity. Conformity would, of course, threaten individuality and social development. To this end, Mill insists on the toleration of differing opinions. The free individual is bound to the discipline of considering both sides of an issue equally; individuality implies an eagerness to know and consider opposing arguments. To Mill, the fact that humans make mistakes indicates that they need to learn from error and experience. Mill describes individuality as the unrelenting search for truth:

> So essential is this discipline to a real understanding of moral and human subjects, that if opponents of all important truths do not exist, it is indispensable to imagine them, and supply them with the strongest arguments which the most skillful devil's advocate can conjure up.[10]

Mill demands much from people: maximum individuality, the abandonment of unjust social patterns, and the mental and moral discipline to avoid insidious conformity. He sets a high expectation for realizing the twin promises of individuality and social equality.

Mill was opposed to all forms of social subjugation, such as slavery. He was an outspoken advocate of women's rights against the despotic power of husbands, and he was also an advocate for children, although in unusual ways. He supported laws that would apply fines to fathers whose children failed to read at a specified level by a particular age. He also favored laws forbidding marriage unless the partners have the means to support a family. He fervently believed in the perfectibility of society, as well as the perfectibility of the individual. Mill's beliefs underlie an American commitment to individualism and social equality that finds expression in modern social reform movements, such as the civil rights movement of the 1960s.

While advocating tolerance, Mill is not free from the challenge that *his* view of society is itself intolerant. He is quite willing to restrict the liberty of persons whose actions may be at variance with his personal view of morality, such as fathers of children who are not reading at grade level or young couples of low income. The limits of Mill's own tolerance may be evident in the ways in which he would restrict others' actions in order to advance his personal sense of morality.[11] Again and again in this chapter we shall see a similar dilemma: how to accommodate the moral claims of different groups under the same umbrella of individualism.

❖ Social Equality in a Contemporary Context: The Civil Rights Movement

The civil rights movement of the 1960s stands as an example of America's fight for social equality. In the following sections we explore the accomplishments and limitations of America's moral commitment to social equality, specifically racial equality, in a 60-year perspective on the civil rights movement. This inquiry draws upon sociological description, political ideas, legislative and judicial history, and current policy dilemmas. The discussion will demonstrate that moral claims can make conflicting demands on social policy, and policymaking frequently centers on competing concepts of individual rights. We shall also see that a moral commitment to social equality, which once anchored the civil rights movement, no longer gives a consistent mandate to social policy.

❖ American Society before the Civil Rights Movement

Two early studies of twentieth-century American society provide a starting point for assessing the impact of the civil rights movement. Both

Middletown in Transition, Robert Lynd and Helen Lynd's study of a Middle American town in the mid-1930s, and Gunnar Myrdal's analysis of race relations in the United States in the 1940s, show an American culture characterized by a limited notion of individualism. These studies establish part of the context and motivation for the demand for social reform in the civil rights era.

Middletown, U.S.A., circa 1936. The Lynds' analysis of a midwestern community in the 1930s was the second of two studies of Muncie, Indiana, a community to which they had given the code name "Middletown."12 This study provides a glimpse into dominant cultural patterns in Middletown and into values widely held by Americans at that time. The exclusiveness of Middletown's culture sets the stage for the reform movements that sought to equalize social rights several decades later.

The term *individualism* captures Middetown residents' positive feelings toward their community. Independence and self-reliance are among the first values evident to the observers of Middletown's dominant culture. In this culture human activity is defined mainly in terms of success and failure, which are believed to be determined solely by one's initiative and hard work. The chance to gain wealth is seen as a necessary spur to initiative. Leading citizens of Middletown view development primarily in quantitative terms, as increases in population and income. Progress, to them, is simply a by-product of wealth.

Most citizens demonstrate a strong sense of social identity. One of Middletown's most pervasive values, according to the researchers, is that people "should be loyal, placing *their* family, *their* community, *their* state, and *their* nation first."13 In this sense, civic pride and community spirit are alive and well in Middletown. The values of independence and community spirit offer only marginal membership and social influence, however, to people outside the central group of business-oriented, white, males. Secondary members of the society are expected to take subordinate roles. The following attitudes, for example, are considered part of the "spirit of Middletown":

- The rich are, by and large, more intelligent and industrious than the poor.
- Men are more practical and efficient than women.
- Most women cannot be expected to understand public problems as well as men.
- A woman who does not want children is "unnatural."
- Protestantism is superior to Catholicism.
- Negroes are inferior.
- Individual Jews may be all right but that as a race one doesn't care to mix too much with them.
- Most foreigners are "inferior."14

Today, the ethnocentricity of these and other attitudes reported as representative of the Middletown community may offend us, and we can see how class, gender, and race consciousness developed for socially marginal persons living among such values and attitudes. In light of the significant social ferment beginning to stir in the United States, Middletown's challenge would be to hold its society together. The Lynds subtitled their book "A Study in Cultural Conflict." Caught between past and future, this emblematic American community moved reluctantly and hesitatingly, in the words of the authors, "backwards into the future."[15]

There are two sides to Middletown in the mid-1930s. On one hand, the positive qualities of the society—a rising standard of living, expanding educational and cultural opportunities, enviable personal and political freedoms for many—coincide with the centrality and influence of business. On the other hand, the values of the dominant group are narrow and exclusive. Had Tocqueville been able to look a hundred years into the future from his vantage point in the 1840s, he might have foreseen that civic pride and participation in society, when they are based on limited notions of membership in that society, could themselves constitute a challenge to social stability. Distribution of rights and privileges between the business class and other citizens was to become the dominant political struggle for the rest of the twentieth century.

Holding a Mirror to Race Relations in American Society. In 1944, Gunnar Myrdal, a Swedish sociologist, published a comprehensive analysis of the disparity between the egalitarian ideals of American society and the reality of its discrimination toward black citizens.[16] *An American Dilemma* is a detailed analysis of race relations in the North and the South of the United States and as thorough a description of blacks' lives, beliefs, political participation, and institutions as could be written at the time by a white male. This book brings into sharp focus the origins, nature, and invidious consequences of the separation of persons and institutions by race in this country.

Myrdal had intended his study to be an examination of African-Americans only. His attention was drawn, however, to the general issue of the disparity between American ideals and social reality regarding race. Ultimately, Myrdal saw the problems of blacks as a function of the culture and values of white American society, as "an integral part of . . . the whole complex of problems in the larger American civilization."[17] His study presented this society with a disturbing picture of its double standards toward blacks and whites.

Myrdal perceives Americans' ambivalence toward the law. On one hand, Americans embody their ideals in the law and look to legislative remedies when reality falls short of these ideals. The Reconstruction amendments, the turn-of-the-century antitrust laws, Prohibition, women's suffrage, and the vast legislation of the New Deal all represent attempts to bring social reality closer to national ideals. On the other hand, Myrdal observes, Americans have a readiness to disregard a given law as "unjust." Americans often rationalize their behavior as being consistent with a "higher order of natural law." This attitude may be a carryover from colonial opposition to British rule. Myrdal also considers that putting oneself outside the law might represent a rebellion against the heritage of Puritanical strictness. In either case, Myrdal sees Americans reserving personal judgment about the law. "America has become a country where exceedingly much is permitted in practice," he observes, "but at the same time exceedingly much is forbidden in law."[18]

Such an ambivalent attitude toward the law, as Myrdal explains, enables the United States to be constitutionally committed to social and political equality and simultaneously to practice racial discrimination. In the 1960s and early 1970s, the tables turned, and the same tendency to call into question the fairness of a given law found expression in the civil rights and antiwar movements.

Writing during World War II, Myrdal saw the United States engaged in an important transition. America's commitment to winning the war against avowedly ethnocentric and dictatorial external regimes made the difference between ideals and social reality within the country painfully and unavoidably obvious. In addition, Myrdal perceived that the strengthening of the black protest movement, rising levels of education, and a more vocal black press placed America, in the mid-1900s, at a crossroads on the issue of race relations. Myrdal expressed optimism that the "better self" of America's split moral personality would take over. By then, barriers of inequality had already begun to fall in two sectors strongly susceptible to government influence: the war industries and the military services.

The next several decades proved Myrdal correct in his forecast of substantial change in the status of blacks in American society following the war. Moral purpose and individualism worked in tandem through the civil rights movement until the early 1970s; since then, these values have become more diffuse and their application has come into dispute.

❖ Individualism and Equality in the Civil Rights Movement

The parameters of Americans' contemporary civil rights were established between the end of World War II and the early 1970s. The popular movement for black civil rights, a sympathetic Supreme Court, and unprecedented federal legislation combined to mandate sweeping institutional changes. Whereas the civil rights movement finally achieved success in the 1960s, it originated much earlier in the twentieth century. Northward migration of blacks and growing concentrations of urban poverty for blacks following World War II strengthened support for the movement.[19] Political organizing by blacks and the effective use of social protest enhanced the movement's political strength and raised public awareness of society's injustices toward blacks. After great physical suffering, psychological struggle, and personal sacrifice on the part of leaders such as Martin Luther King and their followers, by the mid-1960s a significant number of Americans supported the basic principles of social equality for blacks.

This awareness led to national civil rights legislation. The most important of the new laws prohibited discrimination in employment and in public accommodations (1964), abolished poll taxes and ensured voting rights (1964), required fair housing practices (1968), and granted the Equal Employment Opportunity Commission the power to litigate against discrimination (1972). These laws officially affirmed the principle of equality in American private and public institutions.

The Supreme Court played a vital part in the civil rights revolution. Sympathetic to human rights, the Court found the presence of the state in what it might previously have considered private relationships, giving broad equal protection and substantive due process rights to blacks.[20] By discarding the "separate but equal" doctrine of nearly 60 years, the Court created a legal mandate for school desegregation.[21] Through application of the U.S. Constitution's commerce clause, the Court reversed the traditional acceptance of discrimination in services open to the public.[22] And, until the late 1980s, the Court endorsed a more demanding standard for proof of nondiscrimination in employment and education, focusing on the *effects* of practices rather than the *intents* behind them.[23]

Civil rights for African-Americans were the leading edge of social reform. However, the commitment to equal opportunity has been applied even more widely. The values of individualism and equality have been honored, in principle, for other minority groups and women as well. We now turn to examine these principles in practice.

❖ Current Disparities of Race and Gender in the United States

Virtually any statistical measure of social well-being shows wide disparities by race and ethnicity in the United States. Thirty percent of blacks lived below the poverty level in 1989—$6,311 for an individual and $12,675 for a family of four—while 10 percent of whites lived below the poverty level.[24] Further, while 15.4 percent of white children lived below the poverty level in 1989, 38.2 percent of Hispanic children and 43.8 percent of black children lived in poverty.[25] The fact that 18 percent of white children are not covered by health insurance is a sad social commentary; this figure, however, is far lower than the 25 percent of black children and the nearly 35 percent of Hispanic children with no health insurance.[26] And whereas 74 percent of white young people graduate from high school, only 58 percent of blacks and 52 percent of Hispanics do.[27]

Systematic studies of institutional behavior toward black people in particular show a continuing legacy of discrimination in the United States. A 1991 study shows, for example, that even under the oversight of the equal employment opportunity laws, testers—pairs of black and white applicants apparently seeking the same job—receive differential treatment from employers.[28] In Chicago and Washington, D.C., pairs of men, one black and one white, were matched in terms of "age, physical size, education, experience, and other 'human capital' characteristics, as well as such intangibles as openness, apparent energy level, and articulateness."[29] White testers advanced farther in the interviewing process and were offered available jobs more often than their black counterparts. Similarly, differences were found to exist in mortgage lending to blacks and whites, after allowing for income, in a study of bank mortgage lending in ten American cities.[30]

Audits of real estate practices by community activists show similar discrimination, despite open housing laws. Black and white buyers report equal financial resources, education, and creditworthiness; but blacks and whites are treated differently by the real estate industry.[31] The 1989 report of the National Research Council concludes:

> Blacks are more likely to be excluded from renting or buying in certain residential areas, to be given quotations of higher prices and rents, and to be "steered" to areas already primarily populated by blacks. . . . It appears that in many metropolitan areas one-quarter to one-half of all inquiries by blacks are met by clearly discriminatory responses.[32]

The term *glass ceiling* is frequently used to describe barriers to the advancement of women and minorities in organizations. Morrison and Von Glinow define the "glass ceiling" as "a barrier so subtle that it is transparent, yet so strong that it prevents women and minorities from moving up in the management hierarchy."[33] These authors summarize studies from the late 1980s showing that only 3.8 percent of corporate officers in the 500 largest service firms in the United States were women and only 8.5 percent of corporate officers in the health industry were women, although significant numbers of women have been employed in the service and health industries for many years. The figures for women in management positions in government and in higher education are not much more favorable. Further, there are significant salary differences between men and women in management positions.[34]

Prospects for advancement into executive ranks appear even worse for minorities. One 1985 survey of several thousand senior executives showed only four blacks, six Asians, three Hispanics, and twenty-nine women; and a 1986 survey of 40 percent of the Fortune 1,000 companies found less than 9 percent of all managers were minorities.[35] A study of American industry as a whole reports that only 3 percent of the top American managers were women in 1989 and only 1.5 percent were racial minorities—figures virtually unchanged since 1979.[36]

The fact that women are disproportionately represented in certain jobs and men are disproportionately represented in others—in other words, occupational segregation—is easily observed in the United States. The real questions are "Why?" and "With what consequences?" One theory holds that women often choose jobs that have been predominantly "female" jobs because the jobs accommodate family responsibilities more easily. This theory is in sharp contrast with the findings of a recent study in which workers in predominantly "female" jobs are found to be less likely to report that their jobs are flexible or easy to perform.[37] In addition, jobs in which women predominate average less time—27 minutes per day—in unsupervised breaks than jobs in which men predominate, so that women have fewer opportunities to check on children or to do other tasks for the household while at work. The study also concludes that women's inferior wages and benefits, and their limited opportunities for advancement in general, are due to unequal treatment rather than occupational segregation, for women workers in nontraditional occupations also report being disadvantaged in these terms. In fact, ironically, a woman may have to participate in a predominantly "female" occupation in order to have job benefits and promotion opportunities reasonably comparable to those of men.[38] A careful review of available literature led the reviewers in this study to conclude that both individual discrimination and institutional discrimination continue to frustrate the efforts of women and minorities to advance.[39]

❖ Making Morality Claims Specific: Equal Employment Opportunity

Affirmative action programs have been a major instrument for institutional change in American public policy. The Equal Employment Opportunity Commission defines *affirmative action* as "actions appropriate to overcome the effects of past or present practices, policies, or other barriers to equal employment opportunity."[40] Federal contractors were among the first employers required to participate in affirmative action programs when they were directed by a 1965 Executive Order to "take affirmative action to ensure that applicants are employed, and that employees are treated during employment, without regard to their race, color, religion, sex, or national origin."[41] Courts have willingly imposed affirmative action programs on businesses, school districts, and other organizations and institutions to remedy discrimination. As a matter of internal policy in order to reduce the threat of litigation, organizations have often adopted voluntary affirmative action programs. Affirmative action agreements have also arisen as a way for employers to settle pending litigation with aggrieved plaintiffs.

The rationale for affirmative action is that employment disparities between groups tend to perpetuate themselves. Thus, the unequal access of women and minorities to employment opportunities harms the earning ability of members of these groups and damages their ability to compete effectively in the future; if women and minorities compete less effectively, they will continue to be underrepresented in employment, and the cycle will continue. Regardless of whether specific intentional discrimination has occurred, the pattern of imbalance becomes institutional and societal.

The moral imperative that liberty implies social equality compels concerted, positive action to change present imbalances of race and gender in order to break the self-reinforcing cycle.

Such efforts to redress inequities of race and gender, however, often bring to the surface conflicts between the various interests of the groups or individuals involved. Achieving the larger goal may require that opportunities for some individuals, usually white males, be reduced in the transition period toward a color-blind and gender-blind society. At the same time, however, the individuals who are asked to sacrifice their job opportunities also have a moral claim. Neither they nor their employers may have discriminated personally against women or minorities, yet affirmative action programs ask them to assume the burden of correcting an institutionalized system of discrimination.

The Supreme Court provides the forum for final resolution in cases where moral claims and rights conflict. Until the late 1980s, the weight of opinion on the Court favored giving redress to those penalized by institutionalized practices. In order to correct the insidious and subtle effects of bias, the Court required employers in 1971 to delineate specific job qualifications and to show how these qualifications are related to job performance.[42] In 1972, the Supreme Court approved a voluntary employer affirmative action program that established preferences for black workers in order to correct for racial imbalance in traditionally white-only job positions.[43] The Court justified the need to defer access of qualified whites to the training program as a temporary loss. The interests of white employees were not "unnecessarily" abused in the view of the Court majority.

In 1978, the Court ruled that although strict quotas were prohibited, race could be considered one factor in university admission decisions.[44] In 1980, the Court backed numerical remedies to correct racial imbalances in federal contracting;[45] in 1986, it permitted goals for employment of minorities;[46] and, in 1987, it struck down a white man's challenge to a voluntary affirmative action program intended to increase the representation of women and minorities in skilled jobs.[47] Until the late 1980s, the scales of justice usually weighed on the side of members of underrepresented groups.

With changes in the leadership and membership of the Court culminating in a shift toward political conservatism in 1988, the Court majority has frequently shown more sympathy to individual claims of harm from affirmative action programs.[48] In 1989, the Court found that a Richmond, Virginia program setting aside a certain portion of construction jobs for minorities violated the equal protection rights of white contractors.[49] "Societal" discrimination no longer justified this program, in the eyes of the Court; remedies would have to address *specific* acts of discrimination. Later that year, the Court ruled that employers do not have to justify practices that have a disparate impact on women and minorities.[50] The Court said that statistical evidence of racial imbalance does not show discrimination, as there may not be qualified minorities or women in a local labor market. Other decisions restricted the reach of affirmative action programs,[51] limited the time for filing suits alleging discrimination in seniority systems,[52] and narrowed the application of long-standing civil rights laws.[53]

This series of precedent-reversing Court decisions spurred an effort by the Democratic-controlled Congress to reinstate, legislatively, the pre-1989 framework for affirmative action. After several years of controversy, a political compromise was struck between Congress and the Bush administration in 1991 that returned the burden of proof to employers, requiring them to demonstrate the absence of discrimination and to show reason for unequal treatment based on the nature of the business itself. This legislation again legitimized the use of disparate-impact data to indicate discriminatory effects. At the same time, the legislation left the definition of "business necessity" to be resolved by the courts, which could conceivably mitigate some of the impact of the new law. In addition, the results of several state political campaigns in November 1991 in Mississippi and Louisiana indicated that American public opinion was divided over affirmative action, and that civil rights policy would continue to be a contentious political issue.

In the short term, available jobs and university admissions are fixed: One person's success represents another's loss. Rules that perpetuate past inequities may be unjust to minorities and women, and rules that give women and minorities preference may be unjust to white males. Affirmative action alone does not resolve the conflicting moral claims of individuals.

Affirmative action means different things to different people. One observer comments on the double meaning of affirmative action as a means of institutional change: "If civil rights is defined as quotas, it's a losing hand. If it's defined as protection against discrimination and efforts to promote opportunity, then it will remain a mainstream value in American life."[54] The dilemma is that progress on civil rights both restricts and opens opportunity. No single, definitive moral premise exists. Another analyst of the civil rights movement concludes:

> The power of the civil rights movement under Martin Luther King was its universalism. . . . Now, instead of the civil rights movement being viewed as a moral crusade for freedom, it's become an expression of a particular interest group. Once you lose that moral high ground, all you have is a power struggle, and that has never been a persuasive means for the weaker to deal with the stronger.[55]

The dilemma of affirmative action recalls our discussion of the ideas of John Stuart Mill—that what may be wise and noble to one person may be unwise or evil to another. Mill was quite willing to enlist the force of government to establish moral standards essential to *his* sense of individuality, which might, however, constrain the individuality of others. Appeals to individualism and social equality generate conflicting moral claims. As the movement for individualism and social equality in the United States has matured, it appears less capable of resolving the current array of group interests originating in race and gender.

RACIAL ISOLATION: A MODERN PROBLEM OF THE SOCIAL COMMONS

Our second approach to understanding race relations takes its name from a 1968 article by the biologist and ecologist Garrett Hardin, entitled "The Tragedy of the Commons."[56] This concept provides an instructive paradigm for examining contemporary urban population dynamics. *Commons* refers to the village pasture in preindustrial England to which village herdsmen had free access for grazing their sheep. The cost of adding an additional sheep was relatively small for each individual herdsman. Collectively, however, the commons could not support all of the sheep that individual herdsmen might wish to add.[57]

In more general usage, *commons* refers to a tangible or intangible asset that is important to the survival and prosperity of a community. An educated populace, healthy citizens, clean air, and even trust in institutions are all important community assets. An unmanaged commons is any community resource to which individuals have free and unlimited access. A commons deteriorates as individually rational decisions to maximize personal gain combine into overuse or abuse of the community resource. The result is a loss for everyone. Users of a commons may recognize the harmful aggregate effects of their actions even as they face the compelling *individual* logic of adding another "sheep."

Hardin's paradigm is applied to a wide variety of situations in which the collective outcome of individual actions is significant to the community, as in littering, adding another car to an already congested highway, or depleting the ozone layer through overuse of chlorofluorocarbons. Surely, we can all agree that falsifying an insurance claim or income tax report and all other forms of cheating are unsustainable ways of realizing personal benefit in the aggregate because they impose the burdens entailed by one person's actions on all other members of the community.

Responding to the threat of the deterioration of a commons often involves regulations and penalties that force individuals to abstain from socially negative behavior or to absorb the social costs of their actions. Freedom of choice may be another national commons, however, that can itself be threatened by a surfeit of rules, each implemented in response to a different perceived commons problem. Other ways of resolving commons problems include heightening personal accountability to the community through required disclosure of individual actions, restructuring rewards to motivate socially constructive action, and relying on voluntary action and self-restraint.

❖ Racial Integration as a National Commons

We can justify viewing racial integration in each sphere of life as a national commons on grounds both of pragmatism and of principle. In terms of pragmatism, economic prosperity increasingly depends on the abilities of a country's people; no country can afford to neglect the education and development of a significant proportion of its population. In the United States, the current waste of human ability through racial and economic isolation in urban ghettos not only leads to enormous social overhead costs in prisons and welfare programs and differential access to adequate education, but also entails more invisible, indirect lost opportunities for a productive population.

In 1987, the Hudson Institute published a comprehensive and detailed study of trends within the U.S. population, *Workforce 2000* by William Johnston and Arnold Packer.[58] After examining immigration patterns and rates of participation in the work force, Johnston and Packer predict that only 15 percent of new entrants into the labor force by the year 2000 will come from the traditional source of workers, native white males. The American work force will grow slowly, it will become older, and it will depend a great deal more on women and on those who have been socially disadvantaged.

The authors of *A Common Destiny*, a comprehensive study of blacks in American society sponsored by the National Research Council, make a similar point:

> [A]s the twenty-first century nears, demographic conditions will increase Americans' awareness that theirs is a multiracial society. . . . [T]he black population will increase from 11.7 percent of the U.S. total in 1980 to 15 percent in 2020; blacks will be nearly 1 of 5 children of school age and 1 of 6 adults of prime working age (25–54). Rising numbers of blacks will be represented both in influential occupations and positions, and among the poor, the least educated, and the jobless. At the same time, immigration trends are also increasing the numbers and proportions of Asian-Americans and Hispanics in the U.S. population. Thus, the importance of racial and ethnic minorities in general to the nation's well-being is growing.[59]

The future prosperity of America requires us to be more successful in the development of human resources than we are now.

In addition to pragmatism, the commons of integration is also a matter of principle in the United States, as I have argued earlier. The most basic statements of principle regarding equality are the Declaration of Independence and the U.S. Constitution. A civil war was fought, at least in part, in order to maintain these ideals. In this century, Gunnar Myrdal touched a raw nerve by pinpointing the discrepancy between national ideals and social realities with respect to race. In the aftermath of the urban riots of the late 1960s in a number of cities, the Kerner

Commission, appointed by President Lyndon Johnson, drew the conclusion that "our nation is moving toward two societies, one black and one white—separate and unequal."[60] A quarter of a century later in late spring of 1992 urban violence again shocked Americans. Riots in south-central Los Angeles and other American cities erupted in response to a jury's acquittal of four white members of the Los Angeles Police Department in a brutal beating of Rodney G. King, a black male. The riots vividly demonstrated the alienation and rage associated with concentrated poverty, failing educational systems, and high unemployment in urban ghettos. The strong racial and ethnic overtones of the L.A. riots also showed levels of social polarization and hostility had quite possibly increased since the Kerner Commission Report. Racial issues continued to impede Americans' ability to see their society as free and just.

Everyone suffers—even the wealthy—from a segmented and segregated society, for several reasons. A society divided by class and race is inconsistent with values of freedom and justice. In 1968, the Kerner Commission stated that "to pursue our present course will involve the continuing polarization of the American community and, ultimately, the destruction of basic democratic values."[61] A similar argument can be made today. As racial integration relates to an open and democratic society, it represents a national commons. Further, even those with high incomes cannot insulate themselves completely from the ills of the rest of society. Social problems penetrate everyone's experience. One news report in the *New York Times* observes:

> No one suffers more for the decline of the inner city than the people who live there, but the rest of society pays a price as well. . . . Beyond economics, the poverty and disorder of the inner cities lacerate a larger civic fabric, driving people from shared institutions like subways, buses, parks, schools and even cities themselves. . . . Perhaps the most damaging of all is the effect that urban poverty has on race relations. It is like a poison in the national ground water that is producing a thousand deformed fruits, from race-based campaigns for public office to taxicabs that do not stop for black men at night.[62]

In examining the challenge of investing in a decent community life, *New York Times* columnist Anthony Lewis concurs: "In urban society we cannot live in isolated cocoons," Lewis states, "except perhaps for the very rich, and even they feel the effect of spreading ignorance, disorder and squalor in society."[63] The social isolation and personal alienation that accompany segmentation by class and race undermine citizens' ability to realize their aspirations in society.

In the following sections I first discuss residential integration as a national commons, because patterns of living are indicators of the degree of racial isolation. The current debate over multiculturalism, in college curricula and in the environment of higher education in general, presents a second challenge to the national commons of integration. Each is discussed from the perspective that actions that are rational from the individual's or the group's perspective may result in undesired consequences for the wider society.

❖ Residential Living Patterns as an Unmanaged Commons

By 1990, the 39 metropolitan areas of a million or more persons contained nearly 125 million people out of a national population of 249.5 million.[64] A 1988, National Research Council study, *Urban Change and Poverty*, concluded that household income in the suburbs of large metropolitan areas was 34 percent greater than that of the central cities.[65] Central cities have the highest rates of poverty, unemployment, crime, drug abuse, teenage pregnancy, and welfare enrollment in the country.[66] Many other studies have documented the growing concentration of poverty and general deterioration of the quality of life in American cities. A 1989 study evaluated hardship conditions based on housing, educational attainment, welfare dependency, poverty, and employment in the country's 55 largest cities relative to each other and relative to their surrounding suburbs. Researchers Richard Nathan and Charles Adams, Jr., found that, between 1970 and 1980, cities suffered greater hardship relative to their suburbs, and the most distressed cities lost ground relative to other, less distressed cities.[67]

As minorities make up a growing share of central city populations, they bear the brunt of urban economic and social distress. The central cities of the ten largest metropolitan areas were, on average, 47.9 percent white in the 1990 census.[68] Los Angeles is 40 percent Hispanic; New York City is nearly 25 percent Hispanic and nearly 29 percent black. Detroit is more than 75 percent black. There is a strong correlation between poverty and racial isolation in the cities. On the other hand, the fastest-growing areas in the United States are "suburban cities," mostly white areas with populations of more than 100,000 persons near the central cities.[69] Moreno Valley, California, a suburb of Riverside, grew nearly 320 percent between 1980 and 1990. Mesa, Arizona, a suburb of Phoenix, grew 89 percent in the same period, and Plano, Texas, a suburb of Dallas, grew nearly 78 percent. Twenty-two of the 29 communities that passed the 100,000 mark in population for the first time in 1990 are situated beside major urban centers. The new suburban cities do not appear to be socially diverse, however. More than 87 percent of the students in the public schools in Plano, Texas, are white, versus 17 percent white students in the public schools of Dallas.[70]

A group of Ohio researchers has analyzed the ways in which the location of new residential housing interacts with urban decay.[71] A study of the seven largest metropolitan areas in Ohio showed that new construction outpaced the growth of households between 1980 and 1990. On the average, 1.7 new residential units were built for every new household added in these seven areas. Equally significant, the new housing was located mainly within metropolitan areas but *outside* the central cities—

that is, in the suburbs. In the 1980s, the number of households in the suburbs of these seven cities increased by an average of 10.7 percent, whereas the number of households in the central cities declined an average of 4 percent among six of the seven cities. The researchers describe these urban dynamics:

> New housing typically is built at the outer edges of the metropolitan area in suburbs where large tracts of vacant land are available, while the abandoned housing typically is located in old and very worn areas of the central city. The filtering process, therefore, involves a gradual movement outward of the city and metropolitan area; suburbs, as a total group, grow in households and population while the central city declines in households and population and is left with abandoned housing to be demolished.[72]

Housing policy analyst Thomas Bier describes how federal and state policies encourage the decline of the central city.[73] First, interstate highway construction around and through the central city draws higher-income people farther away for residential living. Second, federal tax policy exempts homeowners from capital gains tax on home equity if the equity is reinvested in a new residence. This policy encourages homeowners in the city to reinvest the appreciated value of their homes in more expensive homes, which generally are in the suburbs. Bier also claims that the Federal Housing Administration and Veterans Administration home-loan guarantee programs contribute to neighborhood deterioration through a high rate of foreclosures, in one case 13 times greater than in conventional mortgages. In addition, because new utility installations are not charged the full cost of new service, utility consumers in the city, where relatively few new homes are built, subsidize movement to the suburbs, where most new homes are located. These policies encourage residential real estate to flow away from redeveloping urban areas.

❖ The Social Consequences of How People Choose Where to Live

Social scientist Thomas Schelling has made a careful and wide-ranging study of the aggregate effects of individual persons' motives and behavior.[74] Although he covers many areas of social behavior, from international relations to traffic congestion, Schelling's observations on the social processes of segregation have particular relevance for our discussion.

Schelling describes a hypothetical community in which #'s and 0's—for example, Christians and Jews, French-speaking and English-speaking people, or blacks and whites—are equally represented and randomly distributed. He makes the assumption that, in this community each person wants at least one third of his or her neighbors to have similar characteristics; in short, each wants to avoid minority status. Individuals can move within the community and also into and out of it. New community members are randomly assigned to living locations. Schelling demonstrates mathematically that, in a short time, a highly segregated pattern of living develops in the community.

Schelling shows that segregated living is highly likely, based on reasonable assumptions about the distribution of "tolerance" among #'s and the 0's. In his model, actors are concerned only about the overall ratio between #'s and 0's in the community rather than the group or type of their immediate neighbors. For example, suppose a community includes 100 #'s. Though half of the #'s will live with 0's in equal numbers, the most tolerant are willing to be in a one-third minority and the least tolerant will not accept the presence of any 0's. The 0's in the community have the same tolerance for #'s as the #'s have for them; the only difference is that the initial number of 0's is 50. Schelling's model shows that these assumptions lead to only two stable points of residential composition: all #'s or all 0's. Integrated and stable communities occur under only two possible conditions: that the #'s and 0's become more tolerant of each other, or that the community is limited to the most tolerant members of each type.

Schelling's theoretical analysis parallels the actual racial segregation of America's metropolitan areas. Evidence suggests that Americans have a low tolerance for racial integration. For example, whites living in the 29 largest metropolitan areas in the United States in 1980 lived in neighborhoods that were, on average, 89 percent white.[75] Whites in some metropolitan areas, such as Boston, Pittsburgh, and Milwaukee, lived in neighborhoods that were at least 95 percent white, on average.[76] Blacks living in these metropolitan areas lived in neighborhoods that were, on average, 68 percent black. Indices of residential segregation in the nation dropped between 1960 and 1980, but only slightly.[77] Actual living patterns according to race extensively validate the predictive power of Schelling's models. There is not complete residential segregation in this country because some black and white citizens are willing to live in integrated communities. The fact that the level of segregation is high, however, suggests that the overall level of tolerance is not great in spite of the superficial endorsement of diversity and toleration in the overt American value system.

❖ Multicultural Education: A National Commons

As the United States engages the challenges of a multicultural society, universities will be among the institutions most strongly affected. The quality and accessibility of American institutions of higher learning are admirable. Access to higher education, particularly to public institutions, has helped to lower the artificial social barriers to personal advancement in this country. By challenging the development and expression of individuals' inner resources, higher education supports individualism. American higher education is a manifestation of the classic liberal belief, as articulated by Mill and others, that intellectual freedom leads to social progress. As an institutional sector, universities embody the positive values of individualism and equality. These values represent a precious national commons that exists under the trusteeship of higher education in the United States.

Institutions of higher learning have been integral to America's long struggle for social equality. As social institutions, colleges and universities share the country's history of discrimination and separation; and, like other institutions, colleges and universities are now engaged in adapting to expectations of equal opportunity. Reforms influence recruiting, admission, and retention policies for students, faculty, and staff in the university community. Higher education is a crucial point of access to opportunities, and colleges and universities must be particularly responsible to members of groups that have suffered social exclusion. Because education has a high value in American life, educational institutions play an essential role in helping other institutions, such as business, to bring their own policies into line with social ideals.

The obligation of educational institutions in relation to American society exceeds the requirements of nondiscrimination and promotion of diversity. One result of promoting freedom of thought is that culture and social power themselves become subjects of inquiry and criticism. Increasingly, universities face cultural conflict resulting from the examination of assumptions about race, ethnicity, gender, and sexual orientation that are embedded in the nature of courses offered, in the classroom materials, and in the lessons instructors draw from the materials.[78]

Members of a number of academic institutions are debating whether traditional Western thought, particularly in the humanities and social sciences, is culturally biased or whether it articulates universal values. In the view of some minority groups, virtually all of the social institutions and teachings of Western culture may be unfairly biased in favor of the values and interests of the majority group. Cultural analysis finds biases within the ideas of Milton, Shakespeare, Locke, Jefferson, and other classic Western writers. In this view, few standards of evaluation or interpretations of morality have meaning outside one's personal preference.[79]

Like all institutions, educational organizations are founded on assumptions that are likely to be culturally limited. The constellation of social and cultural values that define educational purpose and content are often perceived as unjust or unfair to people whose experience lies outside the dominant culture. Institutions and the people inside them have little capacity for seeing themselves as outsiders may see them, and change is often infuriatingly slow and painful.

Challenging dominant assumptions and values on the basis of morality can be an outcome of individual inquiry and analysis and a source of social progress. The cultural biases of institutional structures and the exclusiveness of existing arrangements of social power are themselves legitimate topics of inquiry and debate. For example, the underrepresentation of women and minorities on university teaching faculties and especially in university positions of academic administration is itself a valid focus of criticism. A critical perspective on the sources of contemporary culture can inform citizens about choices and can lead to reaffirmation or modification of values. As John Searle notes, the European Enlightenment has shaped the dominant tradition in the United States; nevertheless the dominant culture can be understood only in relation to other traditions and cultures, including those in Europe and America that have been treated unjustly.[80]

Critical analysis of society will inevitably find that the values and experiences of traditionally nondominant groups—racial and ethnic minorities and women—are not well recognized and are not honored as valid to the same degree as the values of the culturally dominant group. Strengthening appreciation for the values of minority groups is a necessary part of becoming a true multicultural society. The path to truth begins with the recognition of diverse perspectives; ideally, it ends, according to Searle, with the development of "intellectual openness, critical scrutiny, and logical clarity."[81]

Racial and ethnic identification also offers people an important source of social support in a complex and often impersonal world. Troy Duster, a professor of sociology at the University of California at Berkeley (a campus that is expected to be 60 percent minority by mid-decade) writes:

> In a diverse nation, [racial, ethnic, nationality] identification[s] can provide a sense of belonging to a recognizable collectivity. It helps give a sense of belonging—of being one with others like oneself—that helps to overcome the isolation of modern life, while paradoxically also allowing a sense of uniqueness.[82]

However, excessive emphasis on individuality within the multicultural movement can have disastrous results. Social organization and collective purpose can exist only within a framework for understanding and action that is provided by a basic set of common cultural expectations and social values. Separatism can lead to chaos, bigotry, social coercion, and loss of individuality. Absolute cultural perspectives in higher education, majority or minority, threaten the national commons of an institutional sector capable of realizing individuality and equality. One participant in the debate on multicultural education comments that minority groups may exchange one form of intolerance for another and that the diversity sought by persons advocating cultural pluralism does not include opinions different from their own.[83]

Attributing the quality of specialness or uniqueness to something implies its opposite: that something else is common. People are distinctive in some ways only because they are similar in others. The notion of difference always implies a frame of reference from which differences are seen. Otherwise, there would exist only chaotic or random experience. A dominant culture that attempts to hold exclusive social power threatens the American values of individualism and egalitarianism. Individuality in the extreme can defeat itself by undermining the common culture on which it ultimately depends. If individuality and the search for distinctiveness lead to exclusiveness, the desirable benefits of diversity, individuality, and openness will be lost.

A successful multicultural society requires appreciation of difference and sameness. In situations of conflict, both challengers and defenders have to be willing to make accommodations to the interests of other groups without conceding their own moral perspective. Each party must be aware that individuality is linked to commonality. Duster has described the emergence of a "third experience" in multicultualism. "In this third experience: the whole is greater than the sum of the various parts," he writes. "Collective problem solving by individuals from different backgrounds produces superior results precisely because of the synergy that develops from different approaches being brought to bear on the same problem."[84] Both majority and minority groups will have to be conscious of individuality *and* the broader community. A multicultural society requires new perspectives, power sharing, and self-restraint in order to maintain a national commons of individualism and community.

CONCLUSIONS

This chapter is concerned with a struggle within America. Unequal access to the opportunities and satisfactions of the society is inconsistent with the society's core value of individualism. Where the dignity and well-being of all people are valued, double standards in treatment are unacceptable. Social behavior in the United States has incompletely conformed to this social ideal. Living by a single standard would be a monumental challenge to any society, and it is a challenge that has been confronted in the United States.

Because individual rights and opportunities are central to the values and ideals of this society, the behavior of one person toward the other or of one group toward other groups is a matter of morality for many people. Unequal treatment of anyone based on personal characteristics is inconsistent with widely shared general values. One person's specific moral claim conflicts with the specific moral claim of another in a variety of settings, however. Conflicting claims of differing parties to limited resources, such as jobs, can each be tied to the fundamental and inviolable value of individualism. In short, the value of individualism alone may be an insufficient guide to resolve the problems of living together and progressing as a diverse society.

The "commons" paradigm applies to aggregate patterns of social isolation and integration in a large society with freedom of association. For many years the United States tolerated discrimination as a natural outcome of individual belief and personal choice. With respect to race in particular, America was a two-class society. After the Second World War, the aggregate result of a society divided by class, race, and gender was eventually perceived to be inconsistent with American ideals. In other words, the pattern itself was found wanting. This national "commons" was in disrepair.

Social reforms of the last 45 years represent reassertion of the collectivity; they constitute efforts to rebuild the commons of universal freedom to an acceptable level. If the primary instruments of change— legal coercion and affirmative action—reduced individual choice, that was the price of restoring the commons. The society judged that the exercise of personal choice to such a degree that it undermined the core value of freedom for all was a situation that could no longer be tolerated. As a matter of public concern, the commons had to be managed differently.

Social patterns of the 1970s and the 1980s in the United States demonstrate that tension between individuality and collectivity in social relationships continues. Differing claims on social morality suggest that the likelihood of agreement between people on opposing sides of questions of social equality is slight, at least in the short term. There is no apparent consensus about the best route to progress; national debate and recourse to legal approaches alone are unlikely to resolve the stalemate.

Progress will result, instead, from the recognition that there are hundreds of thousands of "commons" in the United States, hundreds of thousands of residential communities, school districts, and formal organizations whose members' actions have an effect on patterns of social isolation and on prospects for authentic multiculturalism. Future movement toward racial, ethnic, and gender integration in the United States needs to come as much from the efforts and successes of these distinct organizations and communities as from a national consensus on morality and on legal rights. This country may be experiencing the limits of social progress based on a morality imposed from the top down; social morality that affirms individuality and contributes to social progress must now arise from the grass roots.

The challenge of maintaining social integration amid individualistic values and a diverse society is even more daunting than the challenge envisioned by Tocqueville. Nevertheless, the contemporary challenge leads to much the same conclusion that Tocqueville reached more than 150 years ago: that the potential of the society depends on the generosity of the spirit of individualism is among the people. Will social values span racial, ethnic, and gender differences? The answer to this question will not be found in national policy and Supreme Court decisions alone; it will be found in the specific contexts in which people work, live, and communicate with each other.

[1]"Census Shows Profound Change in Racial Makeup of the Nation," *New York Times*, March 11, 1991, pp. A1, A12.

[2]"The Melting Pot Boils Over," *The Economist*, October 13, 1990, pp. 8–10.

[3]"Asians Spread Across a Land, and Help Change It," *New York Times*, February 24, 1991, p. I22.

[4]Ibid.

[5]*The Road to College: Educational Progress by Race and Ethnicity*, Western Interstate Commission for Higher Education and The College Board (July 1991), pp. 8–9.

[6]"Rise Is Forecast in Minorities in Schools," *New York Times*, September 19, 1991, p. A8.

[7]Alexis de Tocqueville, *Democracy in America*, ed. J. P. Mayer (Garden City, N.Y.: Anchor Books, 1969), p. 503.

[8]Garrett Hardin, "The Tragedy of the Commons," *Science*, 162, December 13, 1968, pp. 1243–1248.

[9]John Stuart Mill, "On Liberty" in *Essential Works of John Stuart Mill*, ed. Max Lerner (New York: Bantam Books, 1961), pp. 312, 318–319.

[10]Ibid., p. 288.

[11]Susan Mendus, *Toleration and the Limits of Liberalism* (Atlantic Highlands, N.J.: Humanities Press International, 1989).

[12]Robert S. Lynd and Helen Merrell Lynd, *Middletown in Transition: A Study in Cultural Conflicts* (New York: Harvest/HBJ Book, 1937), copyright 1937 by Harcourt Brace Jovanovich, Inc. and renewed 1965 by Robert S. Lynd and Helen Lynd, reprinted by permission of the publisher. The Lynds's initial study of Middletown, conducted in 1924–25, was published as *Middletown: A Study in Contemporary American Culture* (New York: Harcourt, Brace, 1929).

[13]Ibid., p. 407.

[14]Ibid., pp. 407–416.

[15]Ibid., p. 510.

[16]Gunnar Myrdal, *An American Dilemma: The Negro Problem and Modern Democracy* (New York: Harper & Brothers, 1944).

[17]Ibid., p. X1IX.

[18]Ibid., p. 17.

[19]National Research Council, *A Common Destiny: Blacks and American Society*, eds. Gerald David Jaynes and Robin M. Williams, Jr. (Washington, D.C.: National Academy Press, 1989), pp. 220–229.

[20]*Shelley* v. *Kraemer*, 334 U.S. 1 (1948); *Burton* v. *Wilmington Parking Authority*, 365 U.S. 715 (1961).

[21]*Brown* v. *Board of Education of Topeka*, 347 U.S. 483 (1954).

[22]*Heart of Atlanta Motel, Inc.* v. *United States*, 379 U.S. 241 (1964).

[23]*Griggs* v. *Duke Power Co.*, 401 U.S. 424 (1971).

[24]" Suffering in the Cities Persists As U.S. Fights Other Battles," *New York Times*, January 27, 1991, pp. 1, 21.

[25]The Center for the Study of Social Policy, *Kids Count Data Book: State Profiles of Child Well-Being* (Washington, D.C.: The Center for the Study of Social Policy, 1991), p. 11.

[26]Ibid.

[27]Ibid.

[28]Margery Austin Turner, Michael Fix, and Raymond J. Struyk, *Opportunities Denied, Opportunities Diminished: Discrimination in Hiring* (Washington, D.C.: Urban Institute, 1991).

[29]Ibid., p. 4.

[30]Association of Community Organizations for Reform Now, "Banking on Discrimination: An Analysis of Home Mortgage Lending in 10 Cities in 1990," October 21, 1991.

[31]National Research Council, *A Common Destiny*, p. 50.

[32]Ibid.

[33]Ann M. Morrison and Mary Ann Von Glinow, "Women and Minorities in Managment," *American Psychologist*, 45, 2 (February 1990), 200–208.

[34]Ibid., p. 201.

[35]Ibid., pp. 200–201.

[36]"Breaking Through," *The Economist*, January 26, 1991, p. 29.

[37]Jennifer Glass, "The Impact of Occupational Segregation on Working Conditions," *Social Forces*, 63, 3 (March 1990), 779–796.

[38]Ibid., p. 792.

[39]Morrison and Von Glinow, "Women and Minorities," pp. 202–204.

[40]Roy L. Brooks, "The New Law of Affirmative Action," *Labor Law Journal* (October 1989), 612.

[41]Ibid., p. 618.

[42]*Griggs* v. *Duke Power Co.*

[43]*United Steelworkers of America, AFL-CIO-CLC* v. *Weber*, 443 U.S. 193 (1979).

[44]*Regents of the University of California* v. *Bakke*, 438 U.S. 265 (1978).

[45]*Fullilove* v. *Klutznick*, 448 U.S. 448 (1980).

[46]*Local 28, Sheet Metal Workers' International Association* v. *Equal Employment Opportunity Commission*, 478 U.S. 421 (1986).

[47]*Johnson* v. *Transportation Agency, Santa Clara County, California*, 480 U.S. 616 (1987).

[48]An overview and discussion of these cases is presented in Samuel Rabinove, "Major U.S. Supreme Court Civil Rights and Affirmative Action Decisions: January–June, 1989," *Journal of Human Rights*, 7 (Symposium 1990), 9–34.

[49]*City of Richmond* v. *J. A. Croson Co.*, 488 U.S. 469 (1989).

[50]*Wards Cove Packaging Co., Inc.* v. *Atonio*, 490 U.S. 642 (1989).

[51]*Martin* v. *Wilks*, 490 U.S. 755 (1989).

[52]*Lorance* v. *AT&T Technologies, Inc.*, 490 U.S. 900 (1989).

[53]*Patterson* v. *McLean Credit Union*, 491 U.S. 164 (1989).

[54]"Rights Movement in Struggle For an Image as Well as a Bill," *New York Times*, April 3, 1991, p. A12. Copyright © 1991 by The New York Times Company. Reprinted by permission.

[55]Ibid., p. A1. Copyright © 1991 by The New York Times Company. Reprinted by permission.

[56]Hardin, "Tragedy of the Commons." In subsequent writings, Hardin has expanded the scope of application of this paradigm considerably. See Garrett Hardin, *Filters Against Folly: How to Survive Despite Economists, Ecologists, and the Merely Eloquent* (New York: Viking Penguin, 1985).

[57]The overgrazing of the commons symbolizes one logical implication of this structure of individual incentives rather than an historical fact. The system

of the village commons in eighteenth-century England succumbed to the interests of members of the landed elite, who gained parliamentary approval to enclose formerly public lands for private use. The enclosure movement was an integral part of political institutional development in England; enclosures destroyed the medieval peasant class, which served in a number of other countries in this period as a reactionary force against the emergence of political democracy. The enclosure movement also showed the growing strength of the Parliament relative to the king. In these ways, the enclosure movement contributed to the development of England's modern democratic institutions. See Barrington Moore, Jr., *Social Origins of Dictatorship and Democracy: Lord and Peasant in the Making of the Modern World* (Boston: Beacon Press, 1966), pp. 20–29. Hardin, on the other hand, uses the notion of the commons to show how incentive structures that privatize benefits and commonize costs, namely, unrestricted access to a public good or resource, are unsustainable.

[58]William B. Johnston and Arnold H. Packer, *Workforce 2000: Work and Workers for the Twenty-first Century* (Indianapolis, Ind.: Hudson Institute, 1987).

[59]National Research Council, *A Common Destiny*, pp. 5–6.

[60]*Report of the National Advisory Commission on Civil Disorders* (New York: New York Times Co., 1968), p. 1.

[61]Ibid.

[62]"Suffering in the Cities," p. 21. Copyright © 1991 by The New York Times Company. Reprinted by permission.

[63]Anthony Lewis, "The Reagan Effect," *New York Times*, July 26, 1991, p. A11. Copyright © 1991 by The New York Times Company. Reprinted by permission.

[64]"Where America Is Growing: The Suburban Cities," *New York Times*, February 23, 1991, p. Y10.

[65]Michael G. H. McGeary and Lawrence E. Lynn, Jr., eds., *Urban Change and Poverty* (Washington, D.C.: National Research Council, 1988), pp. 14–15.

[66]Ibid., p. 13.

[67]Richard P. Nathan and Charles F. Adams, Jr., "Four Perspectives on Urban Hardship," *Political Science Quarterly*, 104, 1 (Fall 1989), 483–508.

[68]U.S. Department of Commerce, Bureau of the Census, Population Division, internal document CPH-L4, 1990 Census.

[69]"Where America Is Growing," pp. 1, 10.

[70]"1990–91 Dallas Independent School District Student Enrollment by School," Dallas Independent School District, October 15, 1990.

[71]"Suburbanization of Ohio Metropolitan Areas 1980–2000," A Report of a Collaborative Research Project Involving Seven Ohio Urban Universities under the Auspices of The Ohio Urban University Program of the Ohio General Assembly and the Ohio Board of Regents, June 27, 1990.

[72]Ibid., p. 2.

[73]Thomas E. Bier, "Public Policy Against Itself: Investments That Help Bring Cleveland (and Eventually Suburbs) Down," in *Cleveland Development: A Dissenting View*, ed. Alvin L. Schorr (Cleveland: David Press, 1991), pp. 43–52.

[74]Thomas C. Schelling, *Micromotives and Macrobehavior* (New York: W. W. Norton, 1978), chap. 4, pp. 135–166.

[75]National Research Council, *A Common Destiny*, p. 79.

[76]Ibid.

[77]Ibid., p. 90.

[78]John Searle, "The Storm Over the University," *New York Review*, December 6, 1990, pp. 34–42; Linda Chavez, "The Real Aim of the Promoters of Cultural Diversity Is to Exclude Certain People and to Foreclose Debate," *Chronicle of Higher Education*, July 18, 1990, pp. B1–B2; Anthony DePalma, "The Culture Question," Calvin Sims, "World Views," and Roberto Suro, "Hispanics in Despair," *New York Times*, November 4, 1990, sec. 4A, pp. 22–25 EDUC; Dinesh D'Souza, *Illiberal Education: The Politics of Race and Sex on Campus* (New York: Free Press, 1991).

[79]This point of view, in addition to the point of view defending the concept of a traditional "canon" of Western culture, are discussed and critiqued in Searle, "The Storm."

[80]Ibid., p. 42.

[81]Ibid.

[82]Troy Duster, "Understanding Self-Segregation on the Campus," *Chronicle of Higher Education*, September 25, 1991, p. B2. Used with permission of Troy Duster.

[83]Chavez, "The Real Aim," p. B1.

[84]Duster, "Understanding Self-Segregation," p. B2. Used with permission of Troy Duster.

Economic Individualism and Social Individualism: The Origins and Consequences of Polarized Values

❖❖❖❖❖

In 1651, the British philosopher Thomas Hobbes articulated a concept of the origin of civil society that has strongly influenced political life and experience in America. In his classic work, *Leviathan*,[1] Hobbes argues that human beings, however inherently selfish they may be, have the redeeming capacity to understand and overcome their own malevolent inclinations. Hobbes theorizes that individual persons in a hypothetical presocietal state of nature foresaw a bleak future, based on their partisan actions toward one another. People have the intelligence and wisdom, Hobbes believes, to take rational action to change their circumstances and, by acting together, to create an agreement or compact with a political ruler. People's desire to establish an orderly, secure existence justifies organized political society, according to Hobbes.

Hobbes's primary intention was to justify obedience to England's monarchs and to convince citizens to subordinate their private interests to those of the state: People should take the sovereign's will as their own. Hobbes readily transferred his personal allegiance among competing royal factions, depending on the consequences of the various contests over the English throne.[2]

Hobbes uses the term *social contract* to convey an abstract notion of the mechanism for ensuring personal self-interest. Personal goals such as safety and order depend on a secure social environment that is possible only through collective agreement. This concept had a lasting impact on subsequent political theory and influenced the development of American political institutions.

Two of Hobbes's intellectual successors, John Locke and Jean-Jacques Rousseau, reconsidered and rejected the need for a powerful sovereign. In contrast to Hobbes, both theorists advocated government by the people. Locke and Rousseau part ways with each other, however, over the primary purpose of the social compact.

John Locke stressed individual rights. For him, private property defines and limits government and ensures political freedom. Locke laid the groundwork for a society organized according to the principle of *economic individualism*. In contrast with Locke's concern for individual liberty, Rousseau focused on the significant social inequities of his day, which he felt must be eliminated in the name of a just society. Rousseau believed that social equality, rather than property rights, offers the means by which to achieve individual well-being. Arguing for a social obligation to the individual person, Rousseau set forth the principle of *social individualism*.

The brief overview of these and related ideas in this chapter admittedly does not do justice to the originality, breadth, and complexity of thinking of these seminal theorists. Our discussion also omits the intellectual contributions of numerous other social and political theorists who have been influential in shaping American political institutions and ideologies. Our more limited objective here, however, is to identify several broad currents of political thought that have contributed to the political development of the United States.

The current ideological environment of business is structured, in general, in terms of the opposing notions of economic individualism and social individualism, deriving, respectively, from the theories of Locke and Rousseau. Each of these values has advocates who vie for influence over the national policy agenda, and the interaction between the two ideologies is played out mainly as a zero-sum game. In this chapter I argue for a different approach, in which both economic values and social values are recognized as *interdependent* and each notion of individualism influences the other. My belief is that a zero-sum political contest inhibits optimal progress toward either value.

The United States may need a new social contract in political thinking that would provide a framework for overcoming the traditional zero-sum relationship between economic values and social values and build on the positive interdependence between the two. Such a framework would require that advocates on both sides emphasize points of mutual agreement rather than points of conflict. It would require proponents of each philosophical position to evaluate their interests in a context that recognizes the necessity of the existence of the other.

Hobbes believed that personal security depends on a social contract in which rational understanding outweighs parochial self-interest. A new social contract for our time would similarly be an effort to change current zero-sum viewpoints into more integrative, positive commitments to economic and social values. In accordance with this positive-sum perspective, we review the roles of economic individualism and social individualism in management theory and thus in management education. Ideological assumptions find their way into management theory, casting the managerial world in ideological terms and distracting managers' attention from the basic task of creating conditions for effective long-term relationships among people and groups in organizations. I argue that such polarization serves neither managers nor employees.

INTELLECTUAL ORIGINS OF THE SPLIT
BETWEEN ECONOMIC RIGHTS
AND SOCIAL RIGHTS

For John Locke, limitations on the authority of the state become the central focus of political theory.[3] Although Locke shares much of Hobbes's suspicious view of human nature, his thinking finds a more constrained role for the state by giving citizens the authority to determine the legitimacy and power of the ruler. To Locke, the sole justification for government, the common interest in the pursuit of which people join together, is to protect their inalienable natural rights—life, liberty, and property—against one another's predatory actions. Civil authority is justified only for the purpose of establishing order, adjudicating conflicts, punishing violators of others' rights, and defending the society against foreign aggression. For Locke, society is a rational agreement among self-interested persons that is intended to preserve their natural liberties rather than a Hobbesian contract between the people and a sovereign for the purpose of creating social order.

John Locke was part of a political movement that was fervently opposed to royal absolutism in late-seventeenth-century England. He was instrumental in the formation of Britain's Whig party and held several government posts in the Whig government after the revolution of 1688. For Locke, the sovereign's powers had to be restrained by consent of the governed. He argued to limit the sphere of the sovereign's rule by sanctifying life, liberty, and property as inviolable and by subjecting public authority to popular election.

Although Locke abhorred Hobbes's belief in the necessity of submitting one's will to that of the sovereign, he joined Hobbes in believing that people must accept some degree of restraint in the interest of social order. Locke considered taxation, for example, to be acceptable for the maintenance of order and for the common defense.

❖ Class Implications of Locke's View
of Political Society

In contrast with the concept of universal natural rights, Locke's vision of democracy grants political rights based on property ownership; for this reason, his critics have pointed out the close tie between Lockean democracy and the interests of the wealthy.[4] Locke's writings imply the acceptance of a two-tiered society, defined by the economic fact of property. As political theorist John Gough describes it:

> Only property-owners were fully members of the community. . . . Landless laborers, on the other hand, though necessary to the community, were not full members of it, so that their consent was not needed. In any case, they were so fully occupied with the struggle for a bare subsistence that they could not be expected to exercise or even possess a rational faculty.[5]

Locke's civil society is designed to limit the sovereign. Because property owners have a direct interest in controlling the powers of the monarch, it is natural to enfranchise them with political rights. People without property, on the other hand, cannot be counted on to ensure economic and political liberties or to maintain social order. This scheme ensures social stability, however, only so long as politically excluded persons accept their subordinate position.

The movement to extend political rights and social well-being to those not holding property shapes a counterideology whose modern realization is social individualism. Jean-Jacques Rousseau's political theory provides an intellectual orientation for this point of view.

❖ Counterpoint: Jean-Jacques Rousseau and the General Will

Social philosopher Jean-Jacques Rousseau provides a contrasting perspective for evaluating the ideological environment of modern business.[6] Writing in the mid-1700s, about 70 years after the publication of Locke's *Second Treatise on Government* and a few decades before the French Revolution, Rousseau passionately opposes social inequities, which, in his view, result from a morally degenerate monarchy and a rigidly class-based European society. Existing European society had demonstrated to him the corruption and injustice of human affairs. Equality is essential to Rousseau's concept of people's natural rights, although his concept of equality does not include equal rights for women.[7] Rousseau's sensitivity to social inequities and his concern for improving society gave support to the popular ideals of the French Revolution of 1789. His ideas on collective decision making also presage the authoritarian excesses of the French Revolution as well as those of twentieth-century coercive regimes based on the later communitarian ideologies of socialism and communism.

For Rousseau, equality promotes a unified society rather than one based on arbitrary social distinctions that deny universal human dignity and inalienable natural rights. Rousseau envisions a society that places equal value on individual freedom and social unity.[8] He sees these two requirements for political organization as

> To find a form of association which may defend and protect with the whole force of the community the person and property of every associate, and by means of which each, coalescing with all, may nevertheless obey only himself, and remain as free as before.[9]

Unfortunately, Rousseau is more successful in stating aspirations than in offering a viable means of realizing them. He proposes resolving the tension between freedom and social order through the concept of the "general will," a somewhat mysterious concept in which each person influences the social body and then subordinates himself to the decisions of the whole. In one sense, Rousseau shares Hobbes's willingness to subordinate the individual to public authority; in another, Rousseau, like Locke, states that only popular democracy can reveal the general will. In Rousseau's vision, however, political rights are not confined to owners of property, but are conferred on all men.

Rousseau seems to have had in mind a great spirit of cooperation in which citizens successfully identify their common interest and voluntarily bind themselves to its authority. His ideas do not safeguard individual rights, however, and regimes claiming to be in concert with his ideals typically require extreme sacrifices of personal freedom. People acting in large numbers generally have not proved themselves capable of realizing a voluntary merging of their wills, a failing ultimately translated into state coercion. The theory of the general will does not anticipate the conflicting agendas and aims of diverse interest groups. Nor does it show that the general will, if it is identified, can be implemented in a fair and reliable manner. Rousseau is strongly idealistic. He makes a valiant attempt to integrate individual and society in formal political theory, but he does not clearly recognize that imputing sovereignty to the general will inevitably restricts some individuals' interests and rights.

Hobbes advocates the idea of a sovereign-oriented social contract to control human selfishness and organize civil society. Addressing the authoritarian implications of this analysis, both Locke and Rousseau formulate versions of political organization based on the importance of the popular will. They differ, however, with respect to the significance of the values of property and equality, and thus on the question of whether the highest rights of individuals are economic or social. These differences lead to important philosophical positions on the role of the state. We now turn to examine ways in which the fundamental issues of economic rights and social rights underlie political ideologies and debates about the role of government within American society.

ECONOMIC VALUES AND SOCIAL VALUES IN THE AMERICAN BUSINESS ENVIRONMENT

Thomas Jefferson's philosophy provides a useful point of departure for considering the evolution of both economic individualism and social individualism in the United States. Jefferson's view of the limited role of government, which later establishes one important framework for public-private relationships, closely parallels Locke's. Jefferson's thinking regarding the functions and purposes of government is conveyed, for example, in his first presidential inaugural address. Consistent with Locke's notion of limited government, Jefferson states:

> What more is necessary to make us a happy and prosperous people? . . . a wise and frugal government, which shall restrain men from injuring one another, which shall leave them otherwise free to regulate their own

pursuits of industry and improvement, and shall not take from the mouth of labor the bread it has earned. This is the sum of good government.[10]

Jefferson shares Locke's antipathy to centralized power, specifically the federal government. Jefferson is not simply an anti-Federalist, however. Within the scope of his background, which includes acceptance of the institution of slavery, he was also committed to education and to the full realization of individual development. Historian Robert McCloskey describes this philosophy:

> The Jeffersonian theory of democracy was rooted in spiritual and humane, rather than material and economic, values.... When he used the term "liberty," the early democrat meant, first of all, freedom of conscience— moral liberty—rather than freedom of business enterprise. His chief interest, in short, was in the right of the individual to realize his moral personality, and not the right to buy and sell and prosper economically.[11]

In this respect, Jefferson adds a humane dimension, absent in the Lockean view, to the American vision of a good society.

The extremely important concept of "moral liberty" is highly ambiguous. To a great extent, evolution of social individualism has been a process of imbuing this notion with specific meaning. In general, moral liberty has come to imply support for society's less powerful and disfranchised persons and the desire that each person's opportunities for personal dignity should not be impaired by economic inequity. Ironically, America would later endorse an active role for government—a role that Jefferson would have opposed—in pursuit of the moral ideals he espoused.

Thus, two basic values, limited government and moral liberty, formed the Jeffersonian vision of society in the first several decades of the nineteenth century. At this time, the United States was a small country with an agrarian economy and a stable social structure. As the nation grew in population, size, ethnic and racial diversity, and economic strength, the Jeffersonian values of limited government and moral liberty would come to be experienced as being less and less compatible with each other and would come to define separate bases for conflicting notions of individualism.

❖ The Emergence of Economic Individualism

Jefferson was most directly opposed by Alexander Hamilton, a strong Federalist and an advocate of banking and manufacturing. As the country's first secretary of the treasury, Hamilton promoted a strong national commitment to economic development, including a national bank, protective tariffs for industry, and the assumption of the states' debts by the federal government. Hamilton must have bristled when

Jefferson asserted in his inaugural address that commerce is the "hand-maid" of agriculture.[12] Nonetheless, much of Hamilton's program, highly favorable to commercial interests, was eventually enacted into law in the early nineteenth century.

As the Jeffersonian ideals of an agrarian economy, moral liberty, and limited government formed the national consensus in the early decades of the nineteenth century, the growth of commerce and industry created forces for social and political change. By the 1830s, an expanding and prosperous business class, often in conflict with agrarian interests, was encouraging a realignment of political views.

Andrew Jackson was the leader of a populist movement, based mainly in the West, that was opposed to national policies that favored commercial interests. Populist President Jackson's veto of the renewal of the charter of the Second National Bank, for example, was based on western and rural citizens' mistrust of industry and of eastern business. In the context of populist influence on public policy, business leaders began to rethink their Hamiltonian belief in the beneficence of government. Populist hostility, and a better developed industrial base than in the early days of the republic, led business to divorce itself from public sponsorship. Historian Arthur Schlesinger comments:

> The politics of the Jackson period was in consequence a traumatic experi-
> ence for businessmen. The result was to make business reconsider the
> whole mercantilist assumption that positive government was a good thing.
> In the new economic context, businessmen no longer saw an economic need
> for governmental activism. Under the stern eye of Jackson, they began to
> discern a belated charm in the Jeffersonian proposition that the government
> was best which governed least.[13]

Political realignments within the emerging industrial state fused the ingredients of contemporary economic individualism: private property, voluntary market-based transactions, and minimal government.

We would be remiss to ignore the role in economic development played by the Supreme Court under the leadership of John Marshall in the first 30 years of the nineteenth century. The Marshall Court clarified issues that the Constitution left ambiguous in ways that fostered economic liberties and a national economy. For example, the Constitution does not explicitly give the Supreme Court power to review national legislation and to void it when necessary. The famous 1803 *Marbury* v. *Madison* case established judicial review of national legislation, a power that was later used to declare business regulation unconstitutional.[14] The finding that the Constitution gives the federal government other powers not specifically designated within it was also instrumental, for example, in validating the legality of the First National Bank of the United States.[15] Finally, where state powers and private property rights were contested, the Marshall Court firmly established the priority of property rights.[16]

These and other decisions shaped a favorable institutional context, consisting of broad powers of the national government and strong individual economic rights, for the emergence of commerce. The states' economic powers were reduced in relation to both the national government and private business activities.

❖ The Emergence of Social Individualism

Populism was focused on the "common man" and sought to reform a system perceived to favor vested interests. Populists wanted to abolish property requirements for voting and for holding office, and they implemented the first limits on terms of office. They also advocated and obtained the selection of presidential electors by the people rather than by state legislators. Populism dignified the individual person by seeking to reduce the political power of commercial interests and by carrying out social and economic reform. Political historian Richard Heffner summarizes the purposes and programs of the populists in this way:

> Determined to cleanse and purify the national life, they enthusiastically devoted their energies to such varied causes as free public education, women's rights, abolitionism, temperance, and the care of criminals and of the insane. With the steady growth of industry in the Northeast the labor movement also received an important impetus, for the squalor and impoverishment of the new urban working class were in striking contrast to contemporary ideals of equality and material well-being for all Americans.[17]

Populism was, fundamentally, a moral and social movement; populists paid specific attention to the people who were alienated from or left behind by the growth and prosperity of the commercial sector. Popular egalitarian sentiment in the 1820s and 1830s drew the attention of a French visitor, Alexis de Tocqueville, and caused him to wonder whether America's egalitarian impulse would bring the country close to disorder and ultimately to despotism, or whether civic spirit would stabilize the society.

❖ The Evolution of Economic Individualism and Social Individualism

Although the outlines of today's ideological polarity between economic individualism and social individualism were established by the latter half of the nineteenth century, economic individualism was the dominant, and virtually unchallenged, social value well into the twentieth century. In the last third of the nineteenth century and the first third of the twentieth, the United States was a major center of industrial innovation, manufacturing development, and economic growth. The nation had pushed to the west and had increased in population, and by the 1920s, it was one of the world's major powers. Increasing industrial and military strength and rising prosperity solidified the business creed—belief in the freedom to acquire and hold property; market-based pricing for capital, labor, and products; and reliance on oneself for economic success or failure.

The ideology of economic individualism draws inspiration from Locke's idea that personal freedom, understood to be the central purpose of society, is best ensured by property rights that limit the reach of government. This belief system grafts Hamilton's emphasis on economic growth and national economic strength onto Locke's declaration, and Jefferson's affirmation, of the merits of limited government.

Social individualism was a less dominant ideology throughout the period of America's rapid industrialization, territorial expansion, and movement onto the center stage of world power. In many respects, the nation's industrial development focused attention on the interests and claims of people who were not immediate beneficiaries of the growing corporate economy. Thus, the negative social consequences of industrialization in the late 1800s spawned the labor movement. Attention to the effects of many negative by-products of economic activity at the turn of the century, such as unsafe food and drugs, led to the growth of the Progressive movement and to the belief that the public sector could regulate, and in some cases supplant, the private economy. A changing society gave rise to the women's suffrage movement and a nascent civil rights movement. The increasing concentration of business resources in many sectors led to public attempts to regulate industrial structure and behavior, resulting in the development of antitrust law.

The various manifestations of social individualism arose largely in response to the nation's evident economic success. To this extent, social individualism grew up as a counterideology, drawing attention to the human consequences of industrial success, casting doubt on economic efficiency as the sole criterion of success, and seeking to increase the perceived fairness of the economic structure of society. The ideology of social individualism draws from Rousseau's belief that ensuring equality is the central purpose of civil society, and it finds inspiration in Jefferson's concern for the humane side of social experience, or what McCloskey calls moral liberty.

Because social individualism was in many respects a countermovement, measures enacted from this perspective required sacrifices from the beneficiaries of the economic status quo. Thus, workers' right to organize in unions and to bargain collectively represented concessions of power by employers. Similarly, social regulation of business, to promote public health or to counteract the threat of monopoly, represented attempts to alter business's existing liberties. As social individualism became more coherent, distinct, and powerful through the late eighteenth and early nineteenth centuries, a zero-sum relationship was established between economic values and social values: More of one meant less of the other.

As America entered the twentieth century, the ideological landscape was occupied by two political ideologies. Basic aspirations for personal political and economic freedom, incorporated into the design of the country's political institutions, characterized the dominant view. An appreciation for economic growth merged with the concept of limited government. An alternative ideology was being molded by the forces and the very successes of industrialization. More uncertain and less coherent, concerns about the fairness and social consequences of the industrial state emerged to compete with accepted premises.

The dominance of the economic rights perspective in this competition is illustrated by the reigning view at the time that the U.S. Constitution defines and defends economic rights. From approximately 1890 to the mid-1930s, for example, the Supreme Court consistently found state attempts to regulate the hours and conditions of work to be unconstitutional. Efforts to legislate in favor of the "general welfare," such as child labor laws or laws to improve women's working conditions, failed most of the time in conflict with the claims of economic liberty, such as freedom of contract, during a 40-year period of judicial conservatism.

❖ The Contemporary Interdependence of Political Ideologies

The period from the 1930s to the 1990s has seen a strengthening of both economic individualism and social individualism; each of these values has become more important and more imperative to society's well-being. Paradoxically, the two notions of individualism draw strength from each other, just as they limit each other. For example, industrialization induces expressions of social individualism:

The greater affluence of some people makes the poverty of others more evident.

The progress of technology exposes the risks of industrialization to public health and safety.

The benefits of industrial progress—greater mobility, affluence, and communication—heighten the social consciousness of women, blacks, and members of other historically subordinated groups.

The system of economic individualism produces conditions that strengthen aspects of social individualism. Social values are expressed in calls for public resources to correct the problems of poverty, illiteracy, crime, and drugs. Social individualism has also resulted in enormous increases in health, safety, and environmental regulation and intense controversy over civil rights.

Similarly, the importance of economic individualism grows as the values of social individualism are accommodated. Government intervention to alter social conditions and ensure the rights of disenfranchised groups has strengthened the arguments for economic rights. For example:

> As society has sought to redistribute and consume available resources, the ability to amass capital and thus to make investments that improve the standard of living becomes increasingly imperative.

> As governmental regulation of business is felt in virtually all aspects of economic activity, the desire for an unencumbered private sector grows stronger.

> As social investments make economic efficiency and innovation more precarious, the struggle of American industry to compete in world markets receives greater attention.

Arguments for economic individualism gain strength from society's commitment to social improvement just as economic success fortifies sentiment for responding to the opportunities and needs of social individualism.

❖ An Uneasy Tension Between the Two Notions of Individualism

The restructuring of institutions to achieve an ideal balance between economic individualism and social individualism is not easily accomplished. For example, the U.S. Constitution and its amendments, the nation's highest legal authority and most basic declaration of individual rights, ensure the right of contracts: the freedom of private parties to make binding agreements among themselves. This clause, in Article I, Section 10, appears to protect private economic freedom. At the same time, however, the Constitution empowers Congress to act for broad national interests by regulating interstate commerce. In doing so, Congress is bound to impinge on private contracts.

The Constitution gives government other powers that may restrain individual freedom. Article 1, Section 8, of the Constitution gives Congress power to provide for the "general welfare." In addition, the power of eminent domain—the ability of public authorities to buy or take private property—is an inherent power of government in the Constitution. Giving meaning to the vague "general welfare" surely involves restraints on some people's economic freedom. There will inevitably be disputes about the government's overreaching its powers and undermining economic freedom.

In the view of many Americans, impoverished life conditions limit some people's potential for experiencing dignity and freedom. In this view, improving the social aspect of personal freedom is an important national priority; however, pursuing this goal inevitably reduces some people's economic liberties. Just as some people envision that an ideal society would maximize economic freedom, others contend that the ideal society would enhance personal freedom by minimizing inequities in life conditions. Sociologist Nathan Glazer makes these observations on the dual nature of individualism in America:

> Two faces of individualism: the more rugged economic and institutional individualism of the United States, hampered and hobbled by a new kind of individualism devoted to self-realization, to the protection of the environment, to suspicion of big business and big organization. . . . Principally, the first kind has contributed to the most marked characteristic of the modern United States, its enormous productivity, while the second clearly places some limits on how this productivity may be realized. Both kinds are suspicious of government, but both are willing to enlist it. The first kind of individualism will enlist government to protect investments overseas, to foster economic growth and profits at home. The second will enlist it to achieve what is felt to be a fairer and more just society, and is relatively indifferent to the claims of production.[18]

American politics pivot on these two dimensions of individualism.

DEBATING THE MERITS OF ECONOMIC INDIVIDUALISM AND SOCIAL INDIVIDUALISM

❖ Philosophical Perspectives

The debate between economic individualism and social individualism takes place in many contexts, one important area being political philosophy. Over the last half-century, a number of conservative political theorists have articulated the reasons economic freedom is important to society. Taking their bearings from Lockean or Jeffersonian views on personal freedom and limited government, individual writers have put forth the following arguments: central planning is inconsistent with individual freedom;[19] state efforts to achieve specific social results or to legislate particular forms of behavior threaten individual liberty;[20] redistribution policies violate an important moral obligation of maximum personal autonomy;[21] and private markets are necessary to the maintenance of personal liberty and economic efficiency.[22] This group of writers sets forth a rationale and justification for the deep American suspicion of centralized public power.

Economist Arthur Okun describes the important contribution of economic liberty to political freedom in his analysis of American institutions and policy choices:

> A market economy helps to safeguard political rights against encroachment by the state. Private ownership and decision making circumscribe the power of the government—or, more accurately, of those who run the government—and hence its ability to infringe on the domain of rights. . . . It is

impressive that the history of nations with fully collectivized economies reveals not a single free election nor one free press.[23]

In this light, it is not surprising that nations in central Europe, as well as many of the states of the former Soviet Union, are going through parallel movements toward political democracy and market economies. It may be difficult to separate the longing for political freedom from the desire for improved standards of living, or to say that one could be achieved without the other.

Social individualists defend contemporary policies that are the legacy of Rousseau's egalitarianism and Jeffersonian morality. In *A Theory of Justice*, philosopher John Rawls justifies a strong government role in resource redistribution.[24] Rawls asks what principles of justice people would accept if removed from their self-oriented biases. To encourage objective thinking on this question, Rawls would ask each of us to decide on basic principles of justice in an "original position," that is, prior to the development of society. Rawls imagines that people would have to decide on principles of justice before they have knowledge of their individual talents, capacities, motives, interests, or attitudes. Behind such a "veil of ignorance," people would have no knowledge of the particular roles or positions they would ultimately assume in society, and they would be in a more objective position to agree on the principles of a just society.

Rawls argues that people behind a veil of ignorance would accept two basic social principles. First, he argues, not knowing their future roles in society, they would agree to unqualified equal rights—that is, no subordination by reason of gender, race, economic status, or other social distinction. Second, Rawls believes that, as a protection against being dealt a hand of impoverishment, people behind the veil would accept the principle that society's disadvantaged persons should also benefit from any action that improves the lot of the well-off. In other words, people in a just society should adopt policies of economic redistribution; the gap between the disadvantaged and the well-off should decrease as a function of continuing efforts of the well-off to improve their own situation.

❖ Constitutional Perspectives

The Supreme Court is a second area for contesting claims of economic individualism and social individualism. Social individualists expect the Court to protect individual persons against legislation that is unfavorable to the rights that are claimed under certain broad concepts, such as privacy.[25] Economic individualists, on the other hand, want the Court to protect individuals against legislation that reduces economic freedom.[26] The views of these two groups correspond to the general philosophical tension concerning the emphasis to be given to economic values and to social values.

Democracy entails conflicting aspirations. First, it is designed to allow national policy to reflect the will of the majority; second, it aspires to protect individual liberty, including that of the minority. The former objective dictates that matters should be determined by elected lawmakers; the latter objective argues to remove decisions from legislative bodies where majorities rule. The U.S. Constitution leaves the boundary between majority rule and minority rights unclear. In practice, the Supreme Court defines this boundary, so that the composition and the philosophical orientation of the Court become a vital political issue. The next sections delineate opposing views of constitutional interpretation that espouse differing priorities in the competition between individual rights and majority rule.

Social Rights The philosophy of "fundamental rights" holds that certain rights not specifically mentioned in the Constitution are nevertheless protected by that document. Such rights can be identified through observation of the conventional sense of social morality, through indications of social consensus, or through philosophical reasoning about the character of personal dignity and autonomy.[27] For example, this perspective finds justification for a general "right of privacy," even though these specific words are absent from the Constitution. One can defend the right to privacy only by understanding the actual words of the Constitution at a relatively high level of abstraction. Thus, a right to privacy, some argue, emanates from stated rights protecting a citizen against the quartering of soldiers without the citizen's consent, against unreasonable searches and seizures, and against self-incrimination.[28]

People who want the Supreme Court to discern social rights in the Constitution distrust the political process in these matters, believing that legislatures and the voting populace are sufficiently misinformed or misguided that such rights may well be subject to legislative abuse. For example, the right to die, the right to terminate a pregnancy, or the right of the accused to retain a public defender could be compromised or denied if the decision is left to legislative expressions of the perceived popular will. Thus, it falls to the Supreme Court to identify these rights in the Constitution or its first ten amendments, the Bill of Rights—to "constitutionalize" them—and thereby remove them from the legislative sphere.

Harvard law professor Laurence Tribe has reviewed various areas in which social rights were restricted legislatively by one or more states in 1961.[29] By 1986, each of these rights had been protected by a Supreme Court ruling. Tribe's list of rights issues includes the exclusion of women from jury duty, the prohibition of interracial marriage, the acceptance of federal wiretapping without a warrant or a reasonable basis to suspect wrongdoing, the use of illegally seized evidence to obtain convictions, the trial and imprisonment of poor people without defense attorneys, and the requirement that state-selected prayers be read in public schools. Each of these state practices was declared unconstitutional in a Supreme Court test between the early 1960s and the mid-1980s. Advocates of constitutional interpretation favoring social rights have urged the Court to fulfill aspirations expressed in such ideals as "human spirit" and "political integrity."[30] Such constitutional values, Tribe argues, "can be discerned and compared only by looking beyond the document's words."[31]

Economic Rights   Those advocating an interpretation of the Constitution favorable to economic rights also distrust legislative processes. In their view, special interests can exert disproportionate influence on the legislative process and its outcome. Laws that impose licensing requirements, product or marketing restrictions, or health and safety regulations inherently restrict economic activity and can often lead to inefficiency and a reduced ability to compete in the market.

Modern proponents of economic rights would have the Supreme Court review the "reasonableness" of economic regulation. For the first third of this century, economic liberties, such as freedom of contract, were interpreted to be constitutional rights that restrained state and federal legislatures' efforts to regulate economic activity in areas such as employee health legislation, for example. Many economic individualists would wish to reintroduce this approach, which was abandoned in the mid-1930s, when President Franklin Roosevelt changed the ideological composition of the Court. In their view, federal courts today leave too much power to regulate economic activity to the legislatures.[32]

The economic rights interpretation of the Constitution is grounded in the Constitution's stated commitment to property rights, and, as we have seen, property rights may be considered the foundation of personal freedom. Legal scholar Bernard Siegan argues this point:

> A free society cannot exist unless government is prohibited from confiscating private property. If government can seize something owned by a private citizen, it can exert enormous power over people. One would be reluctant to speak, write, pray, or petition in a manner displeasing to the authorities lest he lose what he has already earned and possesses.[33]

Conflict between economic rights and social rights is present in differing views on the substantive content of the Constitution as well as in social and political theory.

INDIVIDUALISM AND SOURCES OF RESTRAINT

Typically, the advocates of economic rights and of social rights prefer restraints on one another's liberties. Proponents of economic rights are often ready to support restrictions on individual action in social areas, and proponents of social rights are frequently willing to regulate economic behavior. Examples of each of these positions are readily available. In the regulation of employee health and safety, for instance, advocates of economic rights generally resist new restrictions on business activity. Especially in cases where knowledge about the health effects of working in manufacturing is incomplete, the economic perspective argues for deferring restraint, believing that the burden of proving the danger should lie with those proposing restrictions. In contrast, safeguarding human health is usually the prime consideration for social rights advocates. For them, companies should bear the burden of proving that their activities are safe. Private economic activity should be restrained, in this view, in order to maximize the personal welfare of persons at risk.

In other words, action in both the economic and the social spheres is seen not only as a positive right; the economic and social spheres of behavior are also potential areas of public restraint. Often, economic rights advocates are willing to regulate social behavior according to their view of community interests, and social rights advocates, based on a different view of community interests, readily accept restrictions on economic behavior.

The preferences that people express for economic values or social values as sources of freedom and of restraint roughly delineate their

Dominant Political Orientations Based on Preferences for Individual Freedom or Public Restriction vis-à-vis Economic and Personal Social Rights

		Social Rights	
		As Source of Individual Freedom	As Locus of Restraint on Individuals in the Interest of the Community
Economic Rights	As Source of Individual Freedom	**Libertarianism**	**Conservatism**
	As Locus of Restraint on Individuals in the Interest of the Community	**Liberalism**	**Communitarianism**

personal political ideologies. The accompanying table locates four major types of political and social ideologies on the basis of people's preference for the ways in which issues of freedom and restraint should be reconciled on economic and social questions.

As shown in the table, *libertarians* place individual rights above public restrictions on both economic values and social values. A political orientation is termed *communitarian* if it advocates that restraint, in the name of the community, is judged consistently more important than either economic rights or social rights.

The dominant political ideologies in the United States lie in the upper-right and lower-left quadrants of the table. *Conservatism*, one dominant ideology, generally allows that few social objectives, such as adjusting economic inequities, justify interference with economic liberty. On the other hand, social and community stability is often of concern to proponents of economic rights. If restrictions on freedom are ever justified, limits on personal social freedoms, such as limiting the number of appeals persons convicted of crimes can exercise, are a preferred means of preserving social order.

Liberalism, the second dominant contemporary ideology, views economic inequities as major sources of social injustice, and sees government control over economic activities as a way of enhancing social order. In this view, society should closely regulate corporate behavior and should preserve stability through economic redistribution and adequate public services. Political liberalism also generally favors expanding civil and personal social rights, such as the right to privacy.

No general scheme captures the detail and variety of political orientations or the alignment of political interests on specific issues. Many people undoubtedly perceive finer gradations of conservatism and liberalism than the general types identified in this scheme can suggest. These types are intended only to identify major tendencies, not particular individuals' beliefs. However, this analysis does lead to several conclusions regarding individualism and ideology in the United States. First, though virtually everyone in the United States favors "individualism" and "freedom," these terms mean different things to different people. In practice, differing emphases on economic liberties and social liberties characterize American political orientations, suggesting that there is less unanimity about "individualism" and "freedom" than popular images may convey.

A second conclusion is that each dominant American political ideology not only identifies positive rights but also implies a locus of restraint. Because every society represents a balance between freedom and order, and between individual and community, ideological assumptions about appropriate public restraint are as important as preferences for individual rights. Third, neither conservative ideology nor liberal ideology in the United States explains why the individual takes precedence over the community in one area of freedom and is subordinate to the community in another area. Only libertarianism and communitarianism are consistent approaches to relationships between individual and society, even though these approaches are more extreme and may be less practical. Perhaps the familiar conservative and liberal orientations in American politics represent the ways in which citizens manage to balance economic values and social values without resorting to extremism.

INTERDEPENDENCE BETWEEN ECONOMIC INDIVIDUALISM AND SOCIAL INDIVIDUALISM

The competing ideologies of economic individualism and social individualism pose alternative, "either-or," policy choices in the United States. But the reality is that economic development and social development benefit from one another's advances and ought not to be seen solely in ideological terms. Two contemporary cases in point are parental leave policy and the indexation of financial assets. The next two sections explore ways in which the interdependence between economic values and social values can be obscured by political ideology.

❖ Family and Medical Leave Legislation: A Social Issue with Economic Consequences

The United States has an enormous stake in the quality of the growing-up experiences of each generation of its youth. Unfortunately, according to available indices about the social experiences of many young Americans—adolescent violence, school failure, teenage pregnancy—this country is doing poorly. In *Within Our Reach*, social policy analyst Lisbeth Schorr discusses the extent of these problems and the cost to society as a whole that they impose.[34] She reviews a series of successful intervention programs that have dealt with children whose development is at risk due to poverty, inadequate prenatal and postnatal health care, the absence of family and social support, the presence of physical and psychological abuse, or the lack of adequate schooling. As a matter of long-term social well-being, Schorr argues for services to vulnerable families and children to avoid unplanned pregnancies, improve the quality and availability of care during pregnancy, enhance social support in infancy and during periods of family crisis, and improve education.

The quality of early childhood social experience stands out as an important predictor of later emotional development. Firsthand observations and long-term studies conclude that a connection with a caring adult early in life influences an individual's later ability to form healthy and productive relationships.[35] This concept of human development translates, in part, into a policy of parental and medical leave for employees.

From 1985 to 1991, Congress debated the merits and limitations of legislation concerning parental and medical leave for employees. Parental and medical leave legislation is an example of social individualism responding to human development—in this case, the challenges of creating healthy families in the context of changes in demography and in work force composition. Fifty million women, or 44 percent of the U.S. labor force, worked outside the home in the late 1980s.[36] Moreover, 57 percent of married women with preschool-age children were working, and a full 72 percent of married women with school-age children worked.[37] In addition, about 10 percent of the 1988 U.S. labor force consisted of women supporting families on their own.[38]

These facts suggest the unprecedented pressures on adults as both parents and employees, as well as on their children. Society has an interest in strong families, and, as summarized by Schorr, the involvement of parents early in a child's life is known to be extremely important to the child's subsequent social adjustment. This policy may be one way to reduce the stress of choosing between family and career and to indicate respect for the critical importance of the early years of a child's life. In relation to the magnitude of the problem, it would be a small but perhaps important part of a solution. All of the 12 member countries of the European Community, as well as Japan, have adopted national parental leave policies.[39]

In 1990, Congress passed the Family and Medical Leave Act, which would have covered full-time employees of companies with at least 50 employees. As written, this act permits up to 12 weeks of unpaid leave for an employee for the birth or adoption of a child or the care of a child or parent with a serious medical condition. The act prevents loss of benefits during the absence and requires reinstatement to the same position or an equivalent one upon return.

Estimates of direct costs to employers varied at that time. The General Accounting Office, a generally reliable source, estimated direct costs of $188 million per year for the first three years and $212 million after the third year, when coverage would expand to include companies with 35 employees.[40] Most of these costs would represent the continuation of benefits during the period of absence. Companies would also incur indirect costs, of course, in loss of flexibility, program administration, and the possible dissatisfaction among employees less likely to qualify for the benefit.

While increasing some of a firm's expenses, however, the act might actually save other costs. Without family and medical leave, companies incur the costs of recruiting and training replacements for employees who are terminated or who choose to resign rather than forgo the possibility of spending time with a young child or a sick relative at home. A study of more than 3,000 firms sponsored by the Small Business Administration concluded that the cost of replacing a managerial employee is roughly $3,250 and the cost of replacing a nonmanagerial employee is approximately $1,131 for a company with more than 100 employees.[41] These costs and the associated losses in productivity would be reduced substantially if employees were given unpaid leave instead of being replaced. As an additional consideration, some employees resigning from their positions in order to spend time at home would qualify for public assistance.

A study of 7,000 households estimated that a parental leave policy would save $108 million in additional public assistance expenditures.[42]

Parental leave has been a partisan issue in Congress. A number of representatives of health and child advocacy organizations, such as the Women's Legal Defense Fund, the American Federation of Teachers, the Older Women's League, and the American Federation of State, County and Municipal Employees, supported the proposed legislation.[43] On the other hand, a variety of organizations, including the National Association of Manufacturers, the National Federation of Independent Businesses, the National School Boards Association, and the Concerned Alliance of Responsible Employers, testified against the proposed legislation.[44] The issue reflected, in political terms, the biases of social individualism and economic individualism. In 1990, Congress passed the legislation, President George Bush vetoed the bill, and Congress failed to override the veto.

Economic individualists find the arguments for this legislation based on human development and the needs of a future work force to be vague and unconvincing. They argue that some companies would accrue specific costs today, while the promised benefits not only would lie years in the future but would be available to all firms. Among other objections, opponents of this legislation feel that it would place unreasonable economic burdens on employers that are trying to compete internationally and that it would be an unjustified intrusion by government into private economic affairs.

Overall, the ideological conflict over this bill seems more intense than the facts warrant. Corporate leaders often bemoan the lack of preparation and weak discipline of the American work force. The abilities of the work force are among the most critical issues in corporate competitiveness in the coming decade.[45] Even if the benefits of investment in the social development of future generations of citizens—today's infants—seem too far away and uncertain, business could at least perceive its stake in being able to retain competent, experienced workers who are also committed to caring for their young children. And while other companies would benefit from the costs a particular company incurred in this program, that company also would benefit from other companies' *earlier* investment in the program.

Parental leave, once again, represents a small commitment toward addressing a huge American social challenge. Nevertheless, estimates of direct private and public savings suggest that the economic benefits of parental leave outweigh its costs. In the name of economic freedom, traditional economic individualists apparently reject a policy that may actually be advantageous to business.

❖ The Indexation of Financial Assets: An Economic Issue with Social Consequences

In addition to human resources, the availability of capital affects the competitiveness of the U.S. economy. Improvements in productivity, innovation in products, and economic growth depend on an adequate supply of financial capital; and a low rate of personal savings in the United States has become a national competitive weakness. Americans typically save between 4 and 6 percent of the national income; savings rates are two to three times as high in industrialized European countries and three to four times as high in Japan. International competitiveness and economic growth are important because they increase employment opportunities, reduce the social expenditures associated with a stagnant economy, and allow greater public investment in the social infrastructure, including health and education.

One way to increase the savings rate in the United States may be to improve the real rate of return on financial assets. Inflation decreases the economic value of a financial asset and lowers its real rate of return. Marketing and financial consultant George Nastas provides the following example.[46] Let us say that a person is considering buying a $10,000 government bond that carries an actual rate of return of 8.5 percent. Suppose inflation is expected to run at 5 percent for the coming year. The investor is in the 33 percent federal tax bracket and pays another 4.6 percent in state income tax. At the end of the year, the investor has received $850 in interest payments and has to pay 37.6 percent in taxes (33 plus 4.6), or $319.60. However, 5 percent inflation has reduced the purchasing power of the bond by $500, which is a cost to the investor. Thus, the investor's total cost for the year is the $319.60 in taxes plus $500 in the purchasing power of the asset. The real gain to the investor is income minus cost—$850 minus $819.60, or $30.40. This represents a return of about .3 percent, hardly enough to encourage the investor to save the $10,000 rather than spend all or part of it.

Inflation also reduces the real rate of return on equity assets. Again, Nastas provides an example. Let us assume that an equity investment appreciates 50 percent over a five-year period, but inflation has also increased 30 percent in the same period. Currently, taxes are paid on the 50 percent appreciation, but the real gain to the investor is, of course, only 20 percent. Inflation increases the real rate of taxation and reduces the real return to the investor. The joint effects of inflation and taxation shorten the length of time during which investors are willing to hold equity assets and lead investors to demand higher potential returns in order to protect against future inflation. Such disincentives to investment reduce the supply of available capital.

Some policymakers propose to reduce the rate of taxation on capital gains in order to lessen investment disincentives. However, studies have not demonstrated that positive investment, economic growth, and increases in public revenue can result from the enactment of this proposal alone.[47] A more effective policy measure would diminish the effects of inflation on capital gains by prohibiting taxation on the portion of the increase in asset value that is due to inflation. An even stronger incentive would be to index all financial assets for inflation.

Indexation would, of course, measurably reduce public revenues until the revenue loss would be matched by revenue gains from the economic growth that would be stimulated by lower capital costs. Any such policy with substantial short-term consequences to revenue would have to be implemented in phases.

As with parental leave policy, ideological conflict inhibits movement toward a socially beneficial tax policy. Political liberals oppose tax changes as tax breaks for the wealthy that increase the income of holders of financial assets and imply short-term sacrifices in social programs. The promise of greater employment and increased future public revenues is too distant and indirect to muster liberal support for indexation policies. In the name of personal social freedom, social individualists may reject such policies that are advantageous to all Americans.

❖ The Implications of Polarized Values

The main reason for the severe challenges to the American economy may not be that the precepts of economic individualism are invalid, but that they are not sufficiently broad. A prosperous economic sector relies on high-quality and equitable educational systems and on health care services that provide and sustain the knowledge, skills, and attitudes that an advanced economy requires. The ideology of economic individualism gives little recognition to the role of social institutions in the creation of a favorable environment for economic pursuits, and this ideology pays little attention to the development of human abilities and of the social fabric necessary for the value of economic freedom to thrive.

Similarly, social individualism is insufficient as a stand-alone ideology. Social individualists rarely give recognition to the importance of the economic context of their values or to the contribution of a prosperous American economy to their aspirations. Social values, such as income redistribution, are often seen as absolute; rarely do advocates ask how economic growth enhances human needs. The nation's ability to convey additional social rights or to meet social needs at a higher level depends on its ability to generate greater economic resources. Recognition of the relationship between social needs and economic freedom should be part of a complete vision of social individualism. Our progress as a society may depend on emphasizing ways in which economic individualism and social individualism converge and reinforce each other rather than dwelling on their points of conflict and divergence.

ECONOMIC INDIVIDUALISM AND SOCIAL INDIVIDUALISM IN MANAGEMENT THEORY

❖ Economic Individualism

Modern economic theory provides a framework for understanding and explaining behavior in the business firm. The theory of the firm posits a positive impact of property rights on economic efficiency through the self-interested actions of owners and managers. In this view owner-ship rights in the for-profit corporation direct owners to obtain the most effective and efficient use of assets.[48] Exchangeable property also encour-ages efficiency by allowing the capitalization of expectations for the future into present decisions. The liquidity of ownership shares of the publicly held firm allows the market for corporate control to discipline top man-agers, who, according to this theory, are likely to lose their jobs if they fail to perform adequately and the firm's ownership changes. Property rights lead owners and managers to establish strong standards of efficiency for their own behavior and for that of their employees.

A second aspect of this theory analyzes the structure of the modern corporation from the standpoint of self-interest.[49] First, it is recognized that much corporate work calls for team production, that is, tasks involv-ing collaborative or joint effort. Under conditions of team production, one worker can be a free rider or shirker—that is, he or she does less than a full share of the work, with no reduction in compensation. It is also assumed that if a person can shirk, that person will shirk. Further, the theory states that few team members want to be "suckers" (workers who do not shirk even though others on the team are shirking), and thus the team's performance will be driven to the lowest level of self-oriented behavior. The economic theory of the firm makes the case that monitoring or supervision is needed in order to set and enforce standards for the performance of work involving joint production.

This view of economic behavior finds that managers who are also owners have natural incentives to be efficient supervisors. However, as owners decide to hire professional managers to direct and supervise, profit-dependent mechanisms, such as bonuses, are needed to align a manager's interests with those of owners and to ensure that managers remain efficient monitors of production. Consequently, this explanation of the superior efficiency of the for-profit corporation, the firm's organiza-tional structure, and the function of management is based on two rather simple assumptions: that human beings are motivated purely by material self-interest, and that a system of property rights, that is, owners' claims to the economic results of the firm's activities, is legally enforced.

Organizational sociologist Charles Perrow presents a forceful cri-tique of this view of the firm in *Complex Organizations: A Critical Essay*.[50] Perrow argues that employees are as willing to express trust, reciprocity, and "other-regarding" behavior[51] as they are willing to shirk. The behav-ioral repertoire of most people includes both types of action, and most organizations exhibit both. Perrow suggests that specific conditions within the organization, such as the way work is organized, the measure-ment of performance, the reward systems, and the opportunities for human interaction, will induce more of one kind of behavior or the other.

Perrow also observes that the economic theory of the firm treats the question of shirking from only one perspective. He points out that managers themselves may be no less prone than workers to free-ride on the efforts of others. Employees, communities, and the taxpaying public have already absorbed the cost of special advantages to the owners and managers of a number of financial institutions, such as savings and loans, that have either failed or suffered significant losses in reputation and market share in recent years. By neglecting the possibility of shirking by managers, according to Perrow, proponents of the economic theory of the firm unwittingly reveal hierarchical and managerial biases.

❖ Social Individualism

The ideology of social individualism also reaches into organization and management theory. For example, Patricia Werhane and Michael Keeley propound a moral view of organizations that stresses personal social rights.[52,53] Werhane argues that individual persons, because they have the unique ability to make self-conscious choices, analyze their own actions, act rationally, and affect the interests of others, are moral agents of the highest standing. Organizations have secondary moral standing because they lack the unique qualities of persons. Based on her premises, Werhane advocates the formalization in law of a variety of employee rights, such as the right to retain one's job unless the employer can demonstrate just cause for dismissal.

Keeley places organizations even lower on a scale of moral status. For him, organizations are simply "sets of agreements for satisfying diverse, individual interests."[54] Individuals, on the other hand, have intrinsic worth. Keeley finds that asymmetrical institutional power between workers and managers permits a distribution of costs and benefits that is inconsistent within the framework of personal rights. He argues, for example, that a number of manufacturing plants have been closed unnecessarily and that concessions have been negotiated from workers at times simply because society, in a morally indefensible manner, has given managers disproportionate rights to act upon their self-defined goals for corporations. The established institutional system allows managers to take advantage of workers' weaker rights in spite of the workers' greater moral claim. Keeley favors legislation to strengthen the rights of workers and communities in order to redress the imbalance and to ensure a more just distribution of the costs and benefits of corporate decisions. In this view the primary responsibility of managers is "to facilitate agreements on institutional rights and procedures that respect the human rights of *all* participants."[55]

❖ Implications of the Divergence of Economic Individualism and Social Individualism

Proponents of both economic individualism and social individualism view organizations as contractual systems; however, differing emphases on the property rights and the moral rights of individuals lead to contrasting views of the structure of organizations and the roles of managers.

There may be a conflict over power at the root of differences between economic and social theories of the firm. The economic theory of the firm relegates workers to the position of victims of their own inclination to shirk; the whole system is saved by property rights and the profit motive. Managerial thinking often follows the assumptions of economic individualism. On the other hand, social individualism is an ideological underdog, and social individualists, including Werhane and Keeley, explicitly bid to redress the imbalance of organizational power. Management theory does not benefit from mirroring the wider society's polarized ideological conflict over power.

Organizations, like all social systems, are composed of distinct, but interdependent, persons, groups, functions, and roles. Although the various elements can been seen and experienced separately, rarely will the parts survive if the organization does not work well as a whole. Managers must seek to enhance cooperation between the parts and the whole; this means that each person and group also must see its success in the success of others. The task of management is to avoid debilitating zero-sum processes.

Theories that encourage managers to view the organization from only one perspective serve them poorly. Managers are well advised to reflect closely on the implicit or explicit presence of the ideologies of economic individualism and social individualism in their assumptions, perceptions, and actions. The task is to manage organizations in a way that utilizes several dimensions of individualism and, above all, strengthens both economic and social motives and the forms of behavior resulting from these motives.

A CONCLUDING PERSPECTIVE

Hobbes's social contract was a conceptual innovation that showed people how they might overcome the debilitating consequences of narrow, parochial interests. The essence of this social contract is taken for granted today, for the majority of citizens accept the legitimacy of political authority as necessary for a stable society. What has evolved, however, is a pair of entirely different meanings for the notion of social contract. One interpretation derives from Locke's orientation toward liberty. In this view, economic or property rights are a particularly important representation of and defense for liberty. The other interpretation derives from Rousseau's view that democracy should, above all else, resolve social inequities. Strong ideological differences persist within the broad agreement about the supreme importance of the individual and the legitimacy of democratic government.

In this chapter I have argued that the conflict between economic individualism and social individualism is, in reality, not as conclusive, definitive, or final as political positions on policy questions would have it appear. In fact, an examination of specific issues, such as parental leave and the indexation of financial assets, suggests that, in the long term, economic benefits and social benefits contribute positively to one another. To the extent that corporations are influenced by competing concepts of individualism, it is likely that these organizations will fail to realize the maximum development of available human energy and capacities. Members of organizations who define their interests in terms of the prerogatives of either economic rights or social rights are almost certain to meet with opposition from those with opposing views and thus to end up forgoing opportunities for mutual gain.

The problem in both a political and an organizational sense, is that too few persons speak for an integrative perspective. It is much more familiar, and more natural, to identify one's immediate personal situation more closely with one ideology or the other, and to see the world from its perspective. Accepting a new social contract could expand the limits of our existing definitions of individualism, much as Hobbes's social contract showed that individuals could rise above narrow personal interests. In the notion of a social contract, Hobbes proposed a new understanding of the meaning of government, a concept shaped and modified and ultimately incorporated into society as the idea of democracy. This development of ideas and institutions proved enormously productive as a way of unifying people, while also opening wide spheres of action for the individual expression of abilities and desires.

American society may now have come to a point of excessive partisanship, in which the inherent limitations of each ideology undermine the potential for positive synergies between them. Capitalism and democracy are both constructed on the willingness of all persons to concede some immediate interests for the sake of stable and strong institutions. Integrating self and society is far from an unfamiliar experience in the United States; rather, it is an underacknowledged essence of American institutions. One solution to this country's policy dilemmas is to incorporate full appreciation of the economic and social bases of successful institutions into existing ideologies. The result would be that each view of individualism would broaden its scope, value the future more strongly, and explicitly emphasize points of interdependence between economic values and social values. This perspective would require, however, that we abandon the familiar and secure polarization between the ideologies of economic individualism and social individualism.

[1]Thomas Hobbes, *Leviathan* (1965), reprinted as *Hobbes's Leviathan* (Oxford: Clarendon Press, 1909).

[2]Michael Lessnoff, *Social Contract* (Atlantic Highlands, N.J.: Humanities Press International, 1986).

[3]John Locke, *Two Treatises of Government* (1698), reprinted with introduction by Peter Laslett, 2nd. ed. (Cambridge: University Press, 1967).

[4]C. B. Macpherson, *The Political Theory of Possessive Individualism: Hobbes to Locke* (Oxford: Clarendon Press, 1973), pp. 88–89.

[5]John W. Gough, *John Locke's Political Philosophy* (Oxford: Clarendon Press, 1973), pp. 88–89.

[6]Jean-Jacques Rousseau, *The Social Contract* and *Discourse on the Origin and Foundation of Inequality Among Mankind*, ed. Lester G. Crocker (New York: Washington Square Press, 1967).

[7]Virginia Held, "Mothering versus Contract," in *Beyond Self-Interest*, ed. Jane J. Mansbridge (Chicago: University of Chicago Press, 1990), p. 291.

[8]Rousseau, *Social Contract*, pp. 80–81.

[9]Ibid., pp. 17–18.

[10]Thomas Jefferson, "Jefferson's First Inaugural Address, 1801," in *A Documentary History of the United States*, 4th ed., ed. Richard D. Heffner (New York: New American Library, 1985), p. 74.

[11]Robert G. McCloskey, *American Conservatism in the Age of Enterprise* (Cambridge, Mass.: Harvard University Press, 1951), pp. 2–3.

[12]Jefferson, "Jefferson's First Inaugural," p. 75.

[13]Arthur M. Schlesinger, Jr., "Ideas and Economic Development," in *Paths of American Thought*, eds. Arthur M. Schlesinger, Jr., and Martin White (Boston: Houghton Mifflin, 1963), pp. 114–115.

[14]*William Marbury* v. *James Madison*, Secretary of State of the United States, 5 U.S. 137 (1803).

[15]*McCulloch* v. *State of Maryland*, 17 U.S. 316 (1819).

[16]*The Trustees of Dartmouth College* v. *Woodward*, 17 U.S. 518 (1819).

[17]Hefner, ed., *A Documentary History*, p. 92.

[18]Nathan Glazer, "Individualism and Equality in the United States," in *On the Making of Americans: Essays in Honor of David Riesman*, ed. Herbert J. Gans, Nathan Glazer, Joseph R. Gusfield, and Christopher Jencks (Philadelphia: University of Pennsylvania Press, 1979), p. 32.

[19]Ludwig von Mises, *Human Action: A Treatise on Economics* (New Haven, Conn.: Yale University Press, 1949), and *Planning for Freedom* (South Holland, Ill: Libertarian Press, 1952).

[20]Frederick A. Hayek, *The Constitution of Liberty* (Chicago: University of Chicago Press, 1960).

[21]Robert Nozick, *Anarchy, State and Utopia* (New York: Basic Books, 1968).

[22]Milton Friedman, *Capitalism and Freedom* (Chicago: University of Chicago Press, 1962).

[23]Arthur M. Okun, *Equality and Efficiency: The Big Tradeoff* (Washington, D.C.: Brookings Institution, 1975), pp. 38, 40.

[24]John Rawls, *A Theory of Justice* (Cambridge, Mass.: Belkap Press, 1971).

[25]For example, Laurence H. Tribe, "The Constitution in the Year 2011," *Pacific Law Review*, 18 (1987), pp. 343–349; Ronald Dworkin, *Taking Rights Seriously* (Cambridge, Mass.: Harvard University Press, 1978); and "Law's Ambition for Itself," *Virginia Law Review*, 71, no. 2 (March, 1985), pp. 173–187.

[26]For example, Bernard H. Siegan, *Economic Liberties and the Constitution* (Chicago: University of Chicago Press, 1980); R. Pilon, "Legislative Activism, Judicial Activism and the Decline of Private Sovereignty," *Cato Journal*, 4, 3 (Winter, 1985), pp. 813–833; Calvin A. Kent, "Constitutional Economics," *Baylor Business Review* (Fall 1987), pp. 12–18.

[27]Paul Brest, "The Fundamental Rights Controversy: The Essential Contradictions of Normative Constitutional Scholarship," *The Yale Law Journal*, 90 (1981), pp. 1063–1109.

[28]See, for example, *Griswold et al.* v. *Connecticut*, 381 U.S. 479 (1965).

[29]Tribe, "The Constitution," p. 346.

[30]"The Law's Ambition."

[31]Tribe, "The Constitution," p. 345.

[32]Siegan, *Economic Liberties*.

[33]Ibid., p. 83.

[34]Lisbeth B. Schorr, *Within Our Reach: Breaking the Cycle of Disadvantage* (New York: Doubleday Anchor Books, 1989).

[35]Ibid., 142–150.

[36]U.S. House of Representatives, Committee on Education and Labor, Hearing on H.R. 770. "The Family and Medical Leave Act of 1989," February 7, 1989, 101–2, p. 4.

[37]George L. Stelluto and Deborah P. Klein, "Compensation Trends into the 21st Century," *Monthly Labor Review* (February 1990), p. 41.

[38]Ibid., p. 42.

[39]Kinney Zalesne, "Babies: U.S., European Approaches to Parental Leave," *Europe* (October 1988), p. 30.

[40]U.S. House of Representatives, Hearing on H.R. 770, p. 10.

[41]Eileen Trzcinski and William T. Alpert, *Leave Policies in Small Business: Findings from the U.S. Small Business Administration Employee Leave Survey* (Washington, D.C.: U.S. Department of Commerce, October 1990), p. 44.

[42]Roberta M. Spalter-Roth and Heidi I. Hartmann, *Unnecessary Losses: Costs to Americans of the Lack of Family and Medical Leave* (Executive Summary) (Washington, D.C.: Institute for Women's Policy Research, 1988), p. 5.

[43]U.S. House of Representatives, Hearing on H.R. 770.

[44]Ibid.

[45]Ibid., p. 83.

[46]George Nastas 3d, "Why Limit Indexing to Capital Gains?" *New York Times* September 30, 1990, p. E21.

[47]Herbert Stein, "Taxing Capital Gains," *Society* (March/April 1990), pp. 63–70.

[48]Armen A. Alchian, "Corporate Management and Property Rights," in *Economic Policy and the Regulation of Corporate Securities*, ed. H. Manne (Washington, D.C.: American Enterprise Institute for Public Policy Research, 1969); Eugene F. Fama and Michael C. Jensen, "Separation of Ownership and Control," *Journal of Law and Economics*, 26 (June 1983), pp. 301–325; Michael C. Jensen and William H. Meckling, "Theory of the Firm: Managerial Behavior, Agency Costs and Ownership Structure," *Journal of Financial Economics*, 3, 4 (October 1976), pp. 305–360.

[49]Armen A. Alchian and Harold Demsetz, "Production, Information Costs, and Economic Organization," *American Economic Review*, 62, 5 (1972), pp. 777–795.

[50]Charles Perrow, *Complex Organizations: A Critical Essay*, Third ed., (New York: Random House, 1986).

[51]Ibid., p. 231.

[52]Patricia H. Werhane, *Persons, Rights and Corporations* (Englewood Cliffs, N.J.: Prentice Hall, 1985).

[53]Michael Keeley, *A Social-Contract Theory of Organizations* (Notre Dame, Ind.: University of Notre Dame Press, 1988).

[54]Ibid., p. 12.

[55]Ibid., p. 19.

Alienation, Apathy, and the Role of Self-Interest in American Democracy

❖❖❖❖❖

Chapter 4 addresses the conflict between economic individualism and social individualism in the content of public policy. This chapter focuses on the process of political influence—how public policy content is decided. Our concern here is with the role of self-interest in the formulation of American public policy. In general, we address the apparent disenchantment of the American public with politics and examine some proposals to change the ways in which political influence is exercised.

In 1987 and 1990, the Times Mirror organization published results of its public opinion surveys of Americans' attitudes toward politics and government.[1] The surveys indicate a disturbing degree of cynicism about politics among Americans. For example, 57 percent of respondents agreed "completely" or "mostly" that "people like me don't have any say about what the government does."[2] The public expressed considerable skepticism even toward voting, the defining characteristic of democracy. The proportion of people agreeing that "voting gives some people like me [a] say about how government runs things" decreased from 78 percent in 1987 to 73 percent in 1990.[3]

The current low rate of participation in electoral politics correlates with such negative attitudes. Of the just two thirds of all voting-age Americans who were registered to vote in the presidential election of 1988, only 50.2 percent of those persons actually voted.[4] The 1988 election was marked by the smallest percentage of persons voting for president in more than 50 years. Moreover, only 33 percent of eligible voters voted in the congressional elections of 1990.[5] Voting apparently fails as a meaningful form of political involvement for a majority of Americans.

Americans' answers to other questions in the Times Mirror surveys further demonstrate public pessimism about the responsiveness of those elected to national offices. For example, a full 78 percent of respondents agreed with the statement, "Generally speaking, elected officials in Washington lose touch with the people pretty quickly."[6] The 1990 results were consistently three to five percentage points less favorable than the 1987 results on a number of identical questions about political involvement.

Attitudes measured by opinion surveys, and the associated behavior of voters, may be susceptible to a number of contextual factors—the general economic environment, America's role in international events, or internal political change. The May 1990 Times Mirror study, for example, took place before Iraq's invasion of Kuwait and before the successful U.S.-led international effort to free Kuwait, an event that generated considerable patriotism in America. In addition, the study followed several years of political controversy and scandal in Washington, D.C.; extensive publicity about the Reagan administration's arms-for-hostages deals, which covertly and illegally supplied the Nicaraguan contras; the resignations of Democratic Party leaders Jim Wright and Tony Coelho from Congress following conflict-of-interest charges; and growing awareness of the role of special-interest politics in the savings and loan industry crisis. Both Times Mirror surveys occurred before revelations concerning special privileges of U.S. representatives, including the ability to write checks against negative account balances at an exclusive House bank and to have parking tickets dismissed. Fred Wertheimer, president of the citizens' lobby Common Cause, reported that Common Cause had found sufficient reason to request Ethics Committee investigations of 15 members of Congress between 1987 and 1990.[7]

A study sponsored by the Kettering Foundation in 1991, based on group interviews with a cross section of Americans in ten cities, confirmed many of the statistical findings of the Times Mirror surveys.[8] Americans expressed serious disenchantment with national politics. They felt alienated from political decision making because of special-interest groups, powerful lobbyists, political action committees, and negative media coverage. They experienced frustration, anger, cynicism, and a sense of impotence.[9] Americans interviewed in this study did report a discrepancy between their alienation from national politics and their connection to local projects and citizen action programs. Four of the ten groups in the Kettering project met and were interviewed after the Persian Gulf War early in 1991; the researchers found that the national feeling engendered by the war had little effect on respondents' attitudes toward the political process.

Part of the reason for the public's feeling of alienation from government decision making may be found in the failure of the U.S. savings and loan industry. The effort to rescue this industry will cost American taxpayers between $300 billion and $500 billion over several decades. This enormous sum is being incurred only to avoid financial havoc; it has no redeeming positive value whatsoever as a public investment. The S&L crisis is attributable solely to the workings of the American political system.

How it happened tells us something about the way the political system functions. To begin with, for many years a federal deposit insurance program had supported a stable and prosperous home-financing industry and protected savers by preventing defaults by S&Ls. Historically, these banks had been closely regulated in terms of the rates of interest they could pay on deposits and the types of loans they could make.

Financial institutions faced new and intensified competition for capital in the early 1980s. In order to allow S&Ls to compete for capital, Congress abandoned the regulation of interest rates, and regulatory agencies removed many investment restrictions on S&Ls. Congress also acted to give additional protection to depositors in the new competitive environment by doubling insurance coverage on each account to $100,000. With new freedom to invest widely, S&L owners had the chance to seek high returns. Meanwhile, the deposit insurance program immunized them against losses. The potential for handsome returns and the ability to avoid losses created a climate for excessive risk taking. Deregulation also reduced the public budgets for supervising and auditing S&Ls, and reduced surveillance increased the chances that illegal transactions might go undetected. The industry environment already encouraged excessive risk taking; relaxed auditing occasionally facilitated the extension of risk taking into embezzlement and fraud.

Deposit insurance, market competition for investment, and deregulation are, separately, legitimate instruments of public policy. Each is a powerful idea about the public interest. When combined in the context of the S&L industry, however, they generated perverse incentives.

As the S&L crisis was propelled into the public's awareness in the early 1990s, attention focused on examples of political influence-buying by industry executives. Wide publicity surrounded Jim Wright's resignation as Speaker of the House and a Senate committee investigation into the activities of five senators, the "Keating Five," who had intervened with regulatory agencies to relax application of the rules of good financial management toward Charles Keating's Lincoln S&L. This publicity shed light onto the roles of campaign finance, lobbying, personal ethics, and congressional intervention in the regulatory process. The picture of policymaking that emerged from these hearings was not pretty. Although no member of Congress was charged with illegal conduct in the Keating S&L affair, such political intervention on behalf of S&Ls increased the magnitude and eventual cost of the bailout. The political system had defended and perpetuated unwise and costly policies.

The ability of parochial interests to influence policies that are unwise from a public perspective may not be limited to the savings and loan situation. The U.S. budget, which passes massive costs on to future generations, includes many special-interest claims, leading to a chronic deficit. The political process has also crafted a highly expensive, and embarrassingly inequitable, health care system. Nor can one place much confidence in the political system on the basis of this country's fragmented and incoherent energy policy.

The savings and loan fiasco and other apparent examples of the influence of special interests have produced broad-based criticism of the role of excessive self-interest in American politics. In part, Americans' political alienation may result from the ability of special interests to deflect Congressional attention away from what many people consider the general welfare of society. Unwise and expensive policies, policy paralyzed by standoffs between opposite political forces, and conflicts of interest among elected officials repel many Americans; and the task of overcoming such problems often appears hopeless, leading many people to say they have little influence on government.

The problem of social decision making is not trivial; the challenge is to arrive at an acceptable version of the public welfare from a system based on an array of individual preferences. Another task is to sustain the confidence and participation of the public in a large, diverse society where each person's influence is inherently limited and where some people may abuse positions of trust.

Society as a whole does not agree on the role of self-interest in public affairs. Some people feel that excessive self-interest undermines the integrity of government. Others argue that policy decisions are unrepresentative because many citizens fail to express their interests politically. The latter view implies that policy decisions would improve if self-interest were stronger. Individualistic American society exhibits surprising confusion over the role of self-interest in political affairs.

Problems of the American political system are discussed in several sections of this chapter. First, we will argue against the view that emphasis on self-interest within the political process, per se, lies at the heart of citizens' political alienation. The drawbacks of private interest in public affairs are well stated in theory, and they are evident in practice; yet democracy would not work without strong expressions of individual and group interests. Moreover, evidence that public-spiritedness does exist among citizens and elected officials suggests that there is a need for more citizen involvement in public questions.

Second, we support the popular view that the political action committee system of campaign finance is dysfunctional as an instrument of democracy. The PAC system was created a scant 20 years ago. There is strong evidence that the rules of campaign finance far too often direct the attention of the elected representatives of the people to special interests and thus run contrary to the spirit of democratic politics.

Third, we argue that citizen apathy is a major cause of political alienation. If the laws of campaign finance distort political decisions, public apathy alters democracy itself. Proposals to limit the terms of service of congresspersons are attempts to compensate for political apathy by doing legislatively what the voters appear unwilling to do for themselves—turn incumbents out of office. Limiting length of service involves a paradox: It tries to make the political system more responsive by making it less democratic. Democracy allows citizens the choice of being uninvolved, but to be uninvolved is to undermine the opportunity for choice. People who are discontented with the political system should address the fundamental issue of apathy rather than the superficial issue of incumbency.

Finally, we evaluate whether the political movement toward decentralization of government in the United States—moving decisions away from Congress and the federal courts and toward local and state legislative bodies—increases political participation and reduces citizen apathy. Evidence indicates that the debate over decentralization is independent of the problem of citizen apathy. Although government may need to decentralize certain functions, evidence to date does not suggest that this will remedy the problem of political alienation. It appears, rather, that remedies will have to arise from changes in people's values and in their level of political involvement.

POLITICAL SELF-INTEREST: TOO MUCH OR TOO LITTLE?

The view that self-interest motivates citizens and elected officials has gained substantial currency in political theory over recent decades. A vast accumulation of writing has documented the role of self-interest in public institutions and policy decisions. Self-interest theories are intricate, elaborate, and often highly abstract. Scholars working from this perspective present a skeptical view, at best, of the prospects for public behavior; often, they are outright cynical. The self-interest theory, represented best by the term *public choice*, views the moral basis of society pessimistically: People are willing to exploit others for personal benefit; therefore, we should minimize the number of decisions that are made in the political arena where some people will always be able to capture others' income. Decisions, in this view, should be left in the realm of economic action where self-interest pursuits are thought to generate social benefit.

The literature on public choice views individuals as rational decision makers interested in maximizing their personal preferences. All actions, such as the gathering of information on issues and candidates, have associated cost. Because the cost of obtaining information is high for the typical voter, studying political behavior involves analysis of how people act when they have incomplete information. Individual behavior results from rational consideration of expected costs of and returns from different courses of action, under conditions of imperfect information.

Anthony Downs's *An Economic Theory of Democracy* stands as a landmark in the application of the paradigm of rational decision making to political affairs.[10] Using the concept that people maximize their personal self-interest, Downs assumes that political actors seek solely to obtain the benefits of power, prestige, and income that come with public office, and that policies are only means by which to attain private ends. Downs claims that elections are not won in order to implement policies; rather, policies are formulated in order to win elections.[11]

Private economic markets are efficient because investment projects have to compete with one another on the basis of their marginal economic contributions. However, because votes are more widely distributed in society than is income, officials' efforts to secure votes lead, according to Downs, to the "Robin Hood" function of government. Government officials make public investment decisions on the basis of the contribution of those decisions to electoral support. Consequently, it is rational for governments to be inefficient, that is, to carry out many projects with low utility to the society as a whole.[12]

Some observers have extrapolated from their assumptions regarding selfish human behavior to explain and predict the growth of government, especially in the protection of the environment, in public health, and in public safety. Politicians, for example, are seen as creating a demand for government services that allows them to expand their own wealth and power.[13] In this perspective, public choice analysis leads to the conclusion that "political activists confiscate wealth."[14]

❖ Private Benefits, Public Costs

Downs sets forth the guiding principle that "rational behavior [is] directed primarily towards selfish ends."[15] Surely, evidence of this principle is not hard to identify. Many instances of everyday behavior illustrate the ways in which people benefit privately and spread the costs onto society. It is convenient for me to toss my soft-drink cup into the street, even though doing so imposes a littered street on others in the area. I exceed the positive side of personal choice when I foist the cost of my private interest, whether material gain or simple convenience, onto the community. A society cannot sustain itself for very long without a modicum of cooperation, a minimum of sensitivity to the interests of others.

Examples of self-promoting behavior at public expense are plentiful in the American experience. For example, a federal government policy allows tobacco companies to buy surplus tobacco at discount prices while the government pays tobacco farmers higher prices in order to "stabilize" their income.[16] One program alone cost the public between $660 million and $900 million over eight years.[17] As we can see in the choices of the political system, the American public has been quite generous toward those in the tobacco industry. Americans not only subsidize the tobacco industry; they also pay extra health costs due to the smoking habits of approximately 50 million fellow citizens.

It is difficult to identify an institutional sector in the United States that does not often seek and receive special allocations from the public purse. Members of Congress seem especially willing to sponsor special grants to colleges and universities in their districts, for example. Congress included $493 million for research and construction projects for particular schools in 1990 spending bills.[18] These investments were based solely on the willingness of a congressperson to submit a motion for approval, usually as a rider to another piece of legislation. Such projects, which are not subject to competitive reviews, have been strongly criticized by some observers as "pork barrel science."[19]

It may be more difficult for institutions of higher learning to obtain direct congressional project support for the next few years, however, due to the discovery in 1991 that a number of research universities had been including inappropriate charges in the overhead recovery rates collected on government research grants. Overhead rates are normally calculated as necessary but indirect costs such as the cost of space, electricity, or general administration that are incurred in conducting research. However, Stanford University, for example, apparently was including expenses in research overhead that were difficult to justify as related to research, such as redecoration of the president's home, flowers for university receptions, and depreciation on the university yacht.[20] Early in 1991 Stanford returned $500,000 to the federal government for unwarranted charges for the maintenance of three university residences.[21] Including dubious expenses in the federal overhead recovery rate is a less visible way than direct congressional appropriation for a research university to maximize access to public funds for specific institutional purposes.

❖ Self-Interest and the Elusive Public Good

The reevaluation of commercial bank deposit insurance in 1991 illustrates the difficulty of defining the national interest in the abstract. The Bush administration proposed legislation to eliminate deposit insurance coverage for the deposits of pension funds and brokerage firms in commercial banks. Individuals would still be insured, however, up to $100,000 in regular savings and up to $100,000 in retirement savings per institution.[22] This change was proposed as a way of introducing greater market discipline into the decisions of managers of large funds, who would be led to place their multi-million-dollar deposits in more secure institutions. In order to attract large deposits, banks would have to manage their assets wisely.

This policy proposal encountered immediate challenge, however. One reason advanced by some analysts was that the reduction of deposit insurance would cause funds to move assets away from smaller commercial banks and into large banks, money market funds, treasury notes, and other instruments, thus hurting the 9,000 commercial banks with deposits under $100 million.[23] According to them, the policy change would likely weaken many local banks and local economies; further, the proposed policy would put people holding the assets of pension funds at greater risk. Parties who would be affected negatively by the proposed policy mounted campaigns through their membership organizations, such as the Independent Bankers Association and the American Association for Retired Persons.[24]

It comes as no surprise that retired people and independent bankers would organize politically to advance their interests. Both citizens and elected officials expect that legislators will hear the views and respond to the needs of those affected by policy questions. To the regulated, regulation invariably appears heavy-handed, and legislators offer recourse for citizens who feel they have suffered inappropriate or arbitrary treatment.

The ultimate consequences of one policy or another for the commercial banking industry are unknown, and the best overall policy choice is unclear in advance. In the process, legislators usually lack foreknowledge as to whose claims have merit and whose claims will ultimately be discredited. The nefarious actions of Charles Keating and a number of other executives of the S&L industry were fully exposed only after the extent of the industry crisis became known.

Even as we recognize that the political system cannot guarantee successful policy results, an error of $300 billion to $500 billion still represents a colossal mistake, and the millions of dollars for tobacco farmers and hundreds of thousands for universities do add up. The fact that Charles Keating directly and indirectly supported the political campaigns of key senators with $1.3 million casts serious doubt on any defense of the principle of self-interest in this particular case.[25] While caution about overgeneralizing the faults of political democracy is warranted, Americans have every reason to be concerned about the excessive role of self-interest in politics.

❖ The Unanimity Rule

Building on Downs's assumption that rational behavior is directed toward selfish ends, economic theorists James Buchanan and Gordon Tullock conclude that political decision making should be structured so as to make it harder for special interests to obtain benefits at others' expense.[26] According to them, public decision making should require the *unanimous* agreement of all those affected. This would prevent the tobacco industry, universities, pensioners, and other special interests from obtaining private gains at public expense. Although minimizing the costs of collective action to individuals, however, this perspective locks the society into the status quo distribution of resources.[27] Society as a whole may want to leave itself some latitude to make equity judgments. Why should the status quo have a distinct advantage in social policy simply for being the status quo? Pleas of justice may be able to garner a majority, but they will rarely receive a unanimous vote, even though they may improve the overall quality of life.

Neither the unanimity principle nor the majority rule principle prevents abuse by individuals in positions of high influence. Periodically, we become aware of political appointees giving privileges to themselves that they appear unwilling to grant to others. For example, in May 1991, it was revealed that John Sununu, at the time President Bush's chief of staff, had taken over 70 trips to various parts of the country on executive air force jets that cost taxpayers nearly $4,000 per hour.[28] Some public purpose could be named for each of the trips, but it was also clear that the trips often centered on purely political or personal reasons, such as skiing weekends in Colorado. Sununu apparently reimbursed the government for the cost of a commercial airline ticket for each trip as White House rules specify, but this reimbursement often was only a small fraction of the cost to the public. Even such a fierce skeptic of the concept of the "public interest" as Sununu apparently could identify such an interest in his own case.

Exposés of private benefit obtained at public expense are all too common. It would be difficult to find a single day without news of charges of some form of unfair personalizing of public resources. Elected officials' judgment—and that of many candidates, many senior public administrators, even leaders of private organizations—may often be questionable and too often found wanting.

Do these incidents seem numerous because we are attuned to them, or are we attuned *because* they occur frequently? However they arise, few instances of personal gain at public expense can be successful defended. Once such cases have been exposed, public criticism is a reforming force that changes behavior. After the uproar about overcharging the federal government on research grants, Stanford University and others together returned millions of dollars in overcharges. Sununu's indiscretions and the system of excessive university overhead charges were terminated after they were brought to light. The media act as a watchdog, some would say an overzealous and at times callous one, against those taking advantage of their own position to declare that personal benefit justifies public cost.

❖ Public Benefits and Private Costs

Thus far, we have considered examples in which individuals benefit by doing what is socially undesirable. A second way in which private behavior can conflict with the public welfare is the *failure* of individuals to do what *is* socially beneficial. Political economist Mancur Olson has argued that individuals, in the absence of special incentives, would behave as free riders on the efforts of others in the creation of nonexclusive public goods.[29] For example, it is not possible to prevent people who have not financially contributed to the public radio system from listening to its programs. Those who listen to public radio without contributing are free riders. More public benefit institutions, such as public radio and television, museums, orchestras, theaters, and social agencies, would undoubtedly exist in a world without free riders. Olson argues that the inability of individual persons in large groups to act in their own interest permits small interest groups with high stakes in an issue to have disproportionate influence on public policy and to transfer social wealth to themselves at the expense of others.

For example, financing public elementary and secondary education in the United States depends mainly on a system of local property taxes. It is logical for people with children in public schools to support school tax levies. But in many school districts, a majority of voters are homeowners without children in the public schools. Keeping pace with the increasing cost of education requires voters without children in the public schools to vote for property tax increases that have only distant and indirect returns for them. The difficulty of passing levies in many districts seems to bear out Olson's view.

The disposal of hazardous industrial waste, including nuclear waste, reflects a similar problem of individual cost and public benefit. There are relatively few environmentally safe disposal sites, and people who live near these sites perceive themselves as bearing a substantially greater health risk than persons living farther away. It can be argued that the public benefits from the use of products and services that generate hazardous and nuclear waste and that the public benefits from its safe underground storage. But relatively few persons are asked to bear the risk of living near the storage areas. Many of them object strongly at the time such facilities are sited. Objection to paying the private costs of public benefits has become known, at least in the area of environmental quality, as the NIMBY (Not In My Back Yard) phenomenon.

Organization and social policy seeks to realign individual interests and community interests. Thus, individuals can receive special benefits for participating in a common cause, such as receiving a coffee mug for a $25 contribution to public radio or being listed as a patron in an orchestra program for contributing $250. Reducing taxable federal income by the amount of an individual's personal property taxes decreases the personal cost of school levies to individuals living in a particular district by spreading some of the cost over the entire taxpaying public. The tax deductibility of charitable contributions is also an incentive available only to those who do contribute. Generally, communities that accept hazardous waste are promised considerable economic benefits in return. Sometimes selective incentives are negative, such as penalties for not paying taxes owed to the government. Both positive and negative selective incentives are designed to discourage free riders and to increase the level of personal contribution to collective goods.

The theory of collective action explains why organizations and institutions frequently use selective incentives to encourage participation, and it explains why individual contributions may often be difficult to obtain. At the same time, collective action for the creation of a public good *does* occur: Citizens do pass school levies; nonprofit organizations receive many contributions, with or without selective incentives; and a number of social movements have had huge followings and a substantial impact on public policy. In recent years the theory of collective action has been refined considerably. The probability of collective action has been shown to depend, for example, on differences in interests and resources among members of a group, on whether the cost of providing the public good increases or decreases as the group gets larger, and on whether group members are able to take into account how much others already have contributed.[30] Under these circumstances, individuals do what is socially useful; in other circumstances, the absence of contributions toward a public good presents a difficult challenge to policymakers.

❖ The Worth of Self-Interest

The unavoidable imperfections of democracy, and a large volume of academic literature that is skeptical about self-interest in public affairs, may lead us to overlook the fundamental merits of political self-interest.[31] Some people have argued a positive rationale for self-interest; others have shown that people express their interests in terms of general values and broad ideas, not always in terms of immediate material gains.

Self-Interest: A Public Good   In the United States an organization or group has little standing independent of the satisfactions or advantages it provides specific persons. The individual, not the group, is the "basic philosophical entity" in this country.[32] If the public interest can be defined or reached only through individual efforts, American politics should be organized according to self-interest. There are at least four reasons for the claim that self-interest is good for the U.S. political system.

First, democracy is an absolutely indispensable condition, a sine qua non, for implementing the philosophy of the individual. Inspired by the vision of human dignity, democracy provides the opportunity for political participation that Americans rightly view as fundamental and inalienable. Only in a democracy are people higher than government, at least in principle, and thus only democratic politics accord the individual maximum respect.

Second, governance by self-interest is also the most practical way to resolve conflicting preferences in a large and diverse society. What more reasonable way would there be to balance the thousands of needs and problems of citizens other than by hearing out those helped and those harmed by specific policies? For example, it is impossible to say, in general, which of these programs contributes more to society as a whole—increases in agricultural productivity, preschool education, clean air, support for the unemployed, scientific development, a competitive biotechnology industry, or a balanced budget—other than by regarding the people affected by government action collectively and subjecting them to the admittedly inexact process of advocacy. A dictator, no matter how benevolent, can not understand and weigh particular interests as judiciously as citizens themselves. However imperfect, participatory democracy may best approximate the elusive public interest by deriving policy from the interests of affected individuals and groups.

Third, a political system based on self-interest offers the best chance of protecting small groups of people against abuse by larger, more powerful—and perhaps selfish—interests. For example, if all the industries that would benefit from trade protection were able to act together, the United States would have a massive structure of trade barriers severely damaging to the economy. But differences within this potential coalition prevent common action among these industries, and extreme protectionism has not occurred. People who want protection of the auto industry do not want to pay higher prices for their clothing, and thus they lend weak support, at best, to proposals for additional protection of the textile industry. People affiliated with the textile industry want the cheapest and highest-quality consumer electronics, regardless of country of manufacture, and people affiliated with the manufacture of consumer electronics generally do not want to pay more just to buy an American-made car.

The tendency of special-interest groups, or factions, to cancel out one another was one of the fundamental arguments for a strong national government presented by Alexander Hamilton, James Madison, and John Jay in the influential document *The Federalist Papers*.[33] These men tried to convince the citizens of the various states to adopt the newly written U.S. Constitution. Madison in particular feared that without a strong national government, special interests, such as the textile manufacturers in South Carolina, would be able to gain sufficient political influence to override other South Carolinians' interest in free trade. If trade policy were a national function, however, Madison reasoned, different interests among groups (today, for example, among the automotive, textile, and consumer electronics industries) would cancel one another out and the "public interest" in free trade would prevail. Thus, the U.S. Constitution relegates the setting of tariffs to the federal government alone. The Federalists' argument that the interests of small groups would be protected best by self-interest politics within a national government system remains valid to this day.

A fourth justification for self-interest politics rests on the premise that many individual interests support the general welfare. The corporate tax system allows deductions for corporations that increase their investments in research and development in order to stimulate economic growth, retain jobs, increase tax revenues, and improve the nation's balance of trade. Similarly, the personal tax system maintains a deduction for personal interest paid on home mortgages, avowedly to make homeownership, an important American value, easier for people of moderate income. These examples argue that certain policies proposed by interest groups have the potential to benefit everyone. Tension between private interests and public values is not inevitable; the former can be instrumental in achieving the latter.

The Individual as Public Citizen   Attitude surveys provide us with additional reasons for believing that self-interest is not all-pervasive in politics. Social psychologists David Sears and Carolyn Funk have summarized dozens of surveys concerning political and social issues for the 15-year period from the early 1970s to the mid-1980s.[34] These studies explored the influence of respondents' personal interests on their political opinions. For example, are people more strongly opposed to busing for integrating schools when they have children in public schools and live in districts with busing programs in place or planned? Are attitudes toward property tax reductions, state spending limits, and reductions in state income taxes dictated by the respondent's status as a homeowner, a person with declining family finances, or a public employee?

Several decades of studies on these issues have led Sears and Funk to conclude that there is at best weak support for the view that self-interest alone explains people's political opinions. This conclusion was supported across studies dealing with race, economics, crime, war, women's issues, and energy policy. Nor did these scholars find a substantial tie between people's financial situation and their general voting behavior. Self-interest was most influential when a person faced a severe threat, such as the potential loss of a job.

Rather than self-interest, this body of research suggests that identification with a political party, allegiance to a liberal or a conservative creed, and general values such as racial tolerance or lack of tolerance determine political attitudes and behavior. The authors conclude:

> Self-interest ordinarily does not have much effect on the mass public's political attitudes. There are occasional exceptions, as when there are quite substantial and clear stakes (especially regarding personal tax burdens) or ambiguous and dangerous threats. But even these conditions only infrequently produce systematic and strong self-interest effects, and then, ones that are quite narrowly specific to the interest in question. The general public thinks about most political issues, most of the time, in a disinterested frame of mind.[35]

This line of research supports the view that social decision making suffers most when public involvement is low. The best counterbalance to the influence of special interests in politics is greater public involvement.

❖ Differing Views of the Way Congress Works

The Self-Interest Perspective   A vast empirical literature has documented and tested many of the ideas of public choice theory, and studies have often found what researchers suspected—evidence of narrow self-interest in the policy process. An influential example of this body of work is Morris Fiorina's study of the results of congressional elections.[36] Fiorina probes the fact that the average margin of victory for incumbent U.S. representatives rose by 5 to 10 percent between 1950 and 1970, and the number of contested districts declined. In other words, incumbency increased. Fiorina suggests that the growth of government creates numerous problems for constituents in dealing with public bureaucracies. Constituent problems, in turn, create more opportunities for congresspersons to help constituents, thereby consolidating the political position of the elected officials. Fiorina concludes:

> The Washington system grew up as the public sector expanded. At first the system was an unforeseen by-product of genuine attempts to legislate in the

general interests of the American citizenry. Today the system has become an end in itself. It enables congressmen and bureaucrats to achieve their most dearly held goals [re-election] by giving the appearance of satisfying the goals of the American people. In reality, public policy in this country is hostage to the personal goals of congressmen and the bureaucracy.[37]

Anthony Downs casually accepted selfishness as an "axiom" of his analysis, and this critical assumption became the dogma of the public choice point of view. Fiorina's work is representative of this approach, which, in many respects, has become the received wisdom of political analysis.

Congress as a Public Interest Institution   Self-interest may be an important basis of congressional decisions. However, some observers have argued effectively that Congress is also characterized by public-spiritedness. Just as there are good reasons for valuing self-interest in the American political system, there are several reasons for believing that the level of autonomous self-interest is not excessive.

Political scientist Steven Kelman argues that members of Congress regularly demonstrate public-spiritedness.[38] First, some studies of congressional voting show that senators' and representatives' general personal ideology is a better predictor of voting on strip-mining legislation, for example, than whether or not coal is strip-mined in the elected officials' electoral districts. Second, Kelman points to the presence of large congressional staffs as an influence focused on more general values rather than special interests. Staff members' analyses and opinions can be a counterbalance to the immediate pressure of special interests and politically expedient concessions. Third, the diversity of constituent interests among all members of each body of Congress dilutes the disproportionate influence of narrow interests on committee recommendations. Opposing political forces create room for the official to exercise discretion and independent judgment. Finally, according to Kelman, the desire for positive reputation, an intangible but cherished attribute, encourages public-spiritedness. The scrutiny of the mass media and the public's access to government documents also sensitize elected representatives to the "publicness" of their behavior.

The fact that Congress occasionally passes reform legislation demonstrates a commitment to social values and higher purposes. If Congress were responsive only to self-perpetuating special interests, economic deregulation would never have occurred in the United States, women's suffrage would not have been approved, and legislation protecting consumers, workers, and the environment would not have been enacted. Existing power structures unsuccessfully opposed the movement for each of these reforms. Robert Reich, of Harvard's Kennedy School of Government, refers to political motivation based on widely shared values as "the power of public ideas."[39] Political scientist Gary Orren observes:

The passage of the Voting Rights Act was impossible in 1962. Two years later it seemed inevitable. In that short span, equality of opportunity had become an idea so powerful as to sweep away the organizational inertia and political opposition that had obstructed it. In 1985 few people in Washington thought that a tax reform bill would be passed by Congress. In May 1986 tax reform legislation was unanimously reported out of the Senate Finance Committee, and in June all but three senators voted for it on the floor.[40]

Scholars writing on public choice theory now generally concede that "narrow self-interest is [not] the *sole* motive of political agents."[41] A mutual, albeit grudging, accommodation appears to be at hand between those who see the world in terms of self-interest and those who perceive a moral basis for political behavior. Rather than sharing common ground, however, exponents of the two views seem to occupy adjoining territories.

❖ Conclusions Concerning the Role of Self-Interest in Politics

Discussion of conflicting views of the role of self-interest in policy decisions reveals several important features of policy formulation in the United States. First, the political process tries not to disappoint any constituency: Depositors want deposit insurance, investors and managers want freedom to invest as they wish, universities want new research buildings, and the tobacco industry wants high prices for its product. Resulting policy is often an inconsistent and inefficient patchwork quilt of aims and ideologies: Government subsidizes both the production of tobacco and the health costs of smokers; it tries to give security to depositors and investment freedom to owners. Politicians who want to be reelected find it difficult to say no to anyone who may influence their reelection. Continuing unresolved problems, such as chronic deficit spending, result.

Second, the system is biased toward immediate policy consequences rather than long-term effects. People who would receive immediate harm from a proposed policy, whether they are retired depositors or small commercial bankers, have a loud voice in the political process. Similarly, those who stand to enjoy immediate benefits from a proposed policy, such as savings and loan executives, carry substantial political weight. An ideal political stance is one that promises to avoid immediate harm and to create immediate benefit, that is, both to insure depositors and simultaneously to allow S&Ls to invest freely. Potential future victims of these policies, or potential future beneficiaries of different policies, rarely have strong congressional representation.

On the one hand, these processes resist "public interest" policies. The system has difficulty in getting the real public interest, should it exist, to be recognized. On the other hand, these features mean that the political system responds to the will and interests of many of its members, which may often be public-spirited.

The American political system can become much more effective in structuring decision making to strengthen the role of a person's public-spiritedness. For example, for some time it has been clear to many people that the Pentagon has maintained more domestic military bases than it needs; but proposals to close bases have inevitably run up against a political system designed to respond to individual interests, and individual communities' representatives have successfully protested attempts to close *their* bases. Therefore, few bases were ever closed, although it was clearly in the general interest to reduce their numbers.

Closing unneeded and inefficient bases became possible only when Congress approved a different procedure for making decisions about closings. Under the new system, the Secretary of Defense submitted a list of proposed closings to an independent commission. The commission heard testimony from all interested parties, investigated the circumstances of each base, and made recommendations on closings. Then the President and Congress each had the opportunity to approve or reject the whole list of closings; by prior agreement, the list could not be amended. This procedure structured a process to give priority to the public good while being fair to particular groups. Citizen involvement and the intelligent structuring of specific decision processes can help the system to retain the desired sensitivity to self-interest as well as place self-interest in perspective.

A related issue is whether some aspects of the U.S. political system aggravate the dysfunctional aspects of self-interest. The next section considers a variety of proposals for restructuring political influence in the United States, beginning with the financing of campaigns through political action committees.

PROPOSALS TO ALTER THE SYSTEM OF POLITICAL INFLUENCE

❖ Reforming the System of Campaign Finance

The current system for financing congressional campaigns is one factor that appears to worsen the excesses of political self-interest. Although it was well intentioned, evidence now suggests that the drawbacks of this system, which has been in place since the early 1970s, outweigh its merits. Changing the way in which political campaigns are financed has been a recurrent item on the public agenda in the late 1980s and the early 1990s. A major force behind this issue is the public's perception that campaign financing depends to an excessive degree on special-interest groups, namely, political action committees (PACs).

In the early 1970s, organized labor wanted to protect its ability to raise funds for political uses from union members. In addition, the hidden role of big money in campaign finance came to light in investigations of the Watergate political scandal. In response to these situations Congress rewrote the laws of campaign finance in the early 1970s, establishing tighter reporting and disclosure regulations and limits on the size of contributions. The major innovation, however, was the legitimization of a new vehicle for campaign finance, the political action committee. PACs are organizations created by groups with similar political interests for the purpose of raising and distributing campaign contributions. All PACs must register with the Federal Election Commission and disclose the sources and disbursement of funds. Contribution limits to candidates are established for PACs, as they are for individuals, although at $5,000 per candidate per election, their limits are higher than limits for individual contributions to single candidates. PACs may be affiliated with an organization, such as a corporation or a labor union, or they may be independent of any established organization. PACs affiliated with an organization can have their administrative expenses paid by the organization.

Growth of PACs in numbers and in financial power has been one of the main factors in the story of campaign financing over the last two decades in the United States. In the 1989–90 election cycle, PACs, numbering about 4,500, disbursed $150.6 million to candidates for Senate and House seats, which constituted 32 percent of all campaign contributions.[42] The amount of money raised through PACs between 1979 and 1980 and 1989 and 1990 increased 205 percent in successful Senate races and 239 percent in successful House races.[43] PAC contributions made up 26 percent of the total funds raised by winning Senate candidates and 46 percent of the total raised by winning House candidates in the 1989–90 election cycle.[44]

In theory, the PAC system of campaign finance is politically neutral: PACs are equally accessible to all politically interested parties, and should be as available to challengers as they are to incumbents. In practice, however, PAC contributions distinctly favor incumbents. In 1990, in both the primary races and the general election for Senate and House seats, PACs contributed more than seven times as much to incumbents as to challengers. On the average, an incumbent senator received $912,341 from PACs in the general election campaign; on the average, a challenger for a Senate seat received $277,131 from PACSs.[45] The difference in general election House races was even greater: Incumbents received more than ten times, on the average, what challengers received from PACs.

The fact that PAC giving became strongly skewed toward incumbents is one aspect of the inexorable drift toward the perpetuation of power. Political analysts Al Wilhite and Chris Paul document the influence of PACs on political outcomes."[46] Based on a series of studies assessing the relationship between corporate PAC contributions in particular and congressional voting, these authors explain the commitment to PACs as a rational business decision:

> Contributions do seem to have a rate of return because political decisions can be affected and these decisions can have a large impact on a firm's revenues or costs. Further study is required to measure this return and compare it with other investment alternatives, but the continuing existence and growth of political action committees suggests that it is competitive with alternative investment opportunities.[47]

On one hand, PAC contributions to incumbent elected officials simply reflect the fact that these candidates are likely to be reelected. The PACs' focus on incumbents reinforces and strengthens the incumbency effect even more strongly, however. In 1990, 96 percent of House members and a comparable percentage of senators who chose to run for reelection were successful.[48] Although not inherently or necessarily biased toward incumbency, the PAC system of political campaign finance has evolved into a significant component of the process of self-perpetuation in Congress. In light of public revulsion toward PACs, it is not surprising that banning PAC contributions in campaigns for federal office was a common element of both Republican and Democratic proposals for campaign finance reform in the Senate in 1991, although the constitutionality of such proposals would surely be challenged.

Although less dramatically than recent PAC contributions, individual giving also favors incumbents. In Senate and House campaigns in the 1989–90 election cycle, individual giving favored incumbents over challengers by a ratio of nearly 2.8 to 1.[49] The 1990 election, billed as a voter revolt, had a national turnout of only 33 percent of voting-age people and returned large proportions of senators and representatives to Congress. The main effect of the touted "groundswell" of voter dissatisfaction was merely to reduce the margin of victory of many incumbents.

❖ The Movement to Limit Legislators' Terms

In addition to campaign finance reform, popular disenchantment with the political system is also reflected in proposals to limit the number of terms an elected official may serve in a single office. In the elections of November 1990, strong majorities in California, Colorado, and Oklahoma approved limitations on the terms of state officials, and voters in Kansas City, Missouri, and San Jose, California, likewise approved limits on the terms of municipal officials. In October of that year a nationwide Gallup opinion poll found that 73 percent of respondents favored term limits for members of Congress.[50] In November 1991, term limits were approved by voters for municipal officials in Houston, Cincinnati, and Worcester, Massachusetts, although a term-limit proposal was defeated in the state of Washington. To an American public frustrated by the appearance of invulnerability and insensitivity on the part of elected officials, limiting terms is an appealing way to block incumbency.

The idea of term limits has long been an option in the repertoire of American populism. Along with the popular election of presidential electors and the abolition of property qualifications for office seekers, term limits were part of the agenda of Jacksonian populism in the first third of the nineteenth century. The public seeks a remedy in the limiting of terms whenever it perceives that power lies disproportionately in the hands of an elite that is out of touch with the common person and capable of perpetuating its own position of influence.

Term limits are also a political maneuver. The Twenty-second Amendment to the Constitution, which permits a president to be elected to a maximum of two terms of office, was passed in 1951 with strong support from the Republican party shortly after the unprecedented tenure in office of Democrat Franklin D. Roosevelt, who had been elected to four terms. Likewise, many of the movements for term limits today at the state and local levels appear to be sponsored by Republicans, who have been the minority party for several decades in many legislative bodies.[51] Although term limits are popular with voters, these proposals also have decidedly political implications.

The internal contradiction of term limits, however, is that they seek government responsiveness by restricting the voters' choice; they paradoxically propose to make democracy work by actually reducing citizen influence. Term limits accept the risk of prohibiting able persons from seeking office in order to protect the public from unworthy officials. In the name of populism, they make democracy less popular. In order to compensate for what appears to be a defect of democracy, term limits restrict freedom.

The movement to limit terms is a manifestation of the voters' disaffection with the American political system. It is, however, essentially antidemocratic in that it removes choice in order to strengthen and preserve freedom. Such contradictions are characteristic of efforts to compensate for, rather than to overcome, political apathy.

❖ Decentralizing Governmental Powers

The election of Ronald Reagan ushered in a significant shift away from national government bodies and toward state and local government in the United States. This movement had a democratic rationale: to take decisions out of the hands of centralized congressional and administrative bodies and the Supreme Court and locate decisions closer to the people. Advocates also argued that decentralization would force local governments to compete for residents through lower taxes, and this would constrain the overall size of the public sector.[52] Decentralization was motivated by ideological principles of personal autonomy, local control, and minimal government. Local control was also to represent a needed antidote to political apathy and alienation. The question is whether this trend increased political participation.

Professor David Walker of the University of Connecticut has traced the concentration of government power at the federal level for the years 1964 to 1990.[53] The national government grew in power until about 1978; it then moderated somewhat as a function of the policies of deregulation and decentralization of the Reagan and Bush administrations. Two factors explain why power gravitated to the national government in those years, and why it has been difficult to decentralize governmental power significantly. First of all, national legislation may be the best mechanism for ensuring minimum standards of quality of life for all citizens. Protection of individual rights is a second reason why significant power has been placed in national governmental institutions.

Ensuring Minimal Living Conditions   Government has become increasingly centralized since the early 1960s in areas in which local governments and institutions have been perceived to function below a basic standard of decency. Thus, the federal government initiated social welfare programs for retirement security and for elderly persons' medical care when it became clear that the states were administratively and financially incapable of creating uniform programs to meet these social needs. It is also true that not all states have had the same political will to respond to these needs. In the absence of uniform and basic standards among the states, the federal government has moved extensively to create standards, if not funding, in urban development and housing, education, income assistance, environmental protection, worker safety, consumer protection, and many other areas.

The courts have occasionally intervened in quality-of-life issues at the local level. For example, early in 1991, a district federal court in Boston intervened in the politics of the disposal of sewage into Boston Harbor.[54] The discharge had been in violation of the Federal Clean Water Act for many years, and it had been under litigation by environmentalist groups and the federal Environmental Protection Agency since 1983. In the mid-1980s, the state of Massachusetts pledged itself to an effective and costly treatment plan that would be implemented over 15 years. The first part of the plan, which involved a landfill site for grit, sediment, and sludge, was never put into place, however, due to a political stalemate created by the Not In My Back Yard phenomenon. Thus, the cleanup plan was stalled and the sewage continued to flow unabated into the harbor.

The federal district judge forbade the placement of any new sewer lines into Boston Harbor. Many people saw this action as an unconstitutional imposition of federal power on local decision making. The action was upheld, however, in the court of appeals on the basis of "important state needs and interests." *New York Times* columnist Anthony Lewis concludes: "That we have to look to judges to focus our minds on pollution and decayed hospitals and overcrowded prisons is not a happy fact. But it will go on—it must go on—until we regain the ability to decide such issues for ourselves."[55]

Does this society centralize such decisions because democracy is not working, as Lewis suggests, or is democracy not working because such decisions are centralized?

Valuing Individual Rights   Respect for individual rights is another reason government decisions have become increasingly centralized in the post–World War II period. The Supreme Court's reading of the Constitution on a given issue, more frequently than legislative initiative, is the first step toward greater government centralization. Since 1965, for example, the Voting Rights Act has given the Justice Department authority to supervise state redistricting to prevent inequities based on race. Federal courts were required to supervise busing programs in local school districts because schools had not complied with court-mandated requirements for the desegregation of education. The Supreme Court has determined that working conditions are a legitimate constitutional issue for employees of local governments, as it ruled in 1985 that local government bodies are subject to federal labor legislation.[56] Many of these decisions have been controversial, although consistent with the Supreme Court's willingness in the 1960s and 1970s to interpret the Constitution broadly with respect to individual rights.

Former federal appellate judge Robert Bork, an outspoken critic of such judicial activism, has presented the case for the judicial philosophy of strict constructionism, also called *intentionalism*.[57] In this approach, judges restrict themselves to the core values or premises of those persons who prepared and approved the Constitution and the Bill of Rights and other constitutional amendments as best that these values can be determined. Thus, the Constitution is to be interpreted strictly according the intentions of the framers of the particular statements being interpreted. To expand beyond these core values and intentions is to become a super-legislature of nine persons who are appointed for life and are not directly accountable to the public. Bork writes:

> The Constitution preserves our liberties by providing that all those given the authority to make policy are directly accountable to the people through regular elections. Federal judges, alone among our public officials, are given life tenure precisely so that they will not be accountable to the people. If it were otherwise, if judges were accountable, the people could, when the mood seized them, alter the separation of powers, do away with representative government, or deny basic freedoms to those out of popular favor. But if judges are, as they must be to perform their vital role, unelected, unaccountable, and unrepresentative, who is to protect us from the power of judges? How are we to be guarded from our guardians? The answer can only be that judges must consider themselves bound by law that is independent of their own views of the desirable. They must not make or apply any policy not fairly to be found in the Constitution or a statute.[58]

Legal scholar Mary Ann Glendon believes, for a different reason, that Americans frame too many issues as matters of individual rights. She argues that the tendency in the United States to define virtually every social controversy in terms of legal rights replaces processes of compromise and mutual understanding that require people to deal with each other's needs and opinions.[59] Converting all points of view into claims of rights, Glendon believes, diminishes concern for the community and weakens democracy. She states, "An intemperate rhetoric of personal liberty . . . corrodes the social foundations on which individual freedom and security ultimately rest."[60]

❖ Government Decentralization in the 1980s

The "new federalism" of the Reagan administration decentralized decision making, placing decisions with lower levels of government on a number of substantive issues, such as housing and economic development. It eliminated a number of grant programs at the national level and turned over responsibility for certain regional issues and management of certain environmental programs to the states.[61] Joint federal-state programs were augmented as the national government reduced the number of programs administered entirely from Washington, D.C. On the other hand, the federal government continued to preempt state decisions in certain other areas, as in establishing a national drinking age.

After 1988, the Bush administration continued this general practice of placing responsibility and funding with the states in areas such as wastewater treatment and mass transit, and it continued to propose spending cuts in federal social welfare programs, including child nutrition.[62] Where it made new program initiatives in education reform, for example, it looked to other government units and to the private sector for funding.

Supreme Court decisions in the 1980s showed a distinct, but not uniform, trend toward less judicial activism. The Court upheld federal powers in the application of the Fair Labor Standards Act with respect to state and local employees, and it allowed federal concerns to prevail in the matter of the taxation of interest on state and local bonds. The Court also did not hesitate to find that a number of state systems for financing education were inequitable and violated the Fourteenth Amendment, and it broke new ground in applying the Voting Rights Act to the election of municipal judges.

On the whole, however, by the 1990s the Court had demonstrated a discernible change of course away from the preservation of individual rights. State decision making was gradually given greater weight in the question of terminating an unwanted pregnancy and in the setting of restrictions on incapacitated people's choices as to when to discontinue life-support systems. A series of decisions strengthened the hand of local law enforcement officials and constrained the rights of the accused and the convicted. The Court has been distinctly unsympathetic to affirmative action programs that favor minorities in employment and that use the federal courts to integrate public schools. Its tendency to relegate certain social decisions to local and state authorities created a clear trend by the end of 1991, and, if anything, the Court appeared to be accelerating its deference to legislative bodies on social issues.

The new federalism of the White House and the Supreme Court represents a slow but significant redistribution of government power in the United States. As *New York Times* correspondent Linda Greenhouse writes, these shifts represent powerful forces that, "like the tectonic plates of the earth's surface, can create pressure and stress in unexpected times and places."[63] The following sections review one major positive result and one major negative result of these changes. The critical question for us is whether these changes appear to have stimulated greater public participation in the political process. In other words, has the restructuring of intergovernment powers brought greater democracy to America?

A Positive Result   State governments have shown a strong capacity to absorb additional policymaking functions as national legislative, administrative, and judicial institutions have stepped away from consistently centralized policies. State and local authorities generally have not only shown the will and ability to address issues, but they also have demonstrated considerable originality in providing new solutions to problems.[64] Minnesota, for example, has led the country in school-choice programs. Wisconsin has experimented with a plan for minimum standards for child support and a system tying public assistance payments to children's attendance in school. Oregon, Minnesota, and Arizona have developed novel state-specific plans for health-care insurance. Numerous states have implemented economic development programs involving the financing and development of new businesses and involving improved transfer of technology from universities and government research facilities to industry. In many respects, states have led the federal government in developing imaginative social programs. Decentralization has facilitated to greater responsibility and creativity in these cases.

Major changes in the structure of public finance between 1980 and 1990 tell the story of the new federalism. In 1980, federal grants to state and local governments amounted to nearly $106 billion; by 1990, these expenditures had declined to about $101 billion on an inflation-adjusted basis.[65] In 1980, these grants constituted 15 percent of the federal budget and represented 26 percent of all state and local expenditures. By 1990, federal contributions fell to 11 percent of the federal budget and represented only 18 percent of all state and local expenditures.[66]

A Negative Result   In addition to assuming responsibility for more services, state and local governments have assumed more responsibility for the funding of services. Unlike the federal government, state and local authorities are required to balance their books. The shift in government responsibilities since 1980 and the impact of the 1990–91 economic recession forced state and local governments into financial crisis. For example, in 1984, state and local governments together ran an operating surplus of $20 billion; in 1990, they ran up an operating deficit of $34 billion.[67] The bottom-line result for the American taxpayer was that the total tax bite actually increased over the decade. In 1979, total federal-state-local spending was 30.6 percent of the gross national product; by 1988, it had increased to 34.5 percent.[68] In 1980, taxpayers had to work, on the average, until April 28 to pay all local, state, and federal taxes. By 1990, "Tax Freedom Day" had moved forward to May 8.[69]

The state and local fiscal crises resulted in reduced and more expensive services for the residents of many cities and states. From a strictly conservative, minimal-government perspective, this may be a positive result. From the standpoint of the quality of social and economic life, however, the cutbacks have had negative, sometimes tragic, effects on the lives of individual persons. States are "eliminating programs, freezing hiring, laying off employees, raising college tuitions, increasing fees and fines, using up savings and doing almost anything to avoid raising taxes," according to a press report.[70] (A number of states proved unsuccessful in avoiding increasing taxes in 1991, however.) City governments were particularly hard-hit, being confronted with the responsibility to provide a greater number of services but a declining ability to raise revenue. Bridgeport, Connecticut, declared bankruptcy. Thousands of city employees and teachers were laid off in Philadelphia, New York, and Washington, D.C. Los Angeles and Louisville closed neighborhood health centers.

❖ The Impact of Government Decentralization on Political Participation

The full impact of the legislative and judicial decentralization on political participation remains unclear. On one hand, more people undoubtedly become involved with policy issues as state and local governments deal with the challenges of designing and delivering social services and as these governments implement programs of economic development. Likewise, advocates of particular policies concerning issues such as the right to die, the rights of convicted persons, and abortion should be activated as various state legislatures and courts address these issues.

These forms of decentralization do not appear to go deeply enough into the society, however, to change public involvement in political affairs and overcome people's alienation from policy issues and electoral processes. For example, 52.6 percent of the voting-age population voted in the presidential election of 1980, a date that seems a realistic starting point for evaluating the effort to decentralize governmental power.[71] An even lower proportion of the voting-age public, 50.2 percent, voted in the presidential election of 1988, however, after a decade of decentralization and deregulation.

One might expect a decline in interest in national offices as the center of gravity of government affairs shifts more to the local level; perhaps increases in voting percentages in off-year elections would be a better barometer of citizens' interest and participation. After all, many initiatives are decided, and many local offices are filled, in these elections. Declining participation in presidential election years might mask increasing participation in elections at other levels.

Participation in off-year elections has actually declined slightly since the late 1970s, however. In 1978, with no presidential election, 34.9 percent of the voting-age population voted, and in 1990 only 33 percent.[72] Voting is, of course, only one manifestation of political involvement at the local level. Yet it would be surprising to find citizens involved in advisory committees, local development projects, or special-issue politics who were not also active voters.

APATHY AS A ROOT CAUSE
OF POLITICAL ALIENATION

In *Middle American Individualism*, sociologist Herbert Gans summarizes a career's worth of observations and insights concerning the values held by middle-class Americans.[73] According to Gans, the people of Middle America hold good factory and service jobs; technical, clerical, and administrative positions; and semiprofessional and supervisory positions. These are people of sufficient income to have some degree of choice in their lifestyle and their use of leisure time. This class is largely, but not entirely, white.

Gans coined the term *popular individualism* to refer to the constellation of values of this broad spectrum of middle American society. The desire for personal control is a central value in Middle Americans' search for personal freedom. Gans argues that, most of all, they want to be able to make choices about their own involvement in economic and social decisions. Economic choice among goods and services for comfort, security, and convenience is very important. Socially, they may decide to be neighborly or to be private, to live close to or far from relatives. For them, the personal, immediate part of society, each person's "microsociety," takes precedence over broader ideological and national concerns. At the same time, Middle Americans are intensely patriotic and take pride in national symbols of their freedom.

Middle Americans' desire for personal control expresses itself in the avoidance of obligatory membership in organizations, according to Gans. Middle Americans prefer informal relationships that are directly relevant to their lives. For the most part, they are content to leave the issues of society at large at the periphery of their interest and attention and to avoid political institutions and organizations.

Yet the fundamental mechanism of freedom—democracy itself— calls for a significant degree of involvement in institutions and issues beyond one's microsociety. Democracy demands that its citizens participate, and political organization suffers when participation is seen as being avoidable. Gans observes that "political avoidance conflicts with the democratic ideal," and that "the failure of citizens to participate in accordance with the theory [of democracy] is often ascribed to a moral disease called apathy."[74]

Gans's observations on avoidance and apathy undoubtedly are related to the political alienation identified in surveys of public attitudes such as the Times Mirror polls. On the one hand, apathy breeds alienation. Lack of interest and involvement in political affairs leads citizens to feel they have little say in and little influence over government decisions. On the other hand, alienation fosters apathy. To the extent that government is unresponsive, people lose interest and withdraw from involvement. Apathy and alienation are first cousins. The former originates in public attitudes and habits; the latter comes out of an unresponsive political process. Popular participation is the strongest antidote to apathy, and responsive government can begin to cure alienation.

CONCLUSIONS

We have addressed two primary issues in this chapter. One is the role of self-interest in the American political system. A considerable body of theory and research, as well as numerous everyday examples, argue that the role of self-interest in our politics is excessive. On the other hand, an opposing view recalls that the system is *supposed* to rely on expressions of self-interest. Further, this side presents considerable evidence of public-spiritedness in U.S. politics. Although there are several consistent and significant mismatches between individual and collective interests, we do have ways of dealing with these mismatches. In some cases structural features of the system, such as the role of political action committees in campaign finance, distort the system for representing interests and appear to need an overhaul.

The second focus of this chapter has been the apathy and alienation of many U.S. citizens. Whether people are alienated because they are apathetic, or vice versa, makes less difference than the urgent need to find ways to reverse the trend of low political involvement. People claim to be alienated because government is unresponsive, but it is equally probable that government is unresponsive because people are apathetic. Political systems designed to be sensitive to the expression of people's interests depend on a broad base of involvement; a low rate of participation inevitably makes the system unresponsive. The voters' weak influence must be turned from indifference into activism. Contemporary America needs to draw upon the nation's deeply rooted historical instinct for political activism.

We have also reviewed other structural solutions to the low rate of political participation. Skepticism has been expressed toward proposals limiting the terms of service of congresspersons and other elected officials. Decentralizing and transferring powers from federal to state and local levels has strong justification on democratic principles, although positive results in the promotion of political involvement have not been apparent to date.

In the final analysis the political system based on the expression of self-interest works, but it works imperfectly. An important feature of the system is that it allows for a healthy review of its own performance on a continuous basis. Over time, the system is amenable to restructuring, that is, to changing the procedures and patterns of influence by which rules are made. Although it is true that making changes in procedures or processes will affect results, it appears that changing the input—increasing the variety and intensity of citizens' participation—will be equally, if not more, important to achieving acceptable results. The people of this nation expend considerable effort in defining and clarifying the role of self-interest in political affairs. The current need is for the nation to turn the tools of analysis to the task of enhancing broad-based political participation.

[1]Times Mirror, *The People & The Press*, September 1987, and *The People, the Press & Politics 1990*, October 11, 1990.

[2]Times Mirror, *The People, the Press & Politics 1990*, p. 22.

[3]Ibid.

[4]U.S. Department of Commerce, Bureau of the Census, *Statistical Abstract of the United States 1990*, "Participation of Elections for President and U.S. Representatives: 1932 to 1988," p. 264.

[5]"Incumbents' National Status Breeds Local Distrust," *Congressional Quarterly*, February 23, 1991, p. 484.

[6]Times Mirror, *The People, the Press & Politics, 1990*, p. 22.

[7]Fred Wertheimer, "Restoring the Health of Our Democracy," *Common Cause*, (May/June 1991), p. 44.

[8]Kettering Foundation, *Citizens and Politics: A View from Main Street America* (1991).

[9]Cynicism may be as prevalent in Americans' work lives as in their views of politics. A useful analysis of the causes of cynicism in work and its remedies is Donald L. Kantor and Philip H. Mirvis, *The Cynical Americans: Living and Working in an Age of Discontent and Disillusion* (San Francisco: Jossey-Bass, 1989).

[10]Anthony Downs, *An Economic Theory of Democracy* (New York: Harper & Brothers, 1957).

[11]Ibid., p. 28.

[12]Ibid., pp. 203–204. The field of public choice, generally concerned with institutional decision making that increases economic efficiency, subsumes a num-

ber of conceptual approaches and contributions. For example, a perspective called law and economics advocates basing judicial decisions on the principle of economic efficiency. One party's compensation to another that has been injured, for example, is better decided according to efficiency, that is, the ability of the compensation to reduce the expected costs of future accidents, rather than vague notions of "fairness" or "justice" to the injured party. The case for economic reasoning in judicial opinions is developed in Richard A. Posner, *Economic Analysis of Law* (Boston: Little, Brown, 1986). Another approach to public policy within a related framework of transaction cost analysis, developed by 1991 Nobel prize winner in economics Ronald Coase, has influenced regulatory policy. Instead of viewing the issue of pollution, for example, in terms of rights, Coase analyzes the costs and benefits of different actions to the polluter and to those who suffer the effects of the pollution. Efficient solutions to these problems can be agreed upon simply by reducing the transaction costs associated with negotiations between the parties involved. Coase's ideas have direct relevance for more efficient, market-based pollution-control policies. See Ronald H. Coase, "The Problem of Social Cost," *Journal of Law & Economics*, 3 (October 1960), pp. 1–44.

[13]Armen A. Alchian, "Economic Laws and Political Legislation," in *The Interaction of Economics and the Law*, ed. Bernard H. Siegan (Lexington, Mass.: Lexington Books, 1977), pp. 139–148.

[14]Ibid., p. 148.

[15]Downs, *An Economic Theory*, p. 27.

[16]"Tobacco Aid," *Common Cause* (March/April 1991), p. 9.

[17]Ibid.

[18]"Congress Earmarked $493 million for Specific Universities; Critics Deride Much of the Total as 'Pork Barrel' Spending," *Chronicle of Higher Education*, February 27, 1991, p. A1.

[19]Ibid.

[20]"Stanford U. Embroiled in Angry Controversy on Overhead Charges," *Chronicle of Higher Education*, February 6, 1991, pp. A1, 20.

[21]"Conceding 'Shortcomings' Stanford to Forgo $500,000 in Overhead on U.S. Contracts," *Chronicle of Higher Education*, January 30, 1991, p. A19.

[22]"Banking Overhaul Bill Highlights," *Congressional Quarterly*, March 23, 1991, p. 733; and Thomas Woodward, "Long-Term Deposit Insurance Reform Options," *CRS Review* (May–June 1991), pp. 3–4.

[23]"Banking-Reform Proposals Are Already Rattling the System and Making the Credit Crunch Worse," *Wall Street Journal*, April 16, 1991, p. A16.

[24]Ibid.

[25]"Can You Buy a Congressman?" *The Economist*, November 18, 1989, p. 25.

[26]James M. Buchanan and Gordon Tullock, *The Calculus of Consent: Logical Foundations of Constitutional Democracy* (Ann Arbor: University of Michigan Press, 1962).

[27]Michael H. Lessnoff, *Social Contract* (Atlantic Highlands, N.J.: Humanities Press International, 1986), pp. 126–130.

[28]"White House Details Flights by Sununu," *New York Times*, April 24, 1991, p. A12.

[29]Mancur Olson, *The Logic of Collective Action: Public Goods and the Theory of Groups* (Cambridge, Mass: Harvard University Press, 1965).

[30]Pamela Oliver, Gerald Marwell, and Ray Teixeira, "A Theory of the Critical Mass. I. Interdependence, Group Heterogeneity, and the Production of Collective Action," *American Journal of Sociology*, 91, 3 (November 1985), pp. 522–556; and Pamela E. Oliver and Gerald Marwell, "The Paradox of Group Size in Collective Action: A Theory of the Critical Mass. II.," *American Sociological Review*, 53 (February 1988), pp. 1–8.

[31]See Jeffrey M. Berry, *The Interest Group Society*, 2nd ed. (Glenview, Ill.: Scott, Foresman/Little, Brown, 1989), for a thorough and balanced appraisal of the role of interest groups in contemporary American democracy.

[32]Buchanan and Tullock, *The Calculus of Consent*, p. 11.

[33]Benjamin F. Wright, ed., *The Federalist*, by Alexander Hamilton, James Madison, and John Jay (Cambridge, Mass.: Belknap Press of Harvard University, 1961).

[34]David O. Sears and Carolyn L. Funk, "Self-Interst in Americans' Political Opinions," in *Beyond Self-Interest*, ed. Jane J. Mansbridge (Chicago: University of Chicago Press, 1990), pp. 147–170.

[35]Ibid., p. 170.

[36]Morris P. Fiorina, *Congress: Keystone of the Washington Establishment*, 2nd ed. (New Haven, Conn.: Yale University Press, 1989).

[37]Ibid., p. 76.

[38]Steven Kelman, *Making Public Policy: A Hopeful View of American Government* (New York: Basic Books, 1987).

[39]Robert B. Reich, ed., *The Power of Public Ideas* (Cambridge, Mass.: Harvard University Press, 1990).

[40]Gary R. Orren, "Beyond Self-Interest," in ibid., p. 28.

[41]Geoffrey Brennan and James M. Buchanan, "Is Public Choice Immoral? The Case for the 'Nobel' Lie," *Virginia Law Review*, 74 (1988), p. 181.

[42]Federal Election Commission, "1990 Congressional Election Spending Drops to Low Point," February 22, 1991, p. 1.

[43]Ibid., p. 2.

[44]Ibid.

[45]Ibid.

[46]Al Wilhite and Chris Paul, "Corporate Campaign Contributions and Legislative Voting," *Quarterly Review of Economics and Business*, 29, 3 (Autumn 1989), 73–85.

[47]Ibid., p. 84.

[48]"Incumbents Battle Local Voter Distrust," *1990 CQ Almanac*, p. 903.

[49]Federal Election Commission, "1990 Congressional Election," derived from p. 4.

[50]Thomas E. Cronin, "Term Limits—A Symptom, Not a Cure," *New York Times*, December 23, 1990, p. E11.

[51]Ibid.

[52]Geoffrey Brennan and James M. Buchanan, *The Power to Tax* (Cambridge: Cambridge University Press, 1980).

[53]David B. Walker, "American Federalism from Johnson to Bush," *Publius: The Journal of Federalism*, 21 (Winter 1991), pp. 105–119.

[54]Anthony Lewis, "Why Judges Act," *New York Times*, May 13, 1991, p. A13.

[55]Ibid. Copyright © 1991 by The New York Times Company. Reprinted by permission.

[56]*Garcia* v. *San Antonio Metropolitan Transit Authority*, 469 U.S. 528 (1985).

[57]Robert H. Bork, *The Tempting of America: The Political Seduction of the Law* (New York: Free Press, 1990).

[58]Ibid., pp. 4–5.

[59]Mary Ann Glendon, *Rights Talk: The Impoverishment of Political Discourse* (New York: Free Press, 1991).

[60]Ibid., p. x.

[61]Walker, "American Federalism," p. 111.

[62]Ibid.

[63]Linda Greenhouse, "A Remade Court Shifts The Fulcrums of Power," *New York Times*, April 7, 1991, p. E5. Copyright © by The New York Times Company. Reprinted by permission.

[64]"Midwestern Laboratories: Federalism in Social Policy," *The Economist*, August 25, 1990, pp. 25–26.

[65]"States and Localities May Slow Recovery," *Wall Street Journal*, August 5, 1991, p. A1.

[66]Ibid.

[67]Ibid.

[68]Walker, "American Federalism," p. 113.

[69]"States and Localitites," p. A1.

[70]"80's Leave States and Cities in Need," *New York Times*, December 30, 1990, p. Y10. Copyright © by The New York Times Company. Reprinted by permission.

[71]U.S. Department of Commerce, "Participation in Elections for President and U.S. Representatives, p. 264.

[72]Ibid.; and "Incumbents' National Status," p. 484.

[73]Herbert J. Gans, *Middle American Individualism: The Future of Liberal Democracy* (New York: Free Press, 1988).

[74]Ibid., p. 67.

6

Social and Institutional Factors in the Development and Use of Technology

❖❖❖❖❖

Vast knowledge and skill support the activities of everyday life. Sophisticated systems involving both physical technology and social behavior underlie modern business, politics, education, art, and architecture. People are even connected to religious services through the medium of television. The importance of technology in American life may be matched only by the degree to which Americans are oblivious to its influence.

Technology is not always a silent social partner. The ability to prolong the physical life of an incapacitated person through medical intervention, for example, has led to differences in opinion over the right to die. The ability to transplant human and nonhuman genes divides people over the morality of genetically altering existing lives and the ethics of creating new life forms. Technology is among those features of American life that are most easily taken for granted; it also creates new arenas for emotionally charged conflicts.

American society values scientific discovery and the conversion of scientific knowledge into useful devices. This nation appears less competent, however, in dealing with the economic and ethical consequences of scientific and technological advances. The United States has invested heavily and successfully in the mastery of nuclear power for both peace and war—but that was the easy part. Related problems such as catastrophic reactor accidents, the disposal of highly radioactive used fuel, the proliferation of nuclear weapons, and the prevention of nuclear terrorism have proved to be much harder to solve.

Technology often sets one person's interests against those of another. For example, a new drug, tacrine (or THA), may slow mental deterioration in up to 1.6 million sufferers of Alzheimer's disease.[1] On the other hand, at high dosages the drug may cause liver damage in some patients. Thus, the Food and Drug Administration and other regulatory agencies may face criticism either for accelerating or for slowing the approval process for this drug. Accepting less than definitive knowledge about its health effects and accelerating the process favor the interests of people helped by the drug; waiting for more conclusive evidence on benefits and risks and slowing the approval process favor the interests of people who would be harmed by the drug.

The judicial system, often the setting of last resort for resolving technology-related social conflicts, also faces policy dilemmas in the allocation of risks. Courts can assign the burden of proof to workers who claim that a chemical substance is dangerous to them, or companies, claiming that the substance is safe, may carry the burden of proof. The former policy may put human life at risk unnecessarily; the latter may unnecessarily raise the cost of production, reduce the firm's ability to compete, and hurt the consumer.

Technology variously creates avenues for the expression of individualism, enriches the power elite, threatens individuality, and influences economic growth. Science and engineering, for example, are prestigious occupations that, combined with the strength and openness of the American educational system, can provide routes to upward social mobility regardless of personal background. For many, the route to wealth and social status has involved the ingenuity of inventing and a talent for commerce. Scientific endeavor and accomplishment, and the marriage of technical inventiveness with entrepreneurial capitalism, are themselves important expressions of American individualism.

Others have perceived a different side of technology and industrialization. Karl Marx saw industrial technology as a means of economic manipulation of workers by the capitalist class and predicted that it would ultimately result in a proletarian revolution. Humanists Jacques Ellul and Aldous Huxley feared the antipersonal impact of technology. Huxley warned that systems of production and organization that are designed to be foolproof may also be "spontaneity-proof, inspiration-proof, and even skill-proof."[2] Mid-twentieth-century social philosopher Lewis Mumford argued that technologies can be either authoritarian or democratic.[3] Mumford feared that the scale, mass organization, and centralized control of modern technology would rob people of autonomy and diminish their individuality.

Thirty years of research have established conclusively that technological innovation is a universal, primary source of national wealth.[4] The ability to innovate continuously is the key ingredient in the competitive advantage of nations.[5] Countries, states, and municipalities compete fiercely for the tangible benefits and the social prestige of having strong institutions of science and technology within their borders. Technology also connects economic growth with the ubiquitous phenomenon of globalization. With reference to the intensity of worldwide competition, economists observe that "innovation has become essential to stay even in the marketplace."[6]

If it is true that the quality of social relationships and the vitality of democracy are important factors in people's ability to realize their own goals, technological advances will have to strengthen social relationships to the same degree that they foster independence and autonomy. It matters whether technological change fragments social relations overall or builds social solidarity.

Reacting to some of the uses of technology, people may become more private, less accessible, and more defensive in relation to others. For example, massive data banks of individual health records, credit records, and employment histories improve economic efficiency by allowing health-care providers, lenders, and employers to make better informed decisions. However, they can also create fear that remote bureaucrats will make judgments and decide people's fate based on unreliable information. In addition, the techniques for collection and management of information can produce mounds of junk mail and dozens of irritating telephone sales calls.

Technology enhances personal mobility, independence, and self-sufficiency, but perhaps at a cost to social relationships. Some evidence suggests that America is increasingly becoming a solitary society. For example, in 1960, 88 percent of children under 18 years of age lived with both parents; by 1990, this figure had dropped to 73 percent in general and to 37.7 percent for black children.[7] Overall, nearly 15.9 million children lived in single-parent families in 1990.[8] Solitary living, however, is not confined to children and single parents; it also involves people choosing not to marry or to marry later, a larger number of elderly persons outliving their spouses, and a fourfold increase in the divorce rate since 1960. Overall, 25 million Americans lived alone in 1990, as compared to 7 million in 1960.[9] This represents an increase of nearly 226 percent since 1960; the population as a whole increased 39 percent in the same period.[10] Can these changes be laid at the doorstep of technology? Although it is impossible to show direct causality, it is certainly true that family structure and related social experiences are influenced ultimately by technology.

It is also important to know whether technology strengthens or weakens democracy. Television, that ubiquitous product and form of technology, shapes Americans' perceptions and American political life. Television ought to have the potential to reduce the distance between citizens and political leaders, create wide understanding of issues, and give people ready knowledge of world events. Research has shown, however, that television weakens political parties, discourages serious debate, encourages cynicism, and reduces voter turnout.[11] In large part, politicians' constant need to raise campaign money stems from the rise of the 30-second advertising spot as a major campaign technique. Historian-journalist Theodore White has observed that "the flood of money that gushes into politics to buy television time is the pollution of democracy."[12]

In summary, science and technology play many roles in relation to individual goals. On the positive side, science and technology open vistas for creativity and personal influence. Science and technology improve the conditions and the quality of life, and they raise human aspirations and liberate people's energy. On the negative side, science and technology can put people at physical risk, bring out ethical conflicts, and alienate people within their social and political relationships. Technology equalizes; but it can also be used to preserve invidious social distinctions. Technological advance promotes autonomy, but it just as readily induces isolation.

The fact that technology can have a serious impact on society in so many ways calls for sophisticated decision making concerning technology. I argue in this chapter, however, that in the United States the social impact of technology often receives attention only as an afterthought. Human and social factors receive attention, but usually only in response to stresses and pressures resulting from technological change. Private and public leaders typically face the full implications of technology only after designs have been fixed, investments have been made, and personal stakes have been determined. In large part, managers and policymakers in the United States repeatedly find themselves engaged in the contentious and expensive process of readjusting systems that were initially conceived too narrowly. I argue in this chapter for the importance of avoiding such technological myopia.

The discussion here is divided according to three topics. The first is a historical overview of the development of mass production, the American system of manufacturing that was put into place early in this century. Without question, mass production conferred enormous economic benefits, and, for a time, it represented the best of worldwide industrial practice. Yet today America has reached the upper limits of the gains in efficiency that can be made through the depersonalizing and rationalizing of work. U.S. industry is scrambling to adopt manufacturing concepts from abroad. This dramatic reversal should teach managers to think more broadly about technology in all of its aspects. Many of the policies now being recommended to U.S. managers by academic advisers and business consultants are based on the understanding that technical efficiency and economic rationality must accommodate people, relationships, and social processes. Our point is not to castigate U.S. industry now, with the benefit of hindsight. Rather, we must seek a perspective that respects the interdependence of technology and society. An historical perspective shows the limits of some narrow premises concerning the ways industrial technology has been applied in the past.

The second topic derives from the view that technology is as much an organizational and social phenomenon as an economic phenomenon. Americans demonstrate a strong capacity to invent and discover; all too often, however, the weak point of the American system turns out to be an inability to convert discoveries to practical uses. The reason, again, is the habit of viewing the diffusion of technology too narrowly.

This weakness is seen, first, in the process of commercializing many of today's complex technologies—for example, high-definition television. One root of this problem involves inattention to the roles of nonmarket organizations such as professional societies, trade associations, and independent research organizations. Thinking about technology diffusion within a framework of market incentives alone accounts for only part of the process; nonmarket organizations should also be part of a policy framework. In addition, the commercialization of technology is weakened in the United States because policy prescriptions concerning innovation are in conflict. One policy orientation holds that private interests and the public interest in innovation converge; both firms and society receive positive returns from innovation. Another policy orientation holds that private interests conflict with the public interest; private parties, if permitted to conduct joint research, will collude to raise prices and retard innovation, to the detriment of the general welfare. This discussion will show how conflicting assumptions about economic motives lead to inconsistent and contradictory policies.

A final section dealing with the commercialization of innovation points up the American habit of ignoring the social implications of new technologies. The case of recombinant bovine growth hormone (rBGH) illustrates how intense controversy can surround economically promising innovations. Although justified by strictly economic criteria, this advance in biotechnology has encountered vocal opposition based on possible risks to human and animal health and the impending loss of jobs in dairy farming. The controversy surrounding rBGH demonstrates that the social implications of new technologies are often ignored in the early life of an innovation, setting the stage for later social and political conflict. Society needs mechanisms to reconcile both the social and economic implications of a technology as early as possible in the innovation cycle.

Discussions concerning the American system of manufacturing and the organizational and social aspects of the commercialization of technology demonstrate that industrial success depends on technological systems, broadly conceived. It will be difficult for the American economy to be successful when business values are tied to narrow concepts of the role of individuals and organizations in the development and application of new technology. The proper framework for technology management includes human and social, as well as efficiency-based, factors. Managers will have to recognize that the diffusion and use of technology involve social and organizational processes among interdependent parties, not purely economic transactions among autonomous entities.

HUMAN VALUES
AND MANUFACTURING SYSTEMS

The latter half of the nineteenth century was a watershed period of technological innovation that accelerated the pace of the industrial revolution. The many significant inventions of this era included the internal-combustion engine (1860), telephone (1876), incandescent light (1879), gasoline automobile (1885), diesel engine (1892), and airplane (1902). In many respects, technologies developed during this time defined the economic structure of the United States for the first 50 or 60 years of the twentieth century.

Turning a breakthrough technology into practical use, however, requires at least three additional types of innovation beyond the basic invention. First, a basic invention calls forth myriad innovations that modify, refine, and improve the initial design. For example, though the gasoline engine made automobile transportation possible, the emergence of a large-scale gasoline-powered automotive industry depended on new developments in the internal-combustion engine, such as valve technology, timing devices, and fuel control. A single basic innovation sets off years of creative activity in the development of related technologies. Complementary innovations in the gasoline-powered automobile involved a number of technologies not related to engines, for example, power transmission devices, body construction, and suspension systems.

Second, new technologies also often require complementary developments external to the new device itself. Capitalizing on the invention of incandescent lighting depended on four related system components: a central power-generating station, a transmission network for conducting electricity, a meter to measure each household's consumption of electricity, and a lamp for producing light.[13] The commercial success of such inventors as Thomas Edison and George Westinghouse has been attributed to their recognition of the importance of the wider system to their specific innovations. Widespread acceptance of the gasoline automobile, for instance, depended on improvements in roads, maintenance and repair services, petroleum refining, and systems for storing and supplying gasoline. Each of these components involved a large and complex technical system. The utility of any basic innovation depends not only on a continuous flow of innovation at the level of the specific device but on development at the level of external systems and infrastructure as well.

Third, capturing the benefits to employment and standard of living from a new technology also depends on establishing a favorable cost-to-volume ratio in production and marketing. New technologies often face a chicken-and-egg dilemma: Cost reductions are needed for demand to increase, and increases in demand are needed for costs to be reduced.

The organizational and managerial innovation called mass production overcame this dilemma for many technologies of the early twentieth century. Henry Ford in particular saw that mass consumption of goods and services required ways to reduce costs dramatically by narrowing and specializing the tasks of the production processes. The ability to rationalize manufacturing through task specialization in industrial production was important to the technological promise of the American economy in the early decades of this century, and continues to be important today. Few dispute that "systems" are indispensable to the realization of technological benefits; however, it is not the system, per se, that matters, but the assumptions embedded in a particular system. In the next section we look more closely at the development of the American system of production and its implicit social values.

❖ The American System of Manufacturing

By the early decades of the twentieth century, the United States had emerged as the center of managerial innovation as well as the center of industrial invention. Management systems capitalized on developments in industrial technology to establish this country as the world model of industrial development. In general, organizational innovations extended economic efficiency to its limits through functional specialization and centralized coordination, which simultaneously lowered production costs, improved product quality, and increased production output.

The extraordinary role of Henry Ford in the history of American industrial development has been widely recorded.[14] Ford's zealous pursuit of manufacturing efficiency in automobile production, and his notable success well into the 1920s, place him in the forefront of American industrial pioneers.

Ford presided over the demise of the craft system of manufacturing and pointed the way to the new era of mass production.[15] Where the craft system made use of general-purpose machines capable of drilling, grinding, and performing other operations, Ford introduced machines, each for a single function, in order to reduce changeover and setup times. Whereas a worker would often build, maintain, and repair his own tools under the craft system, Ford designated specialists for these functions. While craft production meant fitting parts together by hand, mass production used standard, interchangeable parts and simple ways of joining them.

In the craft system the assembly process stayed in one place within the workshop, and the workers moved around to obtain components and tools. In mass production workers remained in one place as tools, components, and the product itself moved past them. The craft system generated low volume, and costs stayed high regardless of the number of items produced. Mass production was capable of producing very high volumes and of lowering unit costs with increasing production volumes. The system of craft manufacturing was a decentralized, complex system of entrepreneur-owners. Under mass production contacts with customers, owners, and suppliers became specialized, and staff jobs were created for functions such as product design, production planning, expediting, purchasing, personnel administration, quality control, and inventory management. Coordinating and controlling the enormous complexity of mass production and the new cadre of staff specialists required a well-defined management hierarchy.

We know, of course, that Henry Ford did not single-handedly convert the craft system of manufacturing to mass production; nor did this transformation occur in a few short years at the beginning of the twentieth century. More than a hundred years earlier, Eli Whitney had developed many of the basic elements of high-volume, high-quality process organization in order to manufacture 10,000 muskets for the U.S. government.[16] Nineteenth-century industrialists, including arms manufacturer Samuel Colt and sewing machine pioneer Isaac Singer, put early elements of the mass production system into place. Frederick W. Taylor's ideas about dividing, timing, controlling, and compensating work, known as scientific management, had a profound impact on management philosophy and practice, as did the efforts of time and motion study specialist Frank Gilbreth.[17] Finally, it fell to Alfred P. Sloan to rationalize the development of specific products for separate market segments and to decentralize operating responsibilities within the multidivisional firm.

Still, Ford stands as the father of the American system of manufacturing. According to analysts of this historical period, Ford "presided over the creation of a massive system of production"[18] and established "the model of choice for American manufacturing" through his "ruthless and tireless insistence on the overall rationalization of the manufacturing system."[19]

❖ Questioning the Model

The defects of functional specialization and centralized control became painfully evident to many observers as managers followed these principles through the first half of this century. Disadvantages of the American manufacturing system are widely known and are experienced daily by millions of working Americans: the combative and debilitating division of corporate employees into management and labor, ignorance or neglect of corporate goals by large segments of employees, distrust and animosity between operating personnel and staff advisers, bloated and redundant middle-level organizations, overly centralized decision making, and the costs of delay created by the complexities of bureaucratic coordination. According to a team of researchers from the Harvard Business School, Henry Ford eventually recognized his failure to integrate "the work force into the production process not as a faceless mechanism but as a reservoir of competitively valuable human strengths."[20] Over time, this deficiency appears to have assumed increasing significance. These observers find that the system of mass production pervasive in North America and Europe is now "thwarting the efforts of many Western companies to move ahead."[21]

American managers are now exhorted to abandon the principles of the past and to adopt more complex, holistic views of their organizations.[22] Consultants, academics, and managers themselves variously entreat corporate officials to implement new paradigms of production that treat the manufacturing process as a coherent, integrated system;[23] to apply the methods of "lean," or low overhead, production;[24] or to manage by "walking around" (communicating spontaneously with people throughout the organization).[25] Managing has been compared to making elephants dance.[26] Even the sacred precepts of market segmentation and product specialization may be losing credibility.[27]

Managers are also urged to reduce the amount of time required for specific "cycles" of operations in the firm.[28] Firms that can reduce the amount of time needed to complete a cycle of sales, order processing, and distribution, or a manufacturing cycle, or a cycle of new product development will increase the efficient use of resources, provide better quality and service, and be more competitive. Time itself needs to be a focus of competitive strategy.

Although specific prescriptions for reform are numerous, most reformers basically want corporations to recapture the ability to innovate. They want the range of specialists relevant to new product development to function as a team. They recommend that labor and management cooperate through participation teams, programs in quality of work life, and quality circles (employee problem-solving groups). They seek to break down the walls of departmentalization and specialization, "flatten" the organization, and generate corporate entrepreneurship. It is not uncommon for Americans to draw inspiration for human resources management from Japanese firms. "Americans buy and sell labor," writes a Harvard study team after comparing the U.S. and Japanese auto industries, "[and] the Japanese build a production process around it."[29]

None of these prescriptions even remotely suggests a return to the views and practices of the nineteenth-century Luddites, who were antitechnology, antiorganization, and antisystem. Japanese competitors, for example, have very highly organized production systems. A successful inventory system that calls for the delivery of raw materials at the time they are needed for production, or an effective statistical process control system, requires closely defined procedures and tight coordination between organization members. The Harvard team observes:

> Henry Ford's vigorous emphasis on the design and fabrication of advanced machine tools, his relentless drive to rationalize production and reduce in-process inventory, his push to make all process flows continuous, his reliance on materials handling equipment, and his focus on simple designs and precise machining—all these and more are part of current Japanese practice.[30]

Significant differences between the American and Japanese manufacturing systems lie in organizational processes: how tasks are assigned, how responsibilities are developed, and how roles are defined. Above all, the chorus of voices calling for change in corporate America wants to put personal needs, energy, and creativity back into the system of American management. What American managers are learning from Japanese managers is to incorporate, in the words of the Harvard study team, "the work force as a fully integrated part of the whole production system."[31]

❖ The Path of American Industrialization

Many factors help to explain why the American manufacturing system took the particular form that it did. First, the economic advantages of rationalized production, once evident, were too great to be seriously challenged. For example, assembling components into a complete automobile required 12.5 hours under the craft system in the fall of 1913. Less than a year later, in the spring of 1914, mass production accomplished the same assembly process in 1 hour and 35 minutes, a reduction of 88 percent.[32] The power of these enormous improvements in productivity was verified by increased demand. The modern Japanese system, on the other hand, did not begin to develop until the 1950s. Though much credit for the successes of Japanese industry has been given to the group-oriented Japanese culture, close observers have concluded that the current Japanese commitment to labor-management cooperation was not inherent in that culture; in fact, it emerged after World War II during a tumultuous period of conflict between Japanese employers and labor unions.[33] The Japanese also learned much from observing the American system as it matured and they managed to avoid its weaknesses.[34] If American industrialists also had had the opportunity to look dispassionately at the later stages of the mass production model and to make a fresh start, American industrial history over the last 45 years might have been written very differently.

Another factor in the formation of the U.S. system was that American society had little experience in combining social and human needs with economic advancement. The industrial entrepreneurs of the late nineteenth century—the Carnegies, Rockefellers, and Goulds—had boldly, shrewdly, and energetically developed the nation. They also were domineering, rapacious, self-righteous, and often crude. Historian Richard Hofstadter characterizes the discrepancy between their behavior and the ideals of the age:

> In business and politics the captains of industry did their work boldly, blandly, and cynically. Exploiting workers and milking farmers, bribing Congressmen, buying legislatures, spying on competitors, hiring armed guards, dynamiting property, using threats and intrigue and force, they made a mockery of the ideals of the simple gentry who imagined that the nation's development could take place with dignity and restraint under the regime of laissez-faire.[35]

American social experience provided neither precedent nor guidance to help designers of manufacturing systems to understand and honor the interdependencies between economy and society.

The social reform movement of the early twentieth century addressed itself to the social consequences of American industrialization. The muckrakers pricked the national conscience by drawing attention, for example, to unsanitary and inhumane working conditions in the Chicago stockyards (in Upton Sinclair's *The Jungle*) that led to enactment of the first food and drug regulation in this country. Around the turn of the century, various states made their first forays, largely unsuccessfully, into the regulation of working conditions to try to protect workers' health and safety. Landmark statutes—the Sherman Act

(1890), Clayton Act (1914), and Federal Trade Commission Act (1914)—were enacted to regulate anticompetitive industrial structures and market behavior.

These and most other attempts to identify and deal with the excesses of industrialization were only remedial, however. Social regulation attempted only to cope with the by-products of industrialization. Social reformers rarely offered a coherent vision either for building greater respect for social values into the process of industrialization or for putting concern for people into manufacturing systems.

❖ Intellectually Grappling with Science, Industry, and Society

Social philosophers and social scientists of the late 1800s and early 1900s were alert to the personal and social consequences of industrialization, but in the end they were no more successful than social activists in changing the assumptions and premises of the industrial system. For example, the division of labor into specialized activities was the central focus of the late-nineteenth-century French sociologist Emile Durkheim. Durkheim realized that division of labor not only differentiates one person from another but also makes people more dependent on each other and may ultimately increase their social consciousness. Durkheim wrote, "[T]he individuality of the whole increases at the same time as the individuality of its parts; the society becomes more capable of collective movement, at the same time as each of its elements has more freedom of movement of its own."[36] Durkheim believed that industrialization could simultaneously lead to both greater autonomy and greater social solidarity.

At the same time, Durkheim saw a pathological side to industrialization. A state of social discord and despair, which he called by the French word *anomie*, can arise when people are forced to accept conditions of life below the potential offered by their natural abilities. Durkheim saw the influence of birthright—being born rich or poor—as a primary cause of anomie. "We must introduce greater justice into [social] relationships, " he wrote, "by further diminishing the external inequalities that are the source of our ills."[37] Although they were a provocative commentary on industrialization, Durkheim's ideas did little to modify the premises or the logic of the system of mass production.

Max Weber, the eminent German sociologist and a contemporary of Durkheim, also studied the impact of industrialization on modern society. Weber named bureaucracy as one of the defining characteristics of modern society: administration according to stipulated rules, impersonal criteria for decisions, specialization of positions, separation of official business from private affairs, and a strict hierarchy of authority. However essential bureaucratic administration was to modern industrial society, Weber was also concerned about its negative impact on the individual person. Weber said, in a speech in 1909,

It is horrible to think that the world could one day be filled with nothing but those little cogs, little men clinging to little jobs and striving towards bigger ones . . . the great question is therefore not how we can promote and hasten it, but what can we oppose to this machinery in order to keep a portion of mankind free from this parcelling-out of the soul, from this supreme mastery of the bureaucratic way of life.[38]

The impact of the machine age also preoccupied the American philosopher John Dewey early in the twentieth century. Dewey's ideas accommodated the enormous forces of industrialization, and he did not quarrel with the many economic benefits of industrialization. Rather, his role as a social philosopher led him to try to reconcile the needs and values of a democratic society with the changes wrought by economic development. Dewey saw the vast mechanical forces and impersonal organizations of industrialization diminishing the significance of face-to-face relationships and human communities. For him, industrialization fragmented society and subjected people to forces outside their control. The machine age robbed citizens of a sense of common experience. Industrialization had left society without effective organizations for controlling the social consequences of technology and without the ability to develop a meaningful sense of itself.

Coping with the threat of social disintegration was, for Dewey, the most urgent challenge to society. In this passage from *The Public and Its Problems*, he lamented the impact of social fragmentation on social decision making:

The ramification of the issues before the public is so wide and intricate, the technical matters involved are [so] specialized, the details are so many and so shifting, that the public cannot for any length of time identify and hold itself [together]. . . . There is too much public, a public too diffused and scattered and too intricate in composition. And there are too many publics, for conjoint actions which have indirect, serious and enduring consequences are multitudinous beyond comparison, and each one of them crosses the others and generates its own group of persons especially affected with little to hold these different publics together in an integrated whole.[39]

Along with other social progressives, Dewey searched for ways to retain social and human control over the forces unleashed by industrialization. He recoiled at the philosophy of individualism and "the doctrine of independence of any and all associations,"[40] which he found inadequate to "meet the needs . . . of the new age."[41]

Dewey's views recall the romantic ideals of Thoreau, Emerson, and Whitman. He argued for the development of intelligence and the education of the person as a way of stimulating association, overcoming social disintegration, and reaffirming community. "The Great Society created by steam and electricity may be a society," wrote Dewey, "but it is no community."[42] One commentator summarized the Progressive vision in this way:

The Progressives were prophets of technology, but they were also prophets of a revival of face-to-face community. Science and community were the two poles of their outlook.... Rightly ordered, the new scientific and industrial order would be a series of small communities linked by the technology of modern communications and supported by the abundance made possible by industry. Late industrialism was reassembling a world order that revived the qualities of earlier community life.[43]

Needless to say, the organization of industry did not follow this course. However, this perspective appears to embody a number of the principles of person-oriented management that American industry now tries to learn from observing the practices of its most successful competitors, especially the Japanese.

❖ Extracting Lessons from Experience with the American System of Manufacturing

Inevitably, the significance of a technology, in this case the American manufacturing system, becomes clear only in retrospect. The issue is not whether history might have written itself differently, but what things we accept as lessons from the past and how they can be applied today. The mass production system of manufacturing has created tremendous benefits; it is also now apparent that the system needs to be reconfigured in order to reduce its human, social, and economic costs. What can we learn?

A first lesson returns discussion to focus on democracy. The designing of technology embodies much more choice than may be apparent at first. No matter how tempting they are on the basis of economic criteria, technological solutions that dehumanize people, revert to hierarchy, and create opportunities for autocracy will be self-defeating in the long run. Technology offers potential; design, a human process, searches for, selects, and establishes specific alternatives. It is well worthwhile to ensure that the people who will be affected by technological choices are included in the design process.

Second, twentieth-century industrial history teaches us that we must make technology strengthen personal associations rather than alienate individuals from one another. American industry is currently engaged in a vast, difficult, and uncompleted retrofitting of the organization of work in order to capitalize on the positive benefits of personal interaction and human involvement. As in most such processes, the cost and difficulty of retrofitting are much greater than the costs of making the right decision in the first place. The designing of manufacturing systems has returned to the recognition that people matter. The challenge is to imprint this lesson on our individual and common consciousness.

The American manufacturing system proceeded from the premises of narrow and unfettered individualism. The enthusiasm of industrialists and engineers for mass production may have been shaped, in part, by the fact that greater rationalization of production gave them power, enhanced their status, and increased their economic security. Like mechanical components, workers were often treated as interchangeable. The social premises of mass production were rarely kind. The breadth of consideration was not great.

Even the simple and obvious lessons of this country's experience with mass production have yet to be fully understood and accepted throughout American business and American schools of business and management. In spite of the impressive changes of the last several decades, U.S. business, as a whole, may still be on the rising slope of the curve of incorporating a new philosophy into its activities. The search for innovative techniques—quality circles, just-in-time inventory systems, factory automation, team development of new products—is intense. Unless these changes represent real shifts in the social premises of management, however, the techniques are unlikely to acquire the needed force of fundamental reform. To the extent that managers currently express ambivalence toward lessons from the past, the outlook for maximizing the social and economic value of technology in the future is cloudy at best.

THE COMMERCIALIZATION OF TECHNOLOGY AS AN INSTITUTIONAL PROCESS

We can make two basic observations on the role and functioning of the American science and technology establishment in the context of the globalization of technology today. First, basic innovation is the strong point of the U.S. system. Second, the system's greatest weakness is its limited ability to commercialize the results of technological innovation efficiently and successfully. It is common knowledge that innovations developed in the United States have often been successfully commercialized elsewhere. Pocket calculators, videocassette recorders, and other consumer electronic products were invented in the United States and yet have been more successfully manufactured and marketed elsewhere, primarily by the Japanese. Although it is true that the economic benefits of industrial innovation are not always snatched away from American firms by others, the apparent frequency with which this does happen is disturbing. In this section we examine the growing need for involving a wide variety of organizations in the commercialization of industrial technology. America's relative weakness in this area results from too narrow a perspective within business and government on the complexities of economic individualism and market processes.

❖ The Roles of Diverse Institutions in the Commercialization of Technology

Complementary Technologies and Nonmarket Organizations The development and use of a specific technology often depend on related or complementary innovations. Economist Nathan Rosenberg points out, for example, that development of the compound steam engine required the availability of cheap, high-quality steel. Likewise, the jet engine depended on metallurgical improvements in airplane construction, and the transistor required innovations in the purification of metal.[44] The discovery that glass could be a medium for transmitting concentrated light signals opened up fiber optics communications. Commercialization of this innovation, however, relied on the development of a variety of peripheral devices for converting between electrical and light signals and of electronic devices for accelerating and attenuating light waves. High-definition television (HDTV), an information technology that can offer visual sharpness comparable to that of 35-millimeter film, involves the integration of a number of new technologies: a method for compressing broadcast signals, digital signal processing chips to translate coded signals into configurations of colored dots, extensive software for making the translations, and large-screen display technology. The number of complementary innovations increases further as this technology is combined with advanced digital-audio technology and with computers. In order to find a place in the market, innovations of any significance rarely remain technically independent.

Integrating the many technical aspects of complex systems requires compatibility among the design and the performance requirements of numerous components. Commercialization of technology may also require the creation of a special nomenclature, establishment of minimum performance standards, and development of criteria for testing and inspection.

Because of the number of complementary technologies and the need to coordinate technological development, the commercialization of a technology often involves a wide range of participants.[45] Professional societies, such as the Institute of Electrical and Electronic Engineers, play an important role in defining the language of a new technology and in spreading an understanding of it among various industries. Trade associations, such as the American Electronics Association, need to alert industry members to significant research agendas as they emerge as well as facilitate the intra- and interindustry development of compatibility requirements, performance standards, and testing procedures for specific technologies. Coordination among institutions becomes important when various aspects of a given technology are being developed separately at universities, other independent research organizations, or government research laboratories. Particular technologies also often touch on issues involving regulatory agencies, such as the Federal Communications Commission, the Food and Drug Administration, or the Environmental Protection Agency.

Improvising Organizations for the Diffusion of Innovation   It is not unusual for new organizations to be created or for existing ones to be refocused in order to achieve the widespread use of a specific technology.

Robert Cole, of the University of Michigan, studied the ways in which an important managerial innovation, the quality circle, was adopted in the United States, Japan, and Sweden in the period between 1960 and 1985.[46] The quality circle is a specific technology that draws on employee participation in natural work groups to identify ways to improve work results: to increase the flexibility and speed of work, use resources more efficiently, or reduce errors and mistakes in the work. Quality circles build on the idea of greater satisfaction of needs for employees through involvement in the work, as advocated in the United States by such people as Abraham Maslow, Douglas McGregor, Rensis Likert, Chris Argyris, and Frederick Herzberg. Quality circles also utilize the methods of statistical quality control developed in the United States by W. Edwards Deming, Joseph Juran, and others. Cole explains the different ways that quality circles were adopted in each of the three countries primarily in terms of leadership in the business community to diffuse small-group technology. He attributes special influence to the ways in which each country's national organizational infrastructure responded to this technology.

The quality circle movement in Sweden originated in a larger national political consensus endorsing industrial democracy. By the mid-1960s, the main national business association, the Swedish Employers Confederation, had assumed leadership for implementing the concept of the quality circle. The confederation, representing 30,000 Swedish companies and 40 percent of the country's work force, was a highly respected organization. It created a technical department that encouraged companies to experiment with new approaches to organizing work and publicized successful efforts, and then identified the best practices, generalized from them, and disseminated the results widely. The Swedish Employers Confederation and the two major union federations in Sweden also formed a joint organization to initiate and sponsor pilot cooperative projects.

The Japanese Union of Scientists and Engineers (JUSE) is an organization based on corporate membership that provides services to Japanese companies in the areas of quality and reliability. As early as 1962, this organization had set up a unit to promote quality circles, establishing itself as the leading organization in Japan for the widespread adoption of the technique. JUSE is part of the inner circle of Japanese business leadership. Its chairman, for example, has always been either the current or past chairman of the Japanese Federation of Economic Organizations, the country's most powerful business association. By 1987, JUSE had 1,800 corporate members.

In contrast with the Swedish practice, JUSE democratized the quality circle movement. It set up a national registration system in 1962, welcoming production and office workers into the organization and creating the sense of a mass movement. Participants were offered a variety of training activities, an awards program was initiated, a monthly journal was established, and a program of highly popular local quality circle conventions was begun. In 1987, 250,000 quality circles were registered;

Cole estimates that more than 2 million Japanese employees participated in quality circles in the workplace during that year.[47]

In the United States two organizations strove for national leadership of the quality circle movement. In the late 1970s and early 1980s, a long-standing professional organization, the American Society for Quality Control, sought to spearhead the adoption of quality circles in industry. However, this organization had historically been committed only to individual training and development, it had no corporate members, and its individual professional members tended to be managers at middle and lower levels. Advocates pressing for new initiatives were mainly defeated by bureaucratic inertia and by the fact that the organization itself was not in the mainstream of corporate priorities.

Another organization, the International Association for Quality Circles, was created in 1978 specifically to fill the leadership gap in the quality circle movement. This organization started a series of local chapters, produced a journal, and began holding national conferences that were soon successful in drawing attention to this business technology. But its membership also consisted mainly of members of personnel departments from the middle and lower corporate ranks, and they participated as volunteers. The association gradually turned into a mechanism by which large numbers of consultants gained access to corporations, and not one for the expression of industry's commitment to changing relationships and results within the workplace. Cole's analysis of the relatively weak adoption of quality circles in U.S. industry concludes:

> Ultimately, we can understand [the outcome of the quality circle movement] in terms of the failure of American top management to take a leadership role in supporting the IAQC or any other organization that aimed at leading a national movement for small-group activities. For most of the period in question, top management in America was not seriously interested in small-group activities as a solution to its problems. Even when more interest did develop among some top managers in the early 1980s, their firms were by and large uninterested in building a national infrastructure for diffusing these innovations.[48]

Cole's comparative analysis of the adoption of quality circles by three different nations shows that large-scale organizations (what Cole calls infrastructure) strongly influence the adoption of innovation. A predisposition among leaders within the private sector to create a favorable institutional context for the diffusion of an innovation appears to be as important for managerial technologies such as quality circles as for complex physical technologies such as HDTV. Such a perspective, however, requires that leaders envision the firm as part of a much larger institutional infrastructure rather than as an autonomous entity.

The leadership of the private sector may have been, on the whole, more concerned with the borders of the firm than with its ties to the institutional environment. But what has been the U.S. public policy stance toward issues of technological interdependence and institution building? In the next section we examine the assumptions about the development and commercialization of technology that form the basis of U.S. public policy.

❖ The Limited Tools of U.S. Policy Toward Innovation[49]

***Subsidies for* Innovation** Through a variety of laws and grant programs for research, public policy in the United States has recognized that society as a whole often receives benefits from industrial innovation above and beyond the profits obtained by an innovating firm or person. Handsome profits may accrue to an innovating firm, for example, from the development of ways to recover 10 percent more oil and natural gas from existing wells. But the rate of private return may still be less than the innovation's economic value to society in at least two ways: the preservation of jobs and the payment of both corporate and individual taxes. Such an innovation should also reduce, to a degree, the outflow of dollars for purchasing imported oil, and it may even generate a positive flow of foreign exchange through overseas applications.

Benefits to the public above the cost of an innovation constitute "spillover" gains to society from private innovation. Economists who have systematically evaluated the private and social returns of industrial innovation conclude that economic returns to private parties, on the average, represent only about half of the returns to society as a whole from the innovation.[50] According to one economist, these studies show that "many innovations which would pay handsome social returns are not being carried out, because private rates of return to the innovating firm are unattractive."[51]

If returns to the private sector from innovation are less than the returns to the public, society as a whole would be better off by subsidizing innovation efforts up to the point at which the social cost of public investment in innovation matches the benefit to society from the investment. No one knows exactly where this point is in any given case; nevertheless, this thinking underlies such current policies as protection of intellectual property, grants to university researchers, and tax credits for increases in corporate spending on research and development. Policies for subsidizing innovation are based on a positive view of individuals' economic motives. They assume that because, on the average, firms receive satisfactory returns on investments in innovation, managers have a natural motive to pursue innovation. In this policy perspective, social interests and business interests converge. From this perspective, society as a whole will be better off by helping business do more of what it is naturally willing to do.

Antitrust Restraints on Economic Behavior Antitrust is a second way in which U.S. policy recognizes the social value of industrial innovation, but antitrust laws represent a more pessimistic view of business behavior. Economic assumptions underlying antitrust legislation hold that business competition alone forces individuals and firms to innovate. Without competition, firms have little incentive to innovate and may even try to suppress new technology in order to avoid additional capital investment. Society as a whole would obviously find these tendencies undesirable.

An absence of competition results in negative spillovers to society—higher prices, lower demand and the related loss of jobs, and inefficient allocation of capital. Antitrust law is intended to discourage socially detrimental behavior by preventing, and punishing when appropriate, collusion to gain market power and attempts to monopolize. The antitrust perspective is based on the assumption that society in general and business have conflicting interests. It assumes that society wants competition and innovation; it also assumes that managers look for ways to avoid head-to-head competition between firms and would just as soon not have the survival of a firm, and their own personal accomplishments, tied to the firm's success in innovating.

❖ Consequences of Conflicting Perspectives

Innovation subsidies are based on the view that individual economic actors are predisposed to invest in innovation and create positive social spillovers; antitrust enforcement, on the other hand, is based on the view that economic actors are predisposed to collude and will generate negative social spillovers. In the final analysis public policy conflicts reflect nothing more than conflicting views of individual behavior and differences in how people react to economic freedom. These differences and conflicts create two problems for U.S. policy: ambivalent and indecisive public actions and a lack of attention to the role of nonmarket organizations.

Ambivalent and Indecisive Actions   In the short run opposing views of individual behavior generate ambivalent and inconsistent policy, public policy toward interfirm cooperation being a case in point. The generous view of economic behavior holds that cooperative research, and preferably joint marketing and production among competitors, should be permitted in order to stimulate innovation within a given industry.[52] Because most innovations can be imitated easily, competitive market structures place excessive risk on innovators. In this view leading firms consequently reduce their investment in innovation in order to avoid providing opportunities for free riders to take advantage of their efforts; cooperative research obviates this condition and lets firms' natural tendency to innovate prevail.

The suspicious view of economic behavior arrives at a diametrically opposed conclusion. Cooperative research, from this perspective, is a form of collusion that dulls incentives for individual firms to achieve superior performance by developing proprietary technology.[53] Thus, cooperative arrangements are inherently anticompetitive and will slow, not accelerate, innovation; cooperative research only reinforces firms' natural tendency to avoid the challenge of developing new technology. U.S. public policy toward collaborative research appears to be hampered by conflicting assumptions about how economic motives will be expressed.

Exclusion of Nonmarket Organizations **from Public Policy** Inattention to the role that professional societies, trade associations, independent research organizations, and public interest groups play in the overall policy process for the development and commercialization of technology is the second major problem of current U.S. public policy. Many innovations are created in situations of technological interdependence, and their successful commercialization requires contributions from noncorporate organizations. Public policy risks being ineffective by ignoring the organizational implications of technological complexity. Effective policy might, for example, facilitate standard setting in industry and encourage interindustry information sharing. Public policy might encourage more interaction among industry, professional societies, research and education organizations, labor, public interest groups, and government agencies on the problems of development and coordination of technology.

The issue is less whether to provide public subsidies for research than it is how to build an effective infrastructure for the development and commercialization of innovation. For a radically new technology, an effective infrastructure may take several decades to develop; the Japanese experience with high-definition television can be seen as a 25-year period of infrastructure development.[54] Returns to society as a whole from public investment can be evaluated better through a process that involves a greater number of organizations over a longer period of time. A long time horizon also allows public decisions to be more strategic and less political, that is, more effective in actually facilitating the development and adoption of a new technology.

The working assumption in the United States appears to be that individually oriented market behavior will allocate resources efficiently and integrate the diverse aspects of technology development. In this view nonmarket organizations are only an adjunct to the main activity of innovation within the firm or, at most, within joint ventures. Contributions from industry research associations, for example, are the exception rather than the rule. Inasmuch as little is expected, it is not surprising that industry associations play a relatively weak role in technology development. If Americans view nonmarket organizations as irrelevant or invasive, the motivation to make them work may be weaker. A bias toward economic autonomy makes coordinative and collective action organizations less effective.

TECHNOLOGICAL DECISION MAKING: RECONCILING ETHICS AND ECONOMICS

Researchers typically distinguish between incremental and discontinuous innovations.[55] Incremental innovations are less complex and require fewer changes in existing technological systems. In contrast, discontinuous innovations cause severe dislocations in existing industrial technology, call for many related changes in existing technological systems, and usually involve a wide variety of affected groups. Development of the jet engine, for example, revolutionalized the air transport industry. High-definition television is a current example of a complex, relatively discontinuous technology. The development and widespread use of HDTV will place greater demands on nonmarket organizations than will simpler, more continuous innovations.

The diffusion of innovation is even more complicated in cases where technology may have a highly visible, immediate social impact, such as a potential threat to health or the imminent loss of jobs. The kind of decision-making process that a society uses for a given technology becomes critical in these circumstances.

❖ A Collision Between Economics and Ethics in Genetic Engineering

The process of developing and using a genetically engineered substance, recombinant bovine growth hormone (rBGH),[56] illustrates a contemporary collision between ethics and economics. This hormone, which improves a lactating cow's use of absorbed nutrients, is produced naturally by dairy cows in minute amounts. Recombinant DNA techniques allow the manufacture of the hormone in much larger quantities. Since the early 1980s, researchers have found that daily injections of rBGH increase dairy cows' milk production between 10 and 20 percent.[57] Projecting an estimated global market as large as $1 billion per year for this drug, four U.S. drug companies, Monsanto Agricultural, Upjohn, American Cyanamid, and Eli Lilly, have invested between $100 million and $500 million in its development. In 1985, the Food and Drug Administration judged milk from rBGH-treated cows to be safe for humans beings, and the agency approved large-scale field experimentation with the drug. Thus, rBGH became the first of what is expected to be a long series of genetically engineered drugs promising major increases in the productivity of farm animals. After a fresh review of a series of studies two FDA researchers reiterated the judgment in favor of the drug's safety in August 1990;[58] in May 1991, the Congressional Office of Technology Assessment agreed that the hormone posed no fundamental danger.[59] In September 1990, the editors of the *New York Times* called rBGH a "riskless hormone."[60]

The drug soon became mired in social controversy, however. In 1990, Samuel Epstein, of the University of Illinois School of Public Health, summarized a number of unanswered questions about the veterinary and public health effects of rBGH.[61] Epstein questioned the increased stress and susceptibility to infectious disease of cows treated with the drug. He raised concerns about reduced fertility in treated cows and challenged assumptions about the nutritional quality of rBGH milk. Epstein also disputed the industry's claims that the synthetic rBGH is chemically identical to natural BGH, and he pointed out that no studies had been conducted with synthetic hormones of the potent rBGH type.

Among other reservations about the effect on human health, Epstein pointed to research suggesting a greater incidence of a related hormone, IGF-1, in the milk of rBGH-treated cows. Incremental levels of IGF-1 might, he argued, conceivably stimulate premature growth in infants, cause abnormal growth of mammary glands in male children, or increase the chances of breast cancer in women. The unknown risks of IGF-1 led a highly respected consumer organization, Consumers Union, to oppose the sale of milk from rBGH-treated cows in late 1990.[62] This was a major setback for the drug industry.

As a spokesperson for a variety of consumer, health, and animal rights advocacy groups, Epstein called for a ban on the manufacture and sale of rBGH until the concerns that had been raised could be resolved. Negative publicity surrounding the drug led a number of major dairy products companies and retailers, including Borden, Dannon Yogurt, First National Supermarkets, Kraft General Foods, Kroger, and Safeway, to refuse to accept rBGH test milk.[63] Epstein's recommendations involved intergenerational human-impact studies, which would seriously delay, if not prevent entirely, the commercial use of the drug.

Beyond the health questions, critics faulted the drug's impact on the job security of dairy farmers and on government spending. Additional capital and operating requirements for using rBGH would accelerate the ongoing trend toward consolidation in the dairy-farming industry. One agricultural economist estimated that widespread use of rBGH would cause milk prices to fall 10 to 15 percent and would put between 73,000 and 108,000 dairy farmers out of business.[64] In 1990, two dairy-farming states, Wisconsin and Minnesota, imposed temporary bans on the use of the drug in the industry, and other states began considering mandating the labeling of rBGH milk.

While rBGH represents unnecessary social and personal costs to some people, to others the commercialization of rBGH stands for economic progress. The editors of the *Wall Street Journal*, for example, point out that in 1950 the average American dairy cow produced only 5,314 pounds of milk per year.[65] Technological advances, such as artificial insemination and new feeding methods, introduced over the next 40 years boosted production to more than 14,300 pounds per year by 1991. These advances no doubt created consolidation in the dairy-farming industry and created personal hardship; in the view of the editors of the *Journal*, economic progress should not be held hostage to what is, after all, a relatively small number of farmers.

Some have argued that one way to cushion the impact of rBGH on employment, especially in the main dairy states, would be for the public to further subsidize the price of milk. In 1986, the federal government spent nearly $2.5 billion on dairy price-support programs;[66] Consumers Union estimated that widespread use of rBGH would require the spending of another $1.7 billion per year simply to maintain current milk prices.[67] This might be an acceptable solution to the dairy states and the dairy farmers, but it would probably gain little favor with people who are already concerned about the size and impact of the federal budget deficit.

❖ Social Decision Making About Technology

Overreaction in the Public Sector   The rBGH case illustrates several dimensions of the complex interaction between technology and society. The ability of anti-rBGH forces to mobilize opposition to the commercial use of this drug exemplifies society's sensitivity to health risks, especially risks caused by hormone manipulation. In this sense, the readiness of independent scientists and social activists to challenge the commercial use of rBGH represents, in part, the legacy of this country's regrettable 30-year experience with another synthetic hormone, diethylstilbestrol, or DES.[68] Initially acclaimed as a miracle drug, this chemical was widely used in the treatment of female infertility; as a preventive therapy against miscarriage; as a growth-stimulating additive in chicken, cattle, and hog feed; and as a "morning-after" birth control pill. Some of these uses were continued even after researchers established conclusive evidence of the drug's carcinogenicity. Numerous daughters of women who took the drug to treat infertility are now suffering from vaginal cancer and continue to press litigation against the former producers and marketers of the drug. The DES experience sensitized the American public to the effects of products involving hormone manipulation and, in an important sense, set the stage for the policy battle on rBGH.

Threatening events have made many Americans sensitive to other technologically based risks. The term *nuclear*, for example, has practically achieved code-word status for "unreasonably dangerous." Hiroshima and Nagasaki demonstrated the destructive power of the atom; a near-catastrophe at Three Mile Island, near Harrisburg, Pennsylvania, heightened many Americans' sense of the risk to community and nation; the Chernobyl nuclear accident in Ukraine illustrated how one country's negligence can affect innocent citizens of other countries; and the unsafe handling and disposal of nuclear materials at U.S. weapons facilities demonstrated management's negligence toward employees and nearby communities. These incidents explain the resistance of states and communities to providing sites for the disposal of nuclear waste. Similarly, the human and environmental effects of numerous industrial chemicals had been disputed in the United States until the deaths and suffering of thousands of people in Bhopal, India, in 1984 from the release of the deadly chemical isocyanate heightened public sensitivity to chemical hazards.

The stage is now set for Americans to organize quickly and effectively to combat perceived public health risks. Social activists, some scientists, individual whistle-blowers, and receptive congresspersons see themselves as counterweights to the economic and social influence of industry. Professional societies, government agencies, the media, "public interest" organizations, trade associations, individual companies, self-proclaimed or scientifically credible experts, and a number of politicians stand ready to limit specific technologies. It appears that the public policy arena does not suffer from a shortage of involved participants on technology-based issues; nor is there a shortage of contentious issues to debate.

Dramatic events often shift the center of gravity toward greater social regulation in debates about technological risks and benefits. For example, mounting evidence of the carcinogenic effects of DES played a role in the passage of the Delaney Amendment in 1958, which imposes an absolute ban on adding any substance that causes cancer in humans or animals, in any concentration, to food for human consumption. Safety requirements for the construction and operation of nuclear power plants have virtually brought that industry to a standstill. Bhopal played a role in the Occupational Safety and Health Administration's promulgation, in the mid-1980s, of "community right to know" rules, which established extensive labeling and disclosure standards for the storage, handling, and transportation of many industrial chemicals.

In reaction to perceived technological risks, society bans substances and products, creates regulatory hurdles, makes legal doctrines more punitive, and demands additional social investments. In the process it may also overestimate the extent of a risk, and public officials may act unnecessarily. Through the federal government's overestimation of the risk from an influenza strain known as "swine flu," U.S. citizens incurred an expense of more than $400 million in order to implement an immunization program in the mid-1970s.[69] In spite of early signs that the number of fatalities from reaction to the vaccine itself would be greater than the number of lives it would save, the government proceeded with the unnecessary program. Examples of apparent overreaction to technological risk include the banning of the chemical Alar, used to prevent preharvest fruit drop, improve color, and extend the storage life of apples,[70] and requiring removal of normal building materials containing asbestos from schools and commercial buildings where there is no measurable risk to occupants.[71] Policy analyst Nicolas S. Martin includes the public panic in 1984 over traces of ethylene dibromide (EDB) in food, and he argues that the public overreacted to reports of dioxins in the soil in New York's Love Canal and Times Beach, Missouri.[72] The media, in particular, play a strong role in creating environmental myths and hoaxes, in Martin's view. The actual risks can never be known completely at the moment of decision, and the process of social decision making must be able to account for scientific and technological uncertainty. The readiness of interested parties to respond to technological risk helps society at large to avoid accepting the dangerous as safe; it can also harm society by rejecting the safe as dangerous.

Our system for formulating social policy concerning technology makes few anticipatory decisions. Issues arise as an initiating party, usually industry, develops and commercializes new technology from its perspective. Objections may then come from the media; from health, consumer, or environmental groups; from independent scientists; or from politicians. In the end, the intended technology may go forward, be subjected to regulation, or be banned. Conflicts usually are addressed, however, only after parties have made investments, solidified positions, and drawn conclusions. In addition, the system repeats itself; there is little provision for extracting lessons from past confrontations or avoiding recurrent conflicts. The system seems to suffer from technological myopia, which we may define as an attitude allowing for the formulation of policy toward technology without regard to its full social, economic, and ethical consequences.

Creating "Upstream" Dialogue on the Uses of Technology How can this society avoid technological myopia? Some observers advocate adding a requirement for the evaluation of the social and economic effects of a new drug, such as rBGH, to the FDA's current evaluation of safety and efficacy. Such a review, however, would occur far "downstream," after enormous investments had been made in developing and testing the new product. This proposal would formalize and strengthen social and ethical factors in the approval of new drugs. Companies undoubtedly would consider these factors earlier in their innovation investments, but social concerns would come to a head only after positions on the merits and risks of the drug were well established by the various parties. The proposal would also add to the delay and cost of new technology and thus diminish the economic returns to innovation.

Others have argued for an institutional mechanism capable of evaluating the costs and benefits of new technologies in a broad sense at an early stage in their development. Such a mechanism would also allow consideration of a wide range of perspectives that might influence public sector research priorities. The Office of Technology Assessment's report on rBGH points to the noticeable absence of such an organization within the federal agricultural research establishment:

> Presently, little information about new technologies is available prior to commercialization. There is no institution within the agricultural science policy community that develops information on the benefits and risks of any technology ex ante. There is also no formal structure that provides input to decisionmakers from all affected parties (farmers, marketers, researchers, consumers, etc.). Thus there is no comprehensive information about the benefits and risks of a new technology prior to commercialization and,

therefore, no inclusive criteria to determine how public research resources should be allocated.[73]

An experiment called the Northern Tier Cooperative Land Grant Accountability Project has attempted to implement a similar concept by bringing together citizens and university researchers in Wisconsin, Minnesota, and North and South Dakota.[74] This group involves concerned citizens in discussions about biotechnology research at public universities in these states. The goal is to set priorities among potential research projects that meet both social and economic criteria. The project encourages research on agricultural practices that "require fewer chemical pesticides and fertilizers, [fewer] animal pharmaceuticals, and [less] costly feed."[75] This project has potential for involving the public in the research agenda, building public support for scientific work in agriculture, and avoiding substantial investments in technologies that may ultimately be opposed from a public interest perspective.

The Northern Tier group is embarking on a difficult and ambitious mission. Scientific development is not predictable; success often depends on serendipity. Becoming highly sensitive to public concerns would risk making research programs timid and unimaginative. Also, large-scale cooperative efforts impose high costs for coordination, making these efforts difficult to sustain. Interest in public participation may be vigorous in the wake of intense controversy, as in the case of rBGH. The controversy generated by rBGH will eventually dissipate, however, and the benefits of public involvement may become less visible. The personal and institutional costs of coordination, on the other hand, may become relatively more significant and the time and cost of planning are likely to be significant.

Further, multistate and multiparty organizations such as the Northern Tier Project may lack participation by the appropriate industries. Recombinant BGH was first developed by Genentech in California with a grant from Monsanto Corporation in Missouri. While a citizen-and-university cooperative effort might contribute to socially intelligent research priorities in the Northern Tier states, it still might not have alerted the companies involved to the social implications of rBGH at an early stage. The difficulties of creating and sustaining an encompassing "upstream" organization are greatly magnified in view of the unpredictable nature of scientific discovery, the wide range of innovators, and the physical separation of innovator, commercial agent, and user.

It may be more realistic for industry and government to create national technology-specific ad hoc organizations to evaluate economic and social issues early in the life of a research program. Thus, citizen representatives, commercial agents, users, and independent scientists could be brought together to examine an emerging technology or a specific innovation at an early stage. The perspectives of these groups and the issues they would raise could provide useful input into public and private research priorities.

The rBGH case indicates that the commercialization of innovation is a social and a political process every bit as much as it is an economic process. The social impact of a technology must ultimately be reconciled with the technology's economic potential. The current framework for commercialization, however, views the adoption of innovation as a process initiated by economic factors and calls for social and economic reconciliation at a relatively late stage in the development cycle.

A more productive approach might be for innovators to broaden their thinking about commercialization to test the innovation, on a nonbinding basis, against the variety of perspectives and values that eventually it will have to confront. This way of thinking would serve to gain much-needed public input into technology development and could ultimately be more satisfying and productive for industry and society. It does, however, require interested parties to accept explicitly the fact that technology has many kinds of effects and to recognize the limitations of each individual group's perspective.

CONCLUSION

There can be no doubt about the close and important tie between technology and economics. The American system of manufacturing stands as an excellent example of the positive economic consequences of innovation. Many of the opportunities and satisfactions of contemporary life depend not only on the American commitment to science but also on business's interest in converting innovation to practical use—and its ability to do so.

In this chapter I have argued that Americans' understanding of technology is often unnecessarily, and unfortunately, limited to economics. The social aspects of technology rarely provide the initial rationale and motivating force for innovation, but they do influence the ultimate potential and the limitations of technology. The limits of rationalizing production without regard to human and social processes are now evident. We have seen how the economic assumptions of commercialization, as in cooperative industrial research, are narrow and contradictory; the strength of citizen interest groups and their ability to intervene in the use of biotechnology, as in the case of rBGH, are clear.

These cases do not disconfirm the validity and importance of economic motivation in technology development; they simply point to the need for a broader perspective and greater sensitivity. Limiting one's view of the development and commercialization of technology only to economic incentives and market processes simply defers the day of reckoning. Because economic incentives often initiate and motivate the commercialization process, business has the greatest opportunity to incorporate human and social factors into technological design and to reconcile social and ethical concerns at an early stage of the process. The ideology of individualism does us a disservice if it leads us to view ourselves as autonomous economic actors and encourages us to expect that the process of commercialization to consist solely of economic transactions.

Recognizing and coping with the world's complexity do not inherently require the sacrifice of economic individualism. The real question is whether our coping strategy will be effective. We show breadth of vision and a true understanding of self-interest when we recognize clearly that ultimately technology, and economics itself, are integral parts of a complex, multifaceted society.

[1]"The Alzheimer's Morass," *Wall Street Journal*, March 26, 1991, p. A16; "Second Chance for Alzheimer's," *Wall Street Journal*, July 15, 1991, p. A10; "FDA May Release Drug for Alzheimer's," *Wall Street Journal*, July 15, 1991, p. B1; and "Requiem for Alzheimer's Patients," *Wall Street Journal*, July 19, 1991, p. A12.

[2]Aldous Huxley, "Achieving a Perspective on the Technological Order," in Melvin Kranzberg and William H. Davenport, eds., *Technology and Culture: An Anthology* (New York: New American Library, 1972), pp. 123–123.

[3]Lewis Mumford, "Authoritarian and Democratic Technics," in *Technology and Culture: An Anthology*, pp. 1–8.

[4]Robert U. Ayers, "Technology: The Wealth of Nations," *Technological Forecasting and Social Change*, 33 (1988), pp. 189–201; Ralph Landau and Nathan Rosenberg, eds., *The Positive Sum Strategy: Harnessing Technology for Economic Growth* (Washington, D.C.: National Academy Press, 1986), p. vi.

[5]Michael E. Porter, *The Competitive Advantage of Nations* (New York: Free Press, 1990).

[6]David C. Mowery and Nathan Rosenberg, *Technology and the Pursuit of Economic Growth* (Cambridge: Cambridge University Press, 1989), p. 16.

[7]U.S. Department of Commerce, Economics and Statistics Administration, Bureau of the Census, *Marital Status and Living Arrangements: March 1990*, Current Population Reports, Populations Characteristics, Series P-20, no. 450, May 1991, p. 5.

[8]Ibid.

[9]Ibid., p. 13.

[10]Ibid.; and U.S. Department of Commerce, Bureau of the Census, *Statistical Abstract of the United States 1990*, "Population and Area," p. 7.

[11]Norman J. Vig, "Technology, Philosophy, and the State: An Overview," in Michael E. Kraft and Norman J. Vig, eds., *Technology and Politics* (Durham, North Carolina: Duke University Press, 1988), pp. 21–24.

[12]Quoted in Newton Minow, "The Impact of Television," in Donald L. Robinson, ed., *Reforming American Government: The Bicentennial Papers of the Committee on the Constitutional System*, ed. (Boulder, Colo.: Westview Press, 1985), p. 111.

[13]Nathan Rosenberg, "Technological Interdependence in the American Economy," *Technology and Culture*, 20, 1 (January 1979), p. 29.

[14]Thomas P. Hughes, *American Genesis: A Century of Invention and Technological Enthusiasm 1870–1970* (New York: Viking, 1989), pp. 203–220; and James P. Womack, Daniel T. Jones, and Daniel Roos, *The Machine That Changed the World* (New York: Macmillan, 1990), pp. 21–47, esp. n. 5.

[15]Reprinted with permission of Rawson Associates, an imprint of Macmillan Publishing Company from Womack, Jones, and Roos, *The Machine*, pp. 26–43, copyright © 1990 James P. Womack, Daniel T. Jones, Daniel Roos and Donna Sammons Carpenter.

[16]Comments drawn from William J. Abernathy, Kim B. Clark, and Alan M. Kantrow, *Industrial Renaissance: Producing a Competitive Future for America* (New York: Basic Books, 1983), pp. 30–38.

[17]Hughes, *American Genesis*, pp. 188–203.

[18]Ibid., p. 203.

[19]Abernathy, Clark, and Kantrow, *Industrial Renaissance*, p. 39.

[20]Ibid.

[21]Womack, Jones, and Roos, *The Machine*, p. 30.

[22]Richard T. Pascale and Anthony G. Athos, *The Art of Japanese Management: Applications for American Executives* (New York: Warner, 1982).

[23]Abernathy, Clark, and Kantrow, *Industrial Renaissance*, p. 77.

[24]Womack, Jones, and Roos, *The Machine*, pp. 48–70.

[25]Tom Peters and Nancy Austin, *A Passion for Excellence: The Leadership Difference* (New York: Random House, 1985).

[26]Rosabeth Moss Kanter, *Teaching Elephants to Dance: The Post-Entrepreneurial Revolution in Strategy, Management and Careers* (New York: Simon & Schuster, 1989).

[27]Peter F. Drucker, "The Big Three Miss Japan's Crucial Lesson," *Wall Street Journal*, June 18, 1991, p. A18.

[28]George Stalk, Jr., and Thomas M. Hout, *Competing Against Time: New Time-Based Competition Is Reshaping Global Markets* (New York: Free Press, 1990).

[29]Abernathy, Clark, and Kantrow, *Industrial Renaissance*, p. 78.

[30]Ibid., p. 79.

[31]Ibid., p. 78.

[32]Womack, Jones, and Roos, *The Machine*, p. 29.

[33]Robert E. Cole, *Strategies for Learning: Small-Group Activities in American, Japanese and Swedish Industry* (Berkeley: University of California Press, 1989), pp. 12–13.

[34]Womack, Jones, and Roos, *The Machine*, pp. 48–69.

[35]Richard Hofstadter, *The American Political Tradition and the Men Who Make It* (New York: Vintage Books, 1974), p. 212.

[36]Kenneth Thompson, ed., *Readings from Emile Durkheim* (London: Routledge, 1985), p. 48.

[37]Ibid., p. 57.

[38]Quoted in Reinhard Bendix, *Max Weber: An Intellectual Portrait* (New York: Doubleday, 1960), p. 464.

[39]John Dewey, *The Public and Its Problems* (New York: Henry Holt, 1927), p. 137.

[40]Ibid., p. 87.

[41]Ibid., p. 96.

[42]Ibid., p. 98.

[43]Joseph Featherstone, "John Dewey and David Riesman: From the Lost Individual to the Lonely Crowd," in *On the Making of Americans: Essays in Honor of David Riesman*, ed. Herbert J. Gans et al. (Philadelphia: University of Pennsylvania Press, 1979), p. 21.

[44]Rosenberg, "Technological Interdependence," p. 31.

[45]N. Mohan Reddy, John D. Aram and Leonard H. Lynn, "The Institutional Domain of Technology Diffusion," *Journal of Product Innovation Management*, 8, 4 (December 1991), pp. 295–304.

[46]Cole, *Strategies for Learning*.

[47]Ibid., p. 280.

[48]Ibid., p. 299.

[49]This discussion is drawn from John D. Aram, Leonard H. Lynn, and N. Mohan Reddy, "Institutional Relationships and Technology Commercialization: Limitations of Market-Based Policy," *Research Policy*, in press.

[50]Edwin Mansfield, John Rapoport, Anthony Romeo, Samuel Wagner, and George Beardsley, "Social and Private Rates of Return from Industrial Innovations," *Quarterly Journal of Economics*, 91, (May 1977), pp. 221–240; and J. P. Tewksbury, M. S. Crandall, and W. E. Crane, "Measuring the Societal Benefits of Innovation," *Science*, August 8, 1980, pp. 658–662.

[51]Eric von Hippel, "Increasing Innovators' Returns from Innovation," in *Research on Technological Innovation, Management and Policy*, ed. Richard S. Rosenbloom (Greenwich, Conn.: JAI Press, 1983), pp. 35–36.

[52]Thomas M. Jorde and David J. Teece, "Competition and Cooperation: Striking the Right Balance," *California Management Review*, 31, 3 (Spring 1989), pp. 25–37; Lawrence J. White, "Clearing the Legal Path to Collaborative Research," *Technology Review*, 88, 5, (July 1985), pp. 38–45.

[53]William G. Shepard, "Three 'Efficiency School' Hypotheses about Market Power," *Antitrust Bulletin* (Summer 1988), pp. 395–415; Robert G. Harris and David C. Mowery, "New Plans for Joint Ventures: The Results May Be an Unwelcome Surprise," *American Enterprise* 1, 5, (September–October 1990), pp. 52–55.

[54]Aram, Lynn, and Reddy, "Institutional Relationships."

[55]Michael L. Tushman and Philip Anderson, "Technological Discontinuities and Organizational Environments," *Administrative Science Quarterly*, 31, (September 1986), pp. 439–465.

[56]Recombinant bovine growth hormone is also referred to as bovine somatotropin (bST).

[57]Jonathan Rauch, "Drug on the Market," *National Journal*, April 4, 1987, p. 818.

[58]Judith C. Juskevich and C. Greg Guyer, "Bovine Growth Hormone: Human Food Safety Evaluation," *Science*, August 24, 1990, pp. 875–884.

[59]U.S. Congress, Office of Technology Assessment, *U.S. Dairy Industry at a Crossroad: Biotechnology and Policy Choices—Special Report*, OTA-F-470 (Washington, D.C.: U.S. Government Printing Office, May 1991).

[60]"Riskless Hormone," *New York Times*, September 2, 1990, p. 12E. Copyright © 1990 by The New York Times Company. Reprinted by permission.

[61]Samuel S. Epstein, "Potential Public Health Hazards of Biosynthetic Milk Hormones," *International Journal of Health Services*, 20, 1 (1990), pp. 73–84.

[62]"Use of Growth Hormone in Milk Cows Is Assailed by Two Consumer Groups," *Wall Street Journal*, December 4, 1990, p. B4.

[63]Foundation on Economic Trends, "Information Packet on Bovine Growth Hormone," May 4, 1990.

[64]Robert J. Kalter, "The New Biotech Agriculture: Unforeseen Economic Consequences," *Issues in Science and Technology* (Fall 1985), pp. 125–133.

[65]"Those Terrifying Cows," *Wall Street Journal*, January 7, 1991, p. A12.

[66]Rauch, "Drug on the Market," p. 818.

[67]"Use of Growth Hormone" p. B4.

[68]See, for example, Diana B. Dutton, *Worse than the Disease: Pitfalls of Medical Progress* (Cambridge: Cambridge University Press, 1988), pp. 31–90.

[69]Ibid., p. 168.

[70]Joseph D. Rosen, "Much Ado About Alar," *Issues in Science and Technology*, 7, 1 (Fall 1990), pp. 85–90.

[71]Barbara P. Billauer, Joseph J. Giamboi, Karen S. Jore, and William D. Latza, "The Pull-Out Panic," *ReActions* (March 1990), pp. 41–44.

[72]Nicolas S. Martin, "Environmental Myths and Hoaxes: The Evidence of Guilt Is Insufficient," *Vital Speeches of the Day*, May 1, 1990, pp. 434–437. With respect to the effects of dioxins, see also "U.S. Backing Away from Saying Dioxin Is a Deadly Peril," *New York Times*, August 15, 1991, pp. A1, 12.

[73]U.S. Congress, Office of Technology Assessment, "U.S. Dairy Industry at a Crossroad," p. 12.

[74]Wade Roush, "Who Decides About Biotech?" *Technology Review*, July 30, 1991, pp. 28–36.

[75]Ibid., p. 36.

Personal Reality and Social Development: Implications for Managers

❖❖❖❖❖

Economic historian Elting Morison describes a revealing incident in the development of continuous-aim firing, a new technique in naval weaponry at the beginning of this century.[1] Until the early 1900s, guns were placed in fixed mountings on ship decks, and the inevitable roll of the ship seriously impaired the accuracy of firing. In order to compensate for the delay between a decision to fire and the release of the gun, a gunner had to fire in anticipation of the actual sighting of the target. Gunners also had to wait for the ship to roll back to their side before taking another shot. Hitting a target was, in large part, a matter of luck. In addition, gunners rarely used the telescope that was fastened to the gun because the gun's recoil would cause the telescope to jam the gunner's eye. It is no small wonder that naval gunnery was miserably inaccurate.

Morison tells how these problems were overcome in 1898 by an inventive British admiral, Sir Percy Scott. Scott developed a gear mechanism that allowed the gunner to compensate for the ship's roll by rapidly elevating and lowering the gun. Scott also fitted the telescope in a sleeve so that it did not recoil with the gun. These two modest alterations of existing equipment quickly improved firing accuracy. Morison reports that, in 1899, five ships could put a total of two shells into the sails of a target ship 1,600 yards away after firing five minutes each. Six years later, after the introduction of continuous-aim firing, "one naval gunner made fifteen hits in one minute at a target 75 x 25 feet at . . .1,600 yards; half of them hit in a bull's-eye 50 inches square."[2] Scott had converted an art into a science.

One might think, and hope, that innovations permitting such remarkable improvements in naval weaponry would be eagerly adopted as standard procedure by all naval forces. This was not always the case, however. Morison recounts that a young American lieutenant, William Sims, learned techniques for continuous-aim firing from Scott off the China coast in 1900 but had trouble introducing the techniques in the U.S. Navy. Sims's information about the new method of firing was at first ignored by the navy bureaucracy in Washington, and later the innovation was dismissed as impossible. After repeated rejections by the navy, Sims wrote directly to President Theodore Roosevelt, who appointed Sims instructor of naval target practice; after that, the navy successfully adopted the new firing technique.

Morison argues that U.S. Navy officers' resistance to the new firing system resulted from the way the officers perceived themselves. Officers allied themselves closely with existing naval technology and instruments of firing; changing weapons systems disturbed their established routines, habits of mind, and social relationships. Continuous-aim firing disrupted the miniature society of the navy. Before 1903, for example, the gunnery officer was a minor figure in a ship's hierarchy; with the advent of continuous-aim firing, gunnery officers joined the most powerful members of the ship's command structure. Sims's proposal that the U.S. Navy adopt continuous-aim firing threatened to dislocate the world of the nongunnery officer.

Morison uses the concept of identification to refer to the source of meaning or coherence of an individual's experience. He states, "Our security—much of it, after all—comes from giving our allegiance to something greater than ourselves."[3] In the case of continuous-aim firing, officers identified with existing technology and social arrangements. Although an important source of security to them, this identification was dysfunctional from the standpoint of the broader objectives of accuracy and effectiveness. The threat posed by the new technology to the emotional security of a large number of naval officers explains their reluctance to accept continuous-aim firing.

Morison worries that organizations and society in general can be badly served by the narrowness of their members' identifications. He calls for "enlarging the sphere of our identifications from the part to the whole"[4] in all types of groups—from families to factories to educational institutions. Although narrow identifications in the navy proved to be stronger than officers' allegiance to the main objective of national defense until President Roosevelt's intervention, this example also shows that personal identifications are not fixed permanently. People do broaden their identifications. Morison's account prompts us to think generally about the role of identifications in society and organizations.

"Personal identification" is another way to express explicitly the kind of self-understanding that has also been termed "self-interest" in this book. In the nineteenth century Alexis de Tocqueville expressed concern that individualism would lead to narrow identifications and Americans would withdraw into self-satisfied isolation. Tocqueville found saving grace in the broad identifications demonstrated through the American spirit of voluntarism and civic association. However, recent studies of middle-class American society such as Bellah's *Habits of the Heart* and Gans's *Middle American Individualism* find that Americans generally lack strong social identifications outside their immediate group of family and friends. Bellah and his associates view many Americans as being worried about the apparent absence of social commitments in their lives; Gans simply finds them politically apathetic.

People in all organizations face a choice between narrow and broad identification. A team within an organization is a group of individuals for whom shared goals and activities significantly influence their behavior. Effective teams find ways to make individuals' group identification complement, rather than replace, personal identity. In specializing job functions, the American system of manufacturing arranged for nearly all employees to have narrow identifications, and the system of mass production ignored the liabilities of narrow identifications in the workplace. Coordination of the specialized parts of the system was arranged hierarchically; those at the top of the corporation believed that only they needed to identify with the firm. The drawbacks of this system are now painfully apparent.

As with the adoption of continuous-aim firing, various examples in previous chapters have shown that positive change and successful adaptation in industry require managers to think of organizations broadly. Successful adoption of innovation in the maritime shipping industry depended on cooperative interaction among industry, labor, and government. The development of business associations in the private sector played a key role in those countries where quality circles were widely adopted. In prior chapters I have argued that polarization, whether between blacks and whites, conservative and liberals, or in other situations, results from narrow identifications. Wider identification, leading to collective responsibility, is needed in organizations, social interaction, and political ideology.

The science of economics has played a vital part in formalizing thought about the role of self-interest in organizing society for the benefit and welfare of individuals. The strength of microeconomic analysis is its focus on immediate self-interest. At the same time, evidence concerning the social side of human motivation is plentifully provided in the insights of social psychology and sociology. In previous chapters I have attempted to affirm the validity of both the economic and the social sides of human nature—both narrow and broad identification. In fact, both views contribute to the challenges, dilemmas, and paradoxes of social organization. I have stressed the legitimacy of broad identification without disregarding the relevance and importance of immediate self-interest.

Two contrasting strategies for improving the quality and performance of social institutions follow naturally from this analysis: heightening members' awareness of immediate self-interest and increasing opportunities for acting on this awareness, and broadening people's social identification and feeling of responsibility. For example, those who would allow market forces to guide behavior argue that expanding students' choice of schools will improve the performance of the American educational system.[5] Others argue for changing the social process by increasing the involvement of parents or significant others in children's lives.[6] The former policy assumes that schools function poorly because they operate as local monopolies; giving students a choice is advocated as a way to make schools more responsible by making them compete. Individual choice forces institutions to be more responsive. The latter view assumes that the individual student functions poorly when the social environment is not supportive. Getting relevant adults involved in a child's emotional and academic development, which involves a substantial reorganization of teaching, improves performance. This system would build a stronger support community around each child and breathe new purpose and energy into the school as a whole; institutions would become more responsive by breaking down the narrow roles and identifications of teachers, administrators, and other adults close to the child.

Because of Americans' veneration of political and economic individualism, individual choice and market forces dominate both private and public policymaking. Public debate often centers on choices between market behavior and government control. Officers and employees alike often see private organizations as short-term contractual agreements in a process of career advancement. Too rarely do public and private leaders explicitly concern themselves with the processes that may broaden social identification and thus contribute to the performance of our institutions.

In the following sections we seek to understand how identifications are formed and changed. The intention is not to suggest that broadening identification is the only means of solving America's problems. This discussion simply proceeds from the assumption that broadening identification is often a neglected focus for managers. Nor does this discussion imply that broader identifications are always preferable to narrow identifications. As a source of stability and as an essential value of individualism, narrow identifications, unencumbered by larger social obligations, have great importance. I attempt to balance the attention normally given to narrow self-interest and to argue that a greater range of choices is available to organization and social leaders.

The next section discusses how identifications are developed and how they become broadened. This discussion draws upon the work of social psychologist George Herbert Mead, an early and highly significant theorist among a number of social scientists in this century who have developed the idea that individual identity originates in childhood social interaction. We will review Mead's ideas at some length because of his high standing as a social theorist and because his perspective is particularly relevant to social and organization development. One of Mead's ideas, the concept of rational self-consciousness, is used to summarize much of the discussion in earlier chapters of this book.

Our attention then turns to exploring how important dimensions of organization life can be seen from the standpoint of personal identification and personal views of reality. Three case studies in different organizational settings lend insight into the ways that stability and change in organizations are tied to the identities of organization members. These examples naturally lead to a discussion of leadership. In many cases leaders influence the identifications of citizens and organization members; social movements and rapid organizational change work at the level of the transformation of identifications. Instances of change in organizations and of successful social movements illustrate the importance of these leadership qualities in the task of management today.

The chapter concludes with a discussion of the role of individualism in social development. In this section I argue that increasing individual freedom offers one path to the goal of social development; strengthening collective responsibility offers a second. An analysis of the challenge of development in the states of the former Soviet Union and the countries of Eastern Europe, and an analysis of a case of community development in India, illustrate that the starting point of development varies. These cases also show that both pathways ultimately face the challenge of finding a creative blend of individual values and community values.

THE SOCIAL SIDE OF THE SELF

❖ The Appeal of Common Sentiment

George Herbert Mead was well aware of the exceptional excitement of participating in widely shared emotions, such as the spirit of nationalism that often builds before a country goes to war.[7] He observed that a widely shared emotion provides a break from the daily routine of defending oneself against others by the use of agreements, contracts, rules, and penalties. In this context, neighbors, business associates, and even family members can become rivals and opponents as easily as they can be partners in sympathetic accord. People often set aside their competitive roles and drop the barriers between them when stimulated by a fight against a common enemy.

The occurrence of patriotic sentiment throughout an entire country may be rare, however. More often, group identification occurs on the basis of a small group. Mead would have perceived communal feeling among participants in the Vietnam War protest movement in the early 1970s, a movement that eventually increased significantly in size. In times of social conflict, the meaning of patriotism is up for grabs; both the protesters and the defenders of established policy feel that they are acting in the national interest.

Mead's ideas about the social development of the human personality help to explain the animated enthusiasm often involved in collective action. On the positive side, these ideas explain how broad identification occurs and where it gets blocked, as it did for officers of the U.S. Navy in their deliberations over continuous-aim firing. On the negative side, Mead worried that the exhilaration of group action can also be narrow and destructive. Writing in 1929, Mead looked back at the insanity of World War I and saw the growing signs of nationalism that ultimately led to World War II.[8] He sought ways of achieving a sense of common purpose without militarism and the threat, if not the actuality, of war. Following is a brief description of Mead's ideas about the social development of the self and its influence on social behavior.

❖ Society as Integral to the Self

According to Mead, consciousness of one's self, or of a "me," begins for the child in a process of imitation in play, as the child tries to copy the roles and attitudes of parents and other influential persons in his or her environment. Taking another's role develops and sharpens awareness of one's self; the self forms only as the child imitates the perspective of the other. "Inner consciousness is socially organized by the importation of the social organization of the outer world," writes Mead.[9]

Games are more sophisticated and elaborate experiences that extend the sense of self. Games consist of rules governing the interactions of various roles. The child learns more than to take the role of another; he or she must govern his action according to the various roles of all the participants in the game. The first baseman on a baseball team, for example, has the ability to view his role from the perspective of all the other players. On any particular play, an effective first baseman will fit his actions into his view of how the other players will play their positions. He derives his identity in the role of first baseman from his ability to see his own play from the standpoint of his team members. The notion of a first baseman makes no sense outside the context of the game and the entire team. This role has meaning only in relation to the wider constellation of players. Mead calls the perspective of the society that one maintains in one's consciousness the "generalized other."[10]

What is true for the role of the person playing first base is also true for each of our social roles. Each person's sense of rights and privileges, distinctive capabilities, social positions, and prestige derives from that person's internalization of society's perspective toward him or her. Even a fierce sense of independence derives from the ability to see oneself from the standpoint of the external society. Mead writes:

> What are our peculiar powers and capacities but the facilities by which we perform our parts in common undertakings, and where would they be if others did not recognize them and depend upon them? The proudest assertion of independent selfhood is but the affirmation of a unique capacity to fill some social role. Even the man who haughtily withdraws himself from the crowd, thinks of himself in terms of an ideal community which is but a refinement of the world in which he lives. It is by assuming the common attitudes to each other, which an organized community makes possible, that we are able to address ourselves in the inner forum of thoughts and private purposes.[11]

Mead is a significant figure in the study of the social origins of personality. This perspective, called *social interactionism* or *symbolic interactionism*, generally describes the process by which individuals develop concepts that take into account their own and others' needs, desires, and knowledge. These concepts arise from the interplay of the self both as object and as subject in childhood, and they allow the individual to act on behalf of both the self and the team, organization, or society.

Social interactionism also provides a framework for understanding economic institutions and behavior. For Mead, all institutions arise from social interaction and depend on the internalized presence of other members of society in the individual self. Even the economic institution of property is socially constructed. Owning and exchanging objects depend on the individual's knowledge of the roles of buyer and seller. Mead writes, "Something that can be exchanged can exist in the experience of the individual only insofar as he has in his own makeup the tendency to sell when he has also the tendency to buy."[12] This view asserts that property is socially defined; it remains subject to compatible and reciprocal social agreements between buyers and sellers, between property holders and those who do not hold property. Other ideas, such as the concept of preexisting "natural rights," also depend on meaning created by social agreement. The interactionist perspective draws attention to the social basis of economic institutions and processes.

Saying that the self is socially defined does not necessarily imply, however, that social relationships will always be harmonious. Each person's development in a unique social environment lends tremendous diversity to human experience and makes social unity a persistent challenge. This explains why new social roles must be developed and the old bases of self-consciousness of group members must be replaced in order to facilitate authentic teamwork.

❖ Implications

Social Interaction and Resistance to Innovation   Mead's theory is an abstract way of explaining Morison's insight into the American naval officers' resistance to new technology. What Morison calls the officers' "identities" reflects the way these men had internalized the society of the navy. Continuous-aim firing was rejected not because it was unfamiliar but because it entailed a restructuring of the officers' external society and removed some of the most critical aspects of personal meaning—position and status—from their lives. On the other hand, continuous-aim firing provided an avenue for a welcome change in the self-definition of Lieutenant William Sims. In his role as a junior officer, Sims had internalized a "society" that did not include close association with senior naval officers. Morison shows that continuous-aim firing may have been a vehicle for Sims to make favorable changes in his external society and therefore in his identity. Again, this example shows how the adoption of an innovation can be deeply social and personal.

Mead might add that a state of war could have accelerated the acceptance of Scott's and Sims's firing innovations. Hostile conditions would likely have heightened officers' awareness of their shared destiny and their identification with one another, breaking down the barriers of individual self-perception. External conditions affect the adoption of innovation by reorganizing self-consciousness.

The Origins of Militarism and Ethnocentricism   Mead allowed that both competition and cooperation are basic human impulses. On the one hand, individuals' ability to incorporate others' needs and motives into their consciousness allows them to distinguish themselves from one another and to have a sense of individuality. Instincts of rivalry and competition, self-protection, and mistrust derive from this side of the self. The economic perspective is preoccupied mainly with the issue of how social welfare can be generated from the energy and effort originating in a process of rivalry.

On the other hand, the internal society within each of us stimulates an emotional response to the fact of *belonging*, the "exuberant feeling of being at one with [a] community."[13] People exhibit cooperative, as well as competitive, instincts. Mead identifies a universal human tendency to assist a child who has fallen down, and he calls attention to the spontaneous feeling of unity that people experience in falling in love. He states, "The instinct to helpfulness is just as much an endowment as the impulse of hostility."[14] Observers of American society such as Tocqueville and Bellah have concerned themselves with the presence or absence of this social instinct. Critics of the impact of technology on society such as Aldous Huxley and Lewis Mumford have worried that technology works against the cooperative instinct.

Mead acknowledges that achieving a sense of cohesion and belonging is difficult when external conditions do not provide a visceral charge of what he calls the "fighting spirit." Countries sometimes rely on militarism to overcome internal divisions, and citizens sometimes rely on militarism to give them a satisfying feeling of social unity and cohesion. Militarism may be conspicuous in human affairs just *because* it offers an occasion for the simultaneous expression of both the hostile and the cooperative sides of human nature. Patriotic spirit turned against a common enemy gives people the exhilaration of membership in a larger clan or community while still allowing free rein for the expression of often hostile impulses toward the enemy.

Broadening Identifications Without Militarism   The fighting spirit does broaden identification and create common bonds, but at the expense of other objectives. Internal social cohesion has little worth if it is gained at the huge cost of war. In 1929, observing the Italian dictator Benito Mussolini as he sought to hold his nation together by tapping the hostile impulse under the guise of nationalism, Mead asked, "Can we find outside of the fighting spirit that unifying power which . . . can . . . unite us in the enthusiasms of a common end?"[15] The answer, for Mead, resides in the rational ability of individuals to substitute what might be called a mental nationalism for emotional nationalism. He believes that a "rational self-consciousness," an ability to perceive self-interest in community membership, can control the fighting spirit while attaining social cohesion. He writes that the key to civilization lies in rational thinking, not emotion:

> We can no longer depend upon war for the fusion of disparate and opposing elements in the nation. We are compelled to reach a sense of being a nation by means of rational self-consciousness. We must *think* [of] ourselves in terms of the great community to which we belong.[16]

Mead calls for societies to search their experience for common values in literature, art, science, politics, and industry. "Within our communities the process of civilization is the discovery of these common ends,"[17] he writes.

❖ Extrapolations

Mead's "rational self-consciousness" exemplifies the expanded sense of individualism called forth in discussions in earlier chapters of this book. Rational self-consciousness means the ability to build common purpose out of diversity; it is necessary so that social cohesion can result from the comprehension of interdependence and shared values rather than from the creation of an enemy. It embodies the attitude that Jean Monnet tried to inculcate into relations among European countries for more than four decades. It conveys the quality that Tocqueville admiringly found in American society in the mid-nineteenth century and the quality that the Middletown studies and Myrdal's evaluation of race relations found lacking in the twentieth. American race relations today need a healthy dose of rational self-consciousness to break through the charges and countercharges of conflicting groups. Americans might find that rational self-consciousness could stabilize integrated communities and schools and reduce race and class polarization. Rational self-consciousness might allow for the integration of economic values and social values by breaking down the rigidities of political ideology. It might make the political system more responsive by increasing citizens' involvement in the political process.

Finally, rational self-consciousness should find a welcome place in business. It would enable business to become more competitive by providing a framework for adopting industry-specific innovations such as work reorganization in the maritime shipping industry or multi-industry innovations such as quality circles. Rational self-consciousness could help organizations weigh the social and human aspects of technological change equally with their economic dimensions. In short, the attitude of rational self-consciousness will allow Americans to preserve aspects of individualism that promote independence and privacy and reward initiative and personal effort while recognizing the reality of interdependence and the rewards of community and common effort.

THE RELEVANCE OF IDENTIFICATION
TO ORGANIZATIONS

❖ Organization Development Means
Broadening Identifications

In organizations, one's "society" is a system of positions, activities, and imputed powers. People define their roles in terms of the expectations of other employees; each has the ability to see his or her job from the standpoint of others. For example, describing myself as "worker" means I have internalized the concept of "manager." Being a worker or a manager is a powerful basis of social definition in most organizations and gives numerous behavioral guides to employees. Staff or line roles, departmental affiliations, and division or corporate positions are common forms of identification in organizations.

One's identification in an organization is important because it suggests how each member creates and deals with the great variety of issues facing the organization. Should the navy adopt or reject continuous-aim firing? Should the company modify an old product or drop it in favor of a new model? What should the firm do to retain market share in the face of intense international competition? Can workers trust management? Some people feel the organization should diversify into new markets; others fear that diversification will blur the firm's image. Some members feel that the organization should restructure its divisions; others argue that new leadership is a better solution. Life in an organization is filled with thousands of action possibilities in response to the organization's performance, to changes in leaders or members, to new technologies that challenge formerly distinct industry boundaries, to a competitor's introduction of a new product, and so forth.

Issues and points of view are closely associated with members' identifications. The same event or action often means different things to different participants, and a great deal of organization life involves constructing, dismantling, and reconstructing meanings.[18] Beyond some minimal level of agreement, organizations appear capable of tolerating members' views that are neither wholly in agreement nor wholly in disagreement. Nevertheless, continuity and stability require some minimal level of convergence in the meanings that people attach to issues and events. Gaining this convergence is the task of the process of organizing; disrupting the convergence and creating new forms of convergence are the tasks of changing and adapting organizations. Moments of strong patriotism or team spirit, for example, imply that there is a strong convergence of shared meaning among participants.

Evaluating narrow identifications is the point of departure for improving underperforming organizations. Generally, people in ineffective organizations look out for themselves first and consider their immediate membership groups, such as departments and work groups, second.

These natural, but narrow, identifications heighten the challenge of developing unified action and common purpose. Few people in poorly performing organizations feel responsible for the whole product or have concern for the well-being of other people and other organization groups. Individuals rarely look beyond their own jobs, and they arrange for problems to land on others' shoulders as often as possible. In these circumstances organization development often means identifying communication patterns, leadership styles, organizational structures, and incentive systems that encourage broader identifications and a greater sense of responsibility. Occasionally, improving an organization's performance involves changing a cohesive culture. More frequently, improving organizations entails molding a huge number of narrow and parochial interests into a wider base of coincident, if not shared, identifications.

Leaders of organizations often see lower-level members' narrow identifications as limiting factors in the organization's effectiveness. Lower-level participants often perceive that leaders structure and manage the organization to favor their own narrow identifications and interests. Virtually all the design aspects of organizations induce and reinforce relatively narrow identifications among all participants. Specialization of function, aggregation of tasks by work group, and hierarchical coordination all induce and reinforce narrow identifications. Paradoxically, the logic of an organization's structure often defeats its very effectiveness. Rational organization design may follow principles of bureaucratic segmentation, but effectiveness in an organization calls for thinking in terms of the big picture. Managers often seek an organizational analogue to Mead's plea for rational self-consciousness in national and international thinking.

The following sections exemplify these points through analysis of the experiences of three different organizations involved in long- or short-term processes of change. Each case shows how participants' different views of reality within the organization are tied to the ways they see themselves in the organization. The success of organization change depends on the flexibility of the participants' identifications and their consequent versions of reality. The challenge to management in each case is to understand the tie between members' identifications and the proposed changes in the organization.

Members' Identifications in a Changing Religious Order   Jean Bartunek studied the process of change that took place in a U.S. Catholic religious order between 1966 and 1979.[19] The Second Vatican Council, held in 1962 through 1965, issued directives requiring Catholic religious orders to examine their purposes and methods of organization and to explore new approaches to religious life. Bartunek describes the processes by which a new understanding of its own mission, organization, and activities evolved among the members of a teaching order in the United States. Bartunek calls this type of understanding of the organization an "interpretive scheme." The identifications of members of the order were critical to the substance of change and to the pace at which members changed their interpretive schemes of the order. Over a number of years, the order transformed itself from an organization committed solely to teaching and administered from Rome into a strong national organization with a more diverse set of activities.

In 1965, the order had about 1,000 U.S. members. Before 1967, members working at parochial schools administered by this order were grouped in regional units called vicariates. Virtually all decisions, including those regarding curriculum, were directed from Rome, and vicariates rarely communicated with one another. Following Vatican II, the order redefined vicariates as provinces, to suggest greater autonomy, and gave them substantial decision-making authority. The order decentralized administrative activities and encouraged horizontal communication among provinces.

Encouragement of new expressions of religious life led many members into other forms of service, particularly public education and direct social action. By 1979, only 30 percent of the members were still working in the order's own schools, and the schools themselves had been consolidated and, in some cases, closed. The order suffered an overall membership decline to about 760 in the early 1980s. These developments throughout the 1970s indicated that there was a need to consolidate the provinces into a national organization.

In spite of these changes, for ten years members of various provinces in the United States expressed justifications for maintaining their separateness and resisted merging into a single national organization. Members explained their opposition to a national merger largely in terms of their personal identification. Some felt that a national organization would diminish the international status of their provinces. To many others, a national organization also represented a loss of provincial autonomy, which would also reduce their status. Supporting a national organization would require either a substantial reorganization of members' concepts of themselves or a different interpretation of what a national organization would mean.

Institutional change in this religious order became, then, a story about the evolution of members' interpretations of the order's mission and governance. Gradually, members came to see roles in both education and social justice as equally valid expressions of the values of the order. Thus, members' identification with the order broadened. In addition, over a ten-year period a number of activities were created with interprovincial coordination, planning, and administration. These activities fostered communication across provincial boundaries and weakened sole identification with one's own province. Finally, in the context of an international conference in 1979, provincial leaders recognized the reality of provincial interdependence and the need for national unity. They encountered little opposition to a declaration that a national structure was the best means of supporting the order's corporate mission. This goal was accomplished over the next several years.

The wider changes in the Roman Catholic Church through Vatican II had created considerable uncertainty for members of the order in the United States. Change involved competing interpretive schemes vis-à-vis the organization—education versus social action, provincial organization versus national organization. Groups and individuals addressed this uncertainty with different and conflicting views of the order. Ultimately, the different views were synthesized into a new understanding of the order's mission that incorporated both education and social action as well as a new, national structure for the organization. Bartunek implies that specific actions, such as forming interprovincial coordination and administration groups, influenced the way in which conflicting views of the organization were eventually resolved and translated into organization structures.

Personal identifications influenced the evolution of individuals' understandings of the organization and ultimately determined its structure. Bartunek's report points up the tension between the narrow identification (teaching only, provincial organization) and the broad identification (teaching and social justice activities, national organization), and it suggests that members can eventually alter the ways they think about themselves. Change in the formal mechanisms of governance in this case depended on changes in personal identification and in the way individuals came to understand the organization in relation to themselves.

Failure to Introduce Change in an Insurance Company   The president of an insurance company also sought to encourage new identifications and views of the organization among employees.[20] The company was receiving a growing number of complaints from district sales managers that the home office was handling paperwork inefficiently. Sales agents and sales managers complained about delays and errors in the processing of applications, endorsements, renewals, and claims. Processing delays led field personnel to initiate additional requests, which increased the volume of paperwork and slowed the process even more.

The president addressed this growing problem in May of one year with a special program intended to help the home office become current in its work by the end of June. Borrowing from military language, he declared that the next six weeks would be "Operation June 30," known as "OJ30." Posters emphasizing this special project were placed around the office. The president exhorted employees to exert extra effort over this period and voluntarily work overtime and Saturdays. He requested that departments put aside their normal staffing arrangements and lend each other personnel when needed. On the whole, the president wanted employees to pull together in a common effort to achieve smoothness and harmony to satisfy the urgent organizational need. Basically, he was asking home office employees to suspend everyday definitions of their roles and to cooperate toward the overall organization's need to catch up on its backlog of paperwork. He wanted employees to change their organizational identifications for an urgent project over a short period of time. The president called for the equivalent of a period of "organizational patriotism."

Although the study's authors provide no specific information about the success of OJ30 in reducing the workload at the home office, on July 2 the vice president declared the operation a success, and the president eventually thanked employees for their efforts by hosting a lunch. Personal interviews with various staff members suggested, however, that OJ30 had been less than an outright success. Some people experienced OJ30 as a source of disharmony and noninvolvement. The vice president of operations, for example, privately said he was "fed up" and "agitated by working every Saturday," and he saw "few other people who are helping or anything."[21] This officer had kept a chart of participation in OJ30, and he noted that the director of personnel had not helped out at all. The vice president of operations declared, "We have no team around here."[22]

Nor did executive staff members see themselves as providing tight coordination and helpful behavior. Staff members tolerated the military analogy but remained unmoved and isolated from the management. The staff believed that OJ30 failed to address the fundamental problems of the company. Noncooperative behavior with deep roots was not susceptible to the president's moral exhortations.

Every organization member carries an identity or series of identities that imply expectations for other persons or groups in the organization. Often the perceptions and expectations of different parties come into conflict. Deficient performance on tasks simply "proves" that others have failed to behave correctly and confirms existing identities. In the case of this insurance company, the uneasy structure of identities was not so fragmented as to prevent the organization from functioning. In some ways, conflicts within the office created a kind of stability at a low level of effectiveness; the president's call to cooperation failed to alter the basis of staff members' identities even temporarily.

Identity and Cooperation between Labor and Management OJ30 was only a superficial attempt to broaden the viewpoints of organization members in order to gain their cooperation during a crisis. It may not be too surprising that slogans and posters failed to alter long-standing, ingrained personal identifications and staff members' associated understandings of the organization. Successful efforts to change organizations usually recognize the depth of conflicting views of reality among members and often involve more highly structured activities and processes.

Moch and Bartunek report on the origins, implementation, and results of a program for making changes to increase union-management cooperation at a company called FoodCom.[23] The company initiated the program in the late 1970s at the urging of a national quality of work life organization. The proposed program was a labor-management experiment similar to programs at a number of highly regarded U.S. companies that were receiving favorable publicity. The program's objectives were to use communication and employee-employer problem solving to "reconcile corporate productivity needs with employees' needs for challenging and satisfying work"[24]—in short, both to gain more work productivity and to give the workers more satisfaction.

The program directly addressed the negative consequences of separate and opposing identifications between labor and management. Moch and Bartunek point out that the experimental decision-making process emphasized "cooperation over competition, trust over suspicion, and the well-being of the company over the narrower interests of labor, management, or other stakeholders."[25] The whole effort aimed to "transcend sectarian interests."[26] The success of the program turned on whether the experiment would broaden the participants' identifications and their views of reality or whether these identifications and perspectives would constrain and limit the experiment. Moch and Bartunek, who observed the experiment closely as outside evaluators, conclude that the results fell into the latter category.

The story of this experiment makes clear that participants assigned vastly different meanings to the program. Staff members responsible for labor relations, industrial engineering, and training and development handled the initial invitation and negotiations and defined the program's goals. They saw the experiment as a means of enhancing their job functions and the goals of their departments in the company. People involved in the company-union agreement had a variety of perceptions of the program. Higher company officials saw the experiment as a way to increase the efficiency of operations. The company controller, for example, stated that "productivity is the name of the game," and that the "bottom line" would decide whether the program had succeeded.[27] Officials of the primary union representing company workers saw the experiment as a demonstration of their progressive leadership and as a chance to enhance the reputation and strength of the union within and outside the company.

Early discussions and agreements among these parties failed to surface and identify these basic differences. Differing identifications did not prevent them from agreeing to a program, but the leaders' inability to acknowledge and address the differences may have reduced the program's chances for success from the very start.

An experimental labor-management committee was eventually established in one of the company's factories. Moch and Bartunek identify the following major perspectives bearing on the implementation and evaluation of the program at the plant: those of top company management, local plant management, junior workers who belonged to the international union, senior workers who were members of the international union, plant supervisors and stewards, and members of two smaller unions of electricians and machinists in the plant. Whatever issue the joint labor-management committee considered—synchronizing the clocks in the factory, creating a nonsmoking area in the cafeteria, improving the restrooms and eating areas—the conflicting interests and perspectives of all of these groups came to the surface. The project's costs and the slow pace of progress became controversial issues themselves. The manager responsible for the joint committee often found himself caught between competing identifications and demands. After several years of continuing struggle in which only modest changes were made in the amenities of the plant, the experimental program was reduced to a part of the normal responsibilities of the management. Moch and Bartunek tell the story of a program that got lost amid the widely differing views of reality among the parties involved and gradually lost the capacity to modify those same perspectives.

Overview of the Three Cases These studies of change in a religious order, a special attempt to clear the paperwork backlog in an insurance company, and a labor-management experiment in a food products company illustrate the complex role of personal identification in organization change. In each case perspectives or interpretations or personal views of reality vis-à-vis the organization were closely tied to individual roles and experiences. In each case improving the organization entailed broadening members' identifications and altering their interpretations.

Though the effort to bring about change was most successful in the religious order in the presence of significant environmental pressure, it took more than 13 years for changes involving mission and structure to develop fully. Underlying identifications were not modified easily. The two cases involving businesses further point out the rootedness of existing identifications and their capacity to resist both the banner-waving appeals of the insurance company president and the extensive, deliberate program of planned changed at the food products company. The challenge of improving organizations, of broadening personal identifications, should not be underestimated.

❖ Implications for Social Development

Like an organization, society represents an aggregation of the many identifications and views of reality among individuals and groups. To some, a president's veto of a strong affirmative action bill symbolizes a defense of the work ethic and the rejection of government coercion; to others, the same act compromises of the goals of social justice and institutional reform. The debate over the role of multiculturalism in educational curricula vividly demonstrates the existence of a variety of identities and a variety of social and historical perspectives on society. Some definitions of social reality are less widely shared than others, but that does not automatically make the views of any group less valid than those of another.

As another example of the coexistence of differing interpretations, consider the varying views of the demise of the Bank of Credit and

Commerce International in the summer of 1991. In this case, definitions and perspectives vary across national boundaries. To many westerners, the BCCI case represents the largest bank fraud in world history, the failure of international banking regulation, and the integration of terrorist organizations into established commercial institutions; the bank itself is considered a major money launderer for drug traffickers and an important conduit for financing illicit activities of the U.S. Central Intelligence Agency.[28] But to many people in Pakistan, the bank's home country, the closing of BCCI represents a conspiracy by bankers in the West to eliminate a challenging third world competitor.[29] One Pakistani businessperson asserted forcefully that BCCI was not a criminal bank. "This is a great bank, a Muslim bank that has been so successful that it has provoked the jealousy of the West," he stated.[30] Far from being an exemplar of scandal and fraud, BCCI serves as a symbol of pride and strength to many people in Pakistan and other developing countries.

The FoodCom case points to the existence of varied views of reality in American society. First, the identities of organization members and their associated views of social reality did not have to coincide for FoodCom to function adequately. A labor-management experiment was agreed to, designed, and implemented even though the experiment meant different things to the various actors in the system. Similarly, much social life is based on coexisting, coincident definitions of reality rather than on common experience and unity in the sharing of ideas. Diversity can be a source of creativity in society; in any case, diversity of opinions does not prevent society from functioning. At the same time, identities can be potent centrifugal forces and a democratic society that functions over an extended time may be a near miracle.

The FoodCom experiment fell victim to a debilitating clash of competing individual and group identities. The potential for significant improvement of the organization was constrained by the very kinds of behavior it sought to change. A successful project would not have achieved a merger of identifications; the company needed only to establish a means of understanding people's existing identifications and then evolve a somewhat higher level of identification among members. The need was not to negate narrow identifications, but to create complementary identifications that would be useful in exploring problems and finding more widely acceptable solutions.

Similar conclusions follow for society as a whole. Narrow individual and group identifications are healthy. They add richness to human experience and encourage creativity. Development and growth depend on human differences, and distinct individuals and groups depend on each other. Social development accepts and seeks to integrate these differences. A society becomes more highly developed as it increases its capacity for managing the opposing pulls of separateness and community. Social development means giving rein to the creative and energetic ambitions of individuals while retaining a commitment to a broader identity.

Society has formal and informal methods for blending distinct and shared identities. In one sense, managing the balance is the very function of government and of organized politics. The value of political participation is that as each group attempts to move society closer to its vision, the group accepts the risk of being moved closer to the vision of another group. The give-and-take of open political debate fosters common identification. Closing off the system of give-and-take poses the greatest threat to shared identity and thus also to the distinctiveness of groups and individuals.

Informal social associations also play an invaluable role in blending distinct and shared identifications. Alexis de Tocqueville first articulated the importance of civic spirit in preventing American individualism from turning into isolation and withdrawal. He believed that voluntary civic involvement expands one's horizons and generates a broad view of oneself. There seems to be little reason to challenge his view today.

Initiating a labor-management committee at FoodCom did not require specifying particular areas in which the organization could be improved. Targets for improvement were to grow out of the joint view generated by the various parties, and the creation of a joint view would itself have been a remarkable change—perhaps the most positive change in the plant. If this had come about, many other benefits for distinct groups would have flowed from it. Success in social organization depends on the ability and willingness of participants to avoid the trap of narrow identifications and to use their differences to enrich, rather than limit, experience.

LEADERSHIP IN ORGANIZATION AND SOCIAL DEVELOPMENT

Many observers say that social change is initiated and guided by influential individuals who personally affect the ideas, identifications, perceptions, and actions of others. Thus, understanding leadership is a key to understanding how social behavior changes in society at large.

The processes and dynamics of leadership have attracted many observers. Social psychologists, for example, develop theories to explain interpersonal influence, political scientists study presidential leadership, and many experienced management practitioners do not hesitate to communicate their own ideas of leadership. In the final analysis the strong influence of individual persons in leadership positions on people's perceptions of social and organization reality makes the study of leadership vital.

❖ Transactional Leaders and Transformational Leaders

Transactional Leaders Drawing examples widely from human history, British historian James MacGregor Burns makes a distinction between two types of leadership, which he terms *transactional* and *transformational*.[31] The vast majority of leadership situations are based on a simple transaction, or exchange, between leaders and followers. Followers select leaders who meet the followers' expressed needs; leaders watch public opinion closely and adapt their ideas and images to the sentiment of the moment. These leaders receive the trappings of power and the benefits of "psychic gains"[32] in exchange for responding to followers. Followers receive concrete returns in exchange for their support within the organization or political system.

Burns claims that most leaders in organizations and society involve themselves in exchange transactions. Leaders track the pulse of the public and keep the wheels of bureaucracy turning. Reacting to constituent pressures, decision makers make only incremental adjustments in the system. Transactional leaders may occasionally appeal to the deep convictions and fundamental desires of followers, but they do so only incidentally and unintentionally. Transactions are based exclusively on the need of both leaders and followers to satisfy their self-interest in the exchange. In this sense, the self-interest or market model applies to much of organizational and social life. Burns makes a comparison with the economic marketplace to explain transactional leadership:

> The marketplace is . . . a place of quick connections and quick fixes. It is a place of multiple leaders and followers, a place where leaders can move from follower to follower in search of gratification and followers can respond in the same way to leaders. The moods and styles are quick; they assure reciprocity, flexibility, substitutability of buyers and of sellers, volatility of relationships. *Adaptability* is the rule—to the extent that leaders become hardly distinguishable from followers. Relationships are dominated by quick calculations of cost-benefits.[33]

Transactional leadership accomplishes the vast work of organizations and maintains society. Real social development, however, involves a deeper process.

Transformational Leaders   Occasionally, a leader's ideas and actions articulate the latent or unexpressed aspirations and fundamental values of large groups of people. The leader literally transforms the images, identifications, and behavior of followers and focuses them toward shared experience and collective purpose. People find themselves elevated, inspired, and mobilized. Burns points to Mohandas Gandhi as perhaps the best contemporary example of transformational leadership. Gandhi and other transformational leaders raise the consciousness and aspirations of their followers and also raise the standard for human conduct in the process of change.

A wide variety of leaders and results qualify as transformational in Burns's analysis. Ideas themselves can have an uplifting impact, for intellectual leadership can be transformational. The ideas of seventeenth- and eighteenth-century political theorists—Hobbes, Locke, Rousseau, and others—inspired the imagination of Western societies and led to accomplishments in many areas. American social development is, in part, a story of intellectual richness. Burns traces the reforming effect of the ideas of Presidents Jefferson, Madison, Jackson, and Wilson, among other persons.

The transformational leader may be a reformer, one who changes the system from within, or he or she may be an outside revolutionary who inspires change. Disraeli and Lord Gray in Britain, Theodore and Franklin Roosevelt in the United States, Bismarck in Germany, Golda Meir in Israel, and Alexander II in Russia are examples of the former. Martin Luther, Lenin, Mao Zedong, Joan of Arc, and, of course, Gandhi exemplify the latter. Burns traces the historical context of a number of elements of transformational leadership. He states that "men like Lenin, Gandhi, and Mao brought literally hundreds of millions of men and women out of political isolation and into a new kind of political participation."[34] He also notes that it may be important to differentiate between the personal impact of the charismatic leader and that of the administrative apparatus designed to implement the ideas represented by the leader.

Several aspects of transformational leadership deserve additional attention. First, transformational leadership assumes the existence of social conflict. Individuals, families, nations, races, religions, and economic actors have natural and often deep differences in values and goals for society. On the one hand, a transformational leader heightens followers' consciousness of their own needs, values, purposes, and identities.[35] At the same time, the leader raises people above their conflicts and unites them on a higher plane or value. It is only because of the world's conflicts over narrow identities that transformational leadership becomes possible and is valued. Burns states:

> Conflict is intrinsically compelling; it galvanizes, prods, motivates people. Every person, group, and society has latent tension and hostility. . . . Leadership acts as an inciting and triggering force in the conversion of conflicting demands, values, and goals into significant behavior. . . . Leaders . . . act as catalytic agents in arousing followers' consciousness."[36]

Second, transformational leadership equates with moral leadership. The transformational leader makes followers more aware of their broad or universal, as well as separate, identities. Burns argues that transformational leaders tap into needs and values that elevate followers' concerns toward such values as honesty and selfless commitment to the general welfare.[37] People become "lifted *into* their better selves."[38] Burns restricts his definition of the transformational leader to those whom history will judge to have influenced people for the better.[39] Hitler undeniably transformed social behavior on a wide scale, but he would surely fail the moral test involved in this concept.

❖ Transformational Processes in the Development of Society and Organizations

Other observers' models of social development share the notion of converting conflicting demands into higher levels of conduct. As early as the mid-1940s, community organizer Saul Alinsky understood social development as a process of elevating a group of people above their parochial concerns. Alinsky had an enormous impact on social activism and social reform in the United States, and he would undoubtedly qualify as a transformational leader. He states:

> While it is self-evident that a disorganized people cannot act as a unit, it is also self-evident that a people cannot formulate a philosophy representative of their many diverse loyalties, traditions, and sentiments unless they get together and through a process of interaction achieve a philosophy representative of themselves.[40]

Social change inevitably involves changing perceptions and images. "Challengers [to the status quo] are engaged in battles over meaning," concludes William Gamson in his study of social reform organizations.[41] Influencing social meaning is, of course, exactly what charismatic and transformational leaders accomplish. Other social activists have found that the need to create new meanings applies to a wide variety of organizations committed to more equitable, innovative, productive, and healthy communities and societies.[42] These people find that numerous and conflicting demands threaten to pull apart organizations engaged in social change. Maintaining internal cohesion is their major challenge, and they can best sustain themselves through the mobilizing effects of ideas and values.

Much of the research on the requirements of corporate leadership today supports Burns's views on leadership. Generalizing from the FoodCom project, for example, Moch and Bartunek distinguish between first-order and second-order corporate change. First-order change accepts the underlying adversarial mentality of existing labor-management relationships and simply works to obtain more amenities for plant employees. This level of change parallels transactional leadership. Employees exchange minor forms of cooperation for plant improvements. Managers exchange the resources needed to make improvements for tranquillity in the labor force. In first-order change, none of the basic identifications, values, or levels of conduct within the company is altered to a serious degree. Second-order change does alter the pattern of relationships in the plant. This type of change achieves a greater degree of cooperation among the various parties. A new, shared view of reality develops, out of which projects for real improvement are defined and implemented. Second-order change parallels the outcome of transformational leadership in that it alters the behavioral premises or assumptions of managers and workers.

FoodCom was unable to make a second-order change. Managers never got out of their transactional mode, and the project consultants failed to provide transformational influence. Members of the religious order did experience transformational change. But because there was no single local leader, the change took nearly 15 years. The president of the insurance company wanted transformational change, but he was unable to mobilize employees' energies to accomplish it.

Other researchers have detailed the actions of corporate leaders whom they consider to be transformational leaders,[43] evaluated how managers' ability to construct and reconstruct meanings helps organizations innovate,[44] and described the inspirational impact of highly influential institutional leaders.[45] These approaches, however, appear concerned with the pragmatic aspects of organization change; few deal with the kind of high moral leadership that Burns described.

INDIVIDUALISM AND SOCIAL DEVELOPMENT

Development in organizations and in society has been equated with the broadening of identifications and the elevation of personal aspirations and conduct. This does not mean, however, that individuals must lose their own identities in some kind of "group-mind" or collective mysticism. It does mean strengthening the awareness of interdependencies and shared experience. It means rebalancing the scales of competition and cooperation. It means redefining self-interest, not to exclude the self but to enhance the self as part of a wider social community. Saul Alinsky's perspective on community development, for example, suggests that individual abilities, resources, and opportunities are enhanced, not reduced, through social activism. The process of broadening identifications seeks to strengthen collective values in order to reinforce and heighten individual values.

Identification can be broadened only where individualism already is strong. But how does the process of development work in societies where individualism is weak? In the following sections we discuss two pathways to social development. In the first case individual values had long been suppressed by authoritarian regimes. The eyes of the world are on the former Soviet Union and the countries of Eastern Europe at this moment, as these nations work to re-create their societies and economies. Creating economic and political freedom is one path to improvement. In the second case a rural village in India serves to illustrate another process of social development. The initial path to improvement in this village, in which poverty and demoralization predominated, was the development of a strong system for collective responsibility and community decision making.

❖ Individual Freedom as a Starting Point for Social Development

A major feature of late-twentieth-century political reality has been a high-stakes competition between authoritarian societies and political democracies. The competition has been about military strength, world influence, scientific progress, industrial might, and social justice. The United States and the Union of Soviet Socialist Republics have been the featured contestants, but virtually every nation on earth has played some role in the competition and has been touched by its outcome.

By the mid-1980s, the weight of failure of authoritarian rule in the USSR had become too great for that country to bear, and the soviet premier, Mikhail Gorbachev, initiated a period of economic and political restructuring. Sensing Russia's internal weakness, citizens of the Soviet satellite countries in Eastern Europe—East Germany, Poland, Hungary, Czechoslovakia, Bulgaria, and Romania, as well as the Baltic republics—grasped opportunities for independence from the Soviet empire. The massive change brought by these countries' breathtaking independence movements in 1989 to 1991, plus the formal dissolution of the USSR, declared the East-West competition over. The organization of society according to authoritarian rule, as represented by the USSR, had lost.

The communist system failed for manifestly economic reasons. Its economic failure however, was tied to an even deeper failure which one observer called "moral exhaustion."[46] "It [the source of decline] was the Soviet system's mounting inability to function successfully even on its own terms," writes political analyst William Pfaff, "evident in falling life expectancy, a gradual but visible impoverishment, the bureaucratic stultification of all life."[47] Communism provided the reverse of Burns's notion of moral leadership, degrading rather than elevating individuals and disassociating rather than integrating individual and society.

It is little wonder, then, that many of the peoples of Eastern Europe and the former USSR have, in varying degrees, democratized their governments and moved toward private property and market economies. Political rights and economic individualism hold promise of invigorating disillusioned and apathetic citizens. The market system may improve the efficient use of economic assets, allow participation in international trade, motivate improvements in productivity, and provide incentives for technological change. New economic regimes should provide incentives for effort in work and personal learning, providing reasons for people to participate in legitimate enterprises. A more democratic society should also begin to pay attention to the enormous human and social costs of inhumanely ignoring health, education, and environmental quality. Turning toward individual values has the potential to bring these societies back to life and to improve the quality of life and contributions of their members. Long suppressed, individualism can provide an important starting point toward social development.

Prosperity in these countries will also depend on a reasonable consensus among their citizens about the meaning and value of private initiative, private property, and personal wealth. A public opinion poll taken in June 1990, in the USSR, for instance, indicated that only 28 percent of the population approved of a free market in the sense that Americans would understand that term.[48] This was 3 percent fewer than those who preferred a strictly centralized economy. A full 41 percent of respondents said they wanted the prosperity of capitalism as long as incomes remained roughly equal and jobs were guaranteed. The same survey found that 75 percent of the population resented the owners of the fast-growing cooperative enterprises in Russia. A successful future depends on agreement about the meaning of key values in order to support the institutions of economic and political freedom.

Economic individualism will survive only with difficulty without a strong social consensus. Pfaff describes this challenge to the people of the former USSR in general terms: "The Soviet Union . . . has virtually no national experience of modern economic functioning or of the social and moral foundations of the modern economy."[49]

Knowledgeable observers have made similar points about the pathway to progress in East European countries. The advent of political freedom has the potential to unleash ethnic and religious hostility. These suppressed conflicts may undermine the stability and development of these societies if they express themselves as self-aggrandizement and exclusiveness. One close observer comments on the prospects for successful change in the former Soviet satellites:

> [T]he persistence of political discord at the top, together with nationalist and ethnic animosity and antisemitism below, are cause for serious concern. Most of such negative phenomena should be seen for what they are: the ugly underside of freedom suddenly gained. For while freedom from oppression is already at hand, freedom subjected to sensible, largely self-imposed restraint has yet to take root. When that happens—when freedom begins to coexist with responsibility—the countries of this troubled region will be better positioned to confront the legacy of four decades of totalitarian rule, to cope with the strengths and weaknesses of their procommunist past, to dismantle their command economies and, at the same time, to discover their new identities in a new Europe.[50]

The task of the East European countries, then, is not simply to institutionalize individual rights. They also have to identify, define, and implement a noncoercive, collective basis of society. Vaclav Havel, the first postcommunist president of Czechoslovakia, had already articulated this perspective in an interview in 1986:

> [A] genuinely fundamental and hopeful improvement in "systems" cannot happen without a significant shift in human consciousness. . . . This . . . can be only the natural expression of a more general state of mind, the state of mind in which man can see beyond the tip of his own nose and prove capable

of taking on—under the aspect of eternity—responsibility even for the things that don't immediately concern him, and relinquish something of his private interest in favor of the interest of the community, the general interest. Without such a mentality, even the most carefully considered project aimed at altering systems will be for naught.[51]

Havel's community consciousness is a moral, or noncoercive, social value. Long-standing ethnic, geographic, and religious differences in the countries of Eastern Europe heighten the challenge of achieving this community consciousness. To re-create political and economic systems that value individual freedom and at the same time forge a collective or national consciousness will be a formidable task.

❖ Collective Responsibility as a Starting Point of Social Development

Social development may have several different starting points. Certainly, enlarging the sphere of economic and political liberties of a people offers one way to unleash the energies, ambitions, and powers of individuals. Strong community action is a second path for altering oppressive conditions of social disintegration, discouragement, and apathy. Following is an account of the process of community revitalization in a small village in India.[52]

In 1975, Ralegaon Siddhi, a village of about 2,000 people in western India, was in the throes of extreme poverty. Water was in acute shortage, and agricultural yields were poor. The village lacked the employment opportunities needed to retain its young people. Home-produced alcohol was readily available, and excessive drinking was widely evident. Many people were heavily in debt to moneylenders. Hopelessness pervaded the village.

Fifteen years later, this village was a showcase of rural development. Land under irrigation had increased by 1,600 percent, from 50 to 850 acres. On the average, agricultural yields had increased threefold. The villagers had an enviable standard of living for their district, and people from nearby villages sent their children to school in Siddhi. The town prided itself on its rebuilt temple, a new school, and a new hostel for housing visitors and out-of-town schoolchildren. Agriculture in the village was supported by a series of self-help projects: a repaired percolation tank, an extensive well system, and both drip and lift irrigation systems.

In large part, the revitalization of this village was tied to the charismatic leadership of a young man named Anna who dedicated himself to its reconstruction. But it is also a story about a community taking control of its own life. Anna quickly turned a small group of initial supporters into a youth club in the village. Later, the youth club evolved into a village governing council.

Collective action, rather than individual freedom, per se, provided the starting point for social development in Siddhi. Anna and his supporters first used public recognition to honor people who sacrificed their personal interests for the good of the village as a whole. For instance, those who voluntarily ceased producing liquor were publicly recognized and thanked. The reformers did not hesitate to use force, however, when they felt justified by the needs of the community. The equipment of noncooperating producers of alcohol was smashed by the reformers, and people who refused to give up drinking were publicly flogged and tied up in public places for several days. Later, smoking was banned in the village.

The village council applied strict rules to agriculture as well. For example, the community prevented individual farmers from growing sugar cane, a crop that required substantially more of the scarce water than did other crops. Everyone was required to contribute to the cost of a new dam. Every family was obligated to send a member to work on community self-help projects. Families that did not send anyone were assessed 50 rupees a month for the duration of the project. Poor families were paid 15 rupees per day for sending a family member to work.

In this way, villagers established community control over a number of aspects of their lives and improvement projects. Over time, similar control was implemented in administrative and political affairs. All water and irrigation projects and issues concerning religious matters, youth, women, and education were administered by committees of villagers. Another innovation was that villagers decided together which district political candidates to support after inviting each to speak.

The success of development in Siddhi over 14 years demonstrates the remarkable ability of collective effort to salvage a community from social disintegration. The collectivist, authoritarian approach to community life in Siddhi may have been accepted, however, only because of the village's extreme state of poverty and social degradation. Personal liberties, even the freedom to produce alcohol, smoke, and retain one's wealth, may count more heavily in a more highly economically developed society. The same community-authoritarian approach that was successful in initiating change at the edge of hopelessness may be less acceptable for sustaining change as Siddhi progresses. The saving grace of the youth club was that the moral standards it imposed improved the quality of everyone's life. Anna and the youth club also validated their rules by involving the larger community and worked to institutionalize community decision making.

A fine line may separate the measures needed to energize and improve the community from the dictatorial imposition of the standards of conduct of a powerful minority. Taken to the extreme, Siddhi's collective authoritarianism re-creates the kind of oppressive control maintained under the communist systems recently thrown off by the peoples of Eastern Europe. If Siddhi's leaders truly have the welfare of the village at heart, they will have the foresight to reduce gradually the severe limits on personal freedom. Especially as Siddhi grows in size, the tension between personal freedom and community will mount.

Economic and political freedoms in Eastern Europe ultimately will have to be supported by social consensus on the meaning and limits of these freedoms. In contrast, Siddhi's continuing development may soon require enlarging the sphere of individual freedoms in that village. Individual freedom and community action are two different starting points toward social development; in the final analysis, each must demonstrate an ability to integrate personal freedom with community needs.

CONCLUSIONS

In this chapter I have argued that individuals and society are not distinct entities but, rather, that each incorporates the other. As individuals, we take the very sense of ourselves from people in our immediate and personal world, our miniature "society." And "society" is nothing more than a construction, a highly significant and multifaceted construction, in the minds of individuals.

The universal challenges of stability and adaptation in social organization derive from these facts. Social stability depends on a sufficient convergence of distinct individual identities and views of reality, and adaptation involves a process of creating new, shared identifications. Development is the process by which a society or an organization finds a synthesis in the tension between the convergence and the divergence of identities in a social group. Transformational leadership is the process by which an individual affects the perceptions of reality of participants and make possible a higher level of integration, or synthesis.

This abstract understanding of social behavior, development, and leadership applies to a wide variety of situations. These concepts help to explain why values become polarized and energies become tied up in debilitating conflict in societies and organizations and how organizations are at times structured *against* their own need for broad identification by members. An understanding of how identifications are shaped and changed explains the rarity of excellent organizations.

I also have pointed to processes underlying a number of the situations and problems discussed in earlier chapters: polarization by race, gender, and political ideology; the existence of political apathy; and the lack of competitive commercialization of new technology. In each instance unwanted consequences arise as narrow identifications limit people's alternatives for action. Development in society and in organizations involves integration of the narrow and personal self with the broad and social self. In each case "self-interest" is redefined, away from the struggle for the rights and privileges of the individual and toward the ability to recognize and integrate the various parts of the self.

A number of social scientists have guided our analysis in this chapter, particularly historians such as Morison and Burns and social psychologists such as Mead. But these theorists also have a practical bent. Their work has been useful in the analysis of the adoption of new technologies by organizations—or the failure to adopt new technologies. These writers have cast light on the way in which the positive desire for patriotism can evolve into jingoism and militarism. And they have shown how exceptional leaders have had an impact on the course of human affairs by elevating the identifications of social groups above their existing ways of differentiating and defending themselves. They have shown the nature and importance of such moral leadership to social progress. Here, we have extended these ideas by examining the challenge of social development in formerly communist-authoritarian countries and in a rural village in India. This analysis has permitted us to identify a number of areas of interaction between individual freedom and national development. There are several different paths to social development, and each ultimately faces the challenge of integrating individual values and community values.

[1]Elting E. Morison, *Men, Machines, and Modern Times* (Cambridge, Mass.: MIT Press, 1966), pp. 17–44. Copyright © by the Massachusetts Institute of Technology. Used with permission.

[2]Ibid., p. 22.

[3]Ibid., p. 41.

[4]Ibid.

[5]John E. Chubb and Terry M. Moe, *What Price Democracy? Politics, Markets & America's Schools* (Washington, D.C.: Brookings Institution, 1990).

[6]James P. Comer, *School Power: Implications of an Intervention Project* (New York: Free Press, 1980).

[7]George Herbert Mead, *Selected Writings*, ed. Andrew J. Reck (Indianapolis, Ind.: Bobbs-Merrill, 1964). Used with permission of Andrew J. Reck.

[8]Ibid., pp. 355–370.

[9]Ibid., p. 141.

[10]Ibid., p. 285.

[11]Ibid., p. 357.

[12]Ibid., p. 284.

[13]Ibid., p. 357.

[14]Ibid., p. 358.

[15]Ibid., p. 361.

[16]Ibid., p. 363.

[17]Ibid., p. 365.

[18]Barbara Gray, Michel G. Bougon, and Anne Donnellon, "Organizations as Constructions and Destructions of Meaning," *Journal of Management*, 11, 2 (1985), pp. 83–98. Also see Jeffrey Pfeffer, "Management as Symbolic Action: The Creation and Maintenance of Organizational Paradigms," in *Research in Organizational Behavior*, eds. L. L. Cummings and Barry M. Shaw (Greenwich, Conn.: JAI Press, 1981), pp. 1–52; Louis R. Pondy, Peter J. Frost, Gareth Morgan, and Thomas C. Dandridge, eds., *Organizational*

Symbolism (Greenwich, Conn.: JAI Press, 1983); W. Graham Astley, "Administrative Science as Socially Constructed Truth," *Administrative Science Quarterly*, 30 (1985), pp. 497–513; and Lynn A. Isabella, "Evolving Interpretations as a Change Unfolds: How Managers Construe Key Organizational Events," *Academy of Management Journal*, 33, 1 (March 1990), pp. 7–41.

[19] Jean M. Bartunek, "Changing Interpretive Schemes and Organizational Restructuring: The Example of a Religious Order," *Administrative Science Quarterly*, 29 (1984), pp. 355–372. The specific Order is not identified in this study.

[20] Linda Smircich and Gareth Morgan, "Leadership: The Management of Meaning," *Journal of Applied Behavioral Science*, 18, 3 (1982), pp. 257–273.

[21] Ibid., p. 266.

[22] Ibid.

[23] Michael K. Moch and Jean M. Bartunek, *Creating Alternative Realities at Work: The Quality of Work Life Experiment at FoodCom* (New York: Harper Business, 1990). Used with permission of Harper Business.

[24] Ibid., p. 15.

[25] Ibid., p. 29.

[26] Ibid.

[27] Ibid., p. 32.

[28] *The Economist*, "Curiouser," August 3, 1991, pp. 15–16.

[29] "Pakistan Rallies Behind B.C.C.I.," *New York Times*, August 5, 1991, pp. C1–C2. Copyright © 1991 by The New York Times Company. Reprinted by permission.

[30] Ibid., p. C1.

[31] James McGregor Burns, *Leadership* (New York: Harper & Row, 1978). Copyright © 1978 by James McGregor Burns. Reprinted by permission of Harper Collins Publishers, Inc.

[32] Ibid., p. 258.

[33] Ibid.

[34] Ibid., p. 137.

[35] Ibid., p. 41.

[36] Ibid., p. 38.

[37] Ibid., p. 42.

[38] Ibid., p. 462.

[39] Ibid., p. 426.

[40] Saul D. Alinsky, *Reveille for Radicals* (New York: Vintage Books, 1946 [1969]), p. 47.

[41] William A. Gamson, *The Strategy of Social Protest* (Belmont, Calif.: Wadsworth, 1975 [1990]), p. 147.

[42] L. David Brown and Jane Gibson Covey, "Development Organizations and Organization Development: Toward an Expanded Paradigm for Organization Development," *Research in Organizational Change and Development*, ed. R. W. Woodman and William A. Pasmore (Greenwich, Conn.: JAI Press, 1987), pp. 59–87.

[43]Noel M. Tichy and Mary Anne Devanna, *The Transformational Leader* (New York: John Wiley, 1986); and Bernard M. Bass, *Leadership and Performance Beyond Expectations* (New York: Simon & Schuster, 1985).

[44]Rosabeth Moss Kanter, *Change Masters: Innovation for Productivity in the American Corporation* (New York: Simon & Schuster, 1983).

[45]Warren G. Bennis and Burt Nanus, *Leaders: Strategies for Taking Charge* (New York: Harper & Row, 1985).

[46]William Pfaff, "Redefining World Power," 70, 1 (1991), p. 35. Used with permission of William Pfaff.

[47]Ibid., p. 80.

[48]Richard Pipes, "The Soviet Union Adrift," *Foreign Affairs*, 70, 1 (1991), p. 80.

[49]William Pfaff, "The Well-Intentional Fantasies of Soviet Reform," *International Herald Tribune*, June 8–9, 1991, p. 6. Used with permission of Los Angeles Times Syndicate.

[50]Charles Gati, "East-Central Europe: The Morning After," *Foreign Affairs*, 69, 5 (1990), p. 130. Reprinted by permission of FOREIGN AFFAIRS. Copyright © 1990 by the Council on Foreign Relations, Inc.

[51]Václav Havel, *Disturbing the Peace: A Conversation with Karel Hvízdala* (New York: Alfred A. Knopf, 1990), pp. 17–18.

[52]This account is described in S. Ramnarayan, G. Pangore, and V. Pangore, "From Shindi to Siddhi," Indian Institute of Management, Ahmedabad, 1989 (unpublished). It is summarized in John D. Aram, "Individual and Organizational Interests: Pathways to Integration," *Vikalpa*, 15, 2 (April–June 1990), 13–21.

◆◆◆

8

The Paradoxes and Dilemmas of Individualism: Implications for American Business

◆◆◆◆◆

Discussions in these chapters have ranged widely over contemporary social, economic, political, and technological issues facing American society. My task has been to examine some of the complex interactions among individuals, organizations, and society with an aim of articulating an approach to policy choices that enhances social and organizational development. In these discussions I have assumed that ideas and values are significant determinants of behavior; thus, managerial effectiveness in the long run begins with a study of the role of values in the process of management.

Behavior at one level of analysis is always influenced by factors at a more general level. Thus family dynamics influence individual personality, an organization's culture influences performance in the work group, and social values and norms affect the functioning of political institutions. From this perspective we can gain insight into the tasks of management by studying American social values. Although managers may naturally interpret society from the standpoint of the firm, interpreting the firm from the standpoint of social patterns and values also lends useful knowledge.

In a similar vein, management education focuses predominantly on internal organizational factors that are subject to managers' control. Yet external and uncontrollable forces may pose potentially greater threats to the success of a firm than controllable internal variables. It may be natural for educators to concentrate on that which is controllable rather than on the social and political environment. Managing within an uncertain environment may, however, be as important a skill as the ability to control known factors.

Following these precepts, we have studied American business through the wide lens of the social and political environment of the firm. This focus has led into discussions of social values, political processes, and institutional structures. Because general, value-oriented issues will strongly influence the future of American business, they merit consideration in the preparation of future managers.

The core American value of individualism has provided an entry point for exploring aspects of the business environment. Autonomous self-interest, the most direct expression of individualism, reveals an important and constructive side of human nature. Defended in theory and justified by the political and economic achievements of the United States, traditional individualism has proved an enormously successful principle on which to organize society. I have argued, however, that looking beyond one's own immediate gain to the well-being of the community is a vital, but often a silent, partner in that which economic and political freedom has achieved. Academic studies as well as everyday experiences show that people prosper not only through immediate self-interest; subtle, mostly unwritten, norms of social reciprocity and cooperation are necessary for the success of individual pursuits. The returns to the society as a whole from the existence of personal freedom are great; the benefits of individual commercial, intellectual, and aesthetic achievements are widely available. And the returns to individual freedom from strong communities—emotional support, recognition, social identity—are equally substantial.

Several conclusions derive from placing our attention squarely on the intersection of individuals' interests, that is, on the *community* of interests. First, managers can improve the performance of an organization by understanding how individual behavior depends on social motives and cooperative processes. Behavior in work groups, union-management relationships, and interdepartmental coordination in the firm call for knowledge and skill in managing interdependence. Beyond the firm, the ability to work effectively in nonmarket organizations such as trade associations and policy organizations that span several sectors of the society is increasingly important for effective business leadership.

I have also argued that the perspective of economic self-interest fails to pay adequate attention to the importance of social and political processes to the business system. A vital economic sector is inconsistent, for example, with a society that is strongly segmented by race and by class. A divided society pays dearly in forgone human abilities, it requires unsustainable investments in criminal justice and public assistance programs, and it undermines many citizens' desires for a just society. We need a framework that pays attention simultaneously to individual choice and to the social commons.

If we can become as aware and appreciative of the role of collective action as we are of self-interest, we may be able to overcome unproductive polarities in our thinking. Awareness of social interdependencies encourages a level of self-restraint and cooperation that decreases trade-offs between personal freedom and social control. Recognizing the mutual dependence of material and nonmaterial values reduces polarization between economic individualism and social individualism. In addition, balancing the economic and the human consequences early in the development of new technologies will avoid later conflicts between the need to safeguard people from harm and the need to capture the economic benefits of technological change.

This chapter concludes our inquiry into the role of individualism in the American business environment. Several points serve to summarize perspectives developed through these wide discussions. The following section stresses the contributions of both economic motives and social motives to understanding and addressing private and public policy issues. A society whose managers seek to integrate economic values and social values inherently recognizes the utility of both individual and collective action. In this next section I examine the implications of paradoxes and dilemmas presented by the value of individualism and summarize the qualities of decision making that we need in order to deal with these issues effectively.

In a second section I examine the influence of the term *interests* itself on our thinking as citizens and as participants in organizations. In many respects, this word conveys an outlook or an expectation that people's views are immutable, and the term *interests* may polarize and politicize discussion unnecessarily. How we define our interests derives from how we see ourselves, and experience shows that our identities are relatively amenable to social influence. It takes nothing away from the value of individualism to think in terms of identities as well as in terms of interests.

Finally, I comment on the concept of freedom that has been implicit in this book. Because the value of traditional autonomous individualism is strongly grounded in a quest for personal freedom, any suggestion that we expand the notion of individualism carries with it an obligation to ensure the preservation of freedom. The chapter concludes with a discussion of the kind of freedom that is made possible by a broad definition of individualism.

ECONOMIC MOTIVES AND SOCIAL MOTIVES AS SOURCES OF PROGRESS

Social progress has been defined in these chapters as simultaneous improvement in both individual and collective well-being. Tenets of market capitalism focus on one aspect of social progress: how economic liberty contributes to the general welfare. Without challenging the validity of this view, I have pointed to its limitations. The traditional intellectual framework of business largely neglects the contribution of society as a whole to the opportunities and achievements credited to economic individualism. For example, the ideology of economic individualism depends on social stability but remains silent about the challenges of attaining social unity within a culturally diverse society. The business creed also understates the importance of interdependence—for example, in group decision making within organizations, in interinstitutional collaboration on the adoption of technology, and in multinational collective action that enhances international security and prosperity. In each of these cases collective action benefits the autonomy of the individual and of the firm. In the United States the logic of economic motivation has been emphasized at the expense of the equally important logic of social motivation.

Throughout this book I have identified ways in which social motivation and social participation contribute to progress in organizations and in society: Strong communities permit the expression of autonomy necessary for economic pursuits. Investment in public goods, such as children's emotional development and education, provides a disciplined and able work force for industry in the future. Efforts to avoid racial, ethnic, and gender polarization contribute to the social stability necessary for conducting business. Citizens' involvement in the political process ensures the preservation of economic rights. These forms of social cooperation have to be strengthened in Americans' repertoire of behavioral skills. Avoiding either/or choices between economic motives and social motives would be a significant revision of traditional American values. In a complex and interdependent world, our progress as a society may require us to broaden traditional perspectives without threatening or lessening the ability to capitalize on the enormous potentials of pure economic self-interest.

I have offered a perspective that challenges managers not only to understand issues from the perspective of the autonomous individual but also to expand their view to include the social and institutional structures in which individual action is embedded. Doing so encourages participation in social and institutional processes and heightens a decision maker's concern for the results of these processes. Benefits to be gained from this perspective include the development of more effective work groups, the promotion of adaptive industries, the creation of a multicultural society, the maintenance of responsive democracy, and the promotion of technological advances that will fit society's needs without being condemned for unwanted side effects.

Evidence on the importance of social interdependence is strong enough that advocates of a broad social perspective in policy development should not have to defend the value of their approach. Advocates of traditional autonomous individualism and advocates of the interdependence perspective must join forces if we are to improve the quality of our institutions and create long-term economic prosperity.

❖ Issues for Managers

Many of the values we have identified as relevant to the business environment are interrelated in paradoxical ways. Thus personal autonomy is sustained only by strong communities; however, communities that promote human growth cannot exist without honoring personal autonomy. Society has little value to us apart from its ability to enhance individual freedom and opportunity; yet freedom is ultimately maintained by self-restraint that preserves the society. Democracy allows us to choose to be apathetic; but if we are apathetic, we may forfeit the opportunity to choose. The fact that values are paradoxical and often in conflict means that policymaking for managers in organizations, and in society as a whole, will tax both the depth of our understanding and the flexibility of our behavior. The following sections review aspects of decision making in private and public contexts.

Decision Making in Private Organizations Business organizations depend on the ideas, energies, and skills of individuals. At the same time, the efforts and abilities of separate persons must converge in order for an organization to be effective. Individual members suffer if the organization is not effective as a whole; consequently, patterns of interaction between persons, in addition to the persons themselves, matter. Virtually all organized activity embodies the paradox that collective results depend on individual actions just as individual results depend on collective action. The effectiveness of an organization depends on the sum of its members' abilities, efforts, and interactions, and these individual qualities are supported, to a greater or a lesser degree, by the policies and practices of the organization.

Overcoming the stifling effects of bureaucracy has always been a problem for managers of large organizations. There is a great need to maintain critical thought, originality, and openness in communication at all levels of the organization. Managers must resist the trademarks of conformity—self-censorship, abdication of responsibility, and suppression of conflict—in planning, problem solving, innovation, and day-to-day administration.

Managers employ a variety of techniques to overcome the potential lack of individualism in organizations. They form task forces and other ad hoc work units to undertake special tasks, hoping to promote originality and commitment by giving members new assignments and combining people's skills differently. Managers may separate innovation groups from the main organization both structurally and physically, placing them in special units, often called "skunkworks," in order to free creative effort from the potentially chilling effects of normal supervision and control. Organizations sponsor extensive training programs in human relations skills for supervisors, trying to decentralize responsibility, soften rigid hierarchies, and release employees' constructive energies. Managers also adopt highly individualized reward systems, such as commissions for salespersons and bonuses for senior managers, in order to improve individual performance. They employ a wide variety of changes in structure, personnel, leadership styles, and reward systems to try to keep the flames of personal initiative and innovation alive.

At the same time, managers confront the effects of narrowly defined individualism in their organizations. Personal and departmental parochialism is legendary in large firms. Individuals, work groups, and departments often hoard resources, share information only reluctantly, and seek to pass costs on to others. Petty egoism and debilitating careerism can undermine the effectiveness of relationships and impair work results at all levels of an organization. Managers frequently express frustration with the inability to get employees to act in terms of the broader interests of the organization as a whole. Just as frequently, employees express frustration with the lack of responsibility and variety in their jobs and with the apparent indifference of supervisors to the employees' interest in knowing how their jobs fit into a larger picture. At times, nearly everybody in a large organization may feel that his or her aims are being defeated by others' behavior.

Neither an individual perspective nor a group perspective alone responds adequately to these issues; the individual and the collective consequences of policies must be considered simultaneously. People may become motivated and committed through temporary task teams, innovation skunkworks, or human resource training programs, only to have their enthusiasm dashed when they reenter their regular work groups. Individualized incentive systems, such as commissions and bonuses, reward some people handsomely, but often appear inequitable to those who go unrewarded but have also contributed to the visible success of the few. In other words, we cannot evaluate efforts to strengthen individual motivation and performance apart from their impact on the larger organization.

Managers often seek to create benefits to the organization by humanizing the organization's culture—heightening members' sensitivity to mutual interactions and increasing the level of cooperation. Fostering a humanistic culture typically leads managers to increase communication programs, emphasize the quality of personal interaction, and promote employees' loyalty to the firm. At other times, managers may see the need to increase the organization's efficiency by cutting staff or selling or restructuring divisions. A humanistic culture and an efficient organization are equally important values, but ones that are difficult to realize simultaneously.

It is also true that efforts to humanize the culture of an organization and overcome the debilitating effects of parochialism may lessen the distinctiveness of separate units within the organization. Attempts to enhance employees' loyalty may inadvertently generate a culture of conformity. In short, an effort to strengthen the culture of an organization cannot be fairly assessed without regard to the impact of this effort on behavior of the individuals.

The search for managerial effectiveness at the level of technique alone—building loyalty, restructuring, training, compensating—may often be disappointing. Because the relationship between individual behavior and collective behavior is complex, reliance on faddish, prepackaged solutions invariably oversimplifies reality and can easily mislead managers.

Appreciating the complexity of the situation need not immobilize action-oriented managers, however; grasping the importance of both economic and social motives need not turn managers into indecisive Hamlets. In contrast, recognizing the complexities and ambiguities of organizing should make managers more active in identifying the factors involved in a specific situation and more eager to experiment with alternative solutions. Managers should put greater effort into defining problems and exploring their potentials and limitations from a variety of perspectives. If problems are defined effectively, less effort will be needed to deal with the unwanted consequences of canned solutions. In addition, managers may find it necessary to discover the experiences and ideas of other people in new ways in order to define a problem effectively. Consequently, the process of defining problems itself may become an important step toward realizing an effective balance between seeming opposites.

An Integrative Perspective on Social Issues As leaders of institutions and as citizens, managers have a significant stake in the outcome of public policy deliberations. Few persons or institutions will remain unaffected by choices we make as a society among economic, social, and political values. Here, again, I have argued that managers must broaden the scope of their thinking, defining the quality of social life for all citizens as a business issue, seeing business's stake in the functioning of democracy, and perceiving the social dimensions of technological change. Each of these issues depends on allowing our identities to reach beyond immediate and parochial concerns.

Like the expression of individual values and social values within the firm, relationships between values in political thinking give rise to a number of complicated policy choices. For example, reducing marginal tax rates heightens incentives for economic pursuits that should raise society's long-term standard of living. In the short run, however, reducing tax rates makes less money available for meeting pressing social needs, such as education, public health, housing, and improvements in environmental quality. Conversely, seeking to alleviate personal hardship through short-term income transfer programs requires more public funds and higher taxes that, in turn, reduce long-term economic efficiency. Short-term programs for transfer payments, though justified by immediate needs, may at times increase social dependency and work against long-term community interests. Due to the trade-offs between the long term and the short term, policy preferences depend on one's value preferences and time perspective.

Ultimately, economic values and social values, often translated into claims of economic rights and social rights, are interdependent. A high standard of living and a society worth living in are equally desirable; however, anxiety and isolation result if members of society pay attention only to their personal economic status, and human opportunity is sacrificed if people give inadequate attention to economic pursuits. We should not neglect one value at the expense of the other. I have argued that we must avoid debilitating political and social polarization between citizens without losing the value of competing ideas, ambition for personal advancement, or the desire to influence the world according to one's own vision.

❖ Implications for Decision Making

Recognizing the paradoxes, dilemmas, and value conflicts in organizational and social issues can change the perspective of managers, as leaders of organizations and as citizens, in three ways. First, when one accepts the belief that abstract ideas and conflicting values are directly and indirectly relevant to business, the process of framing or defining problems becomes as important as solving them. However, awareness of the subtle and complex role of values will make the task of definition anything but easy, and solutions will not be self-evident or instantaneous.

Second, openness to the role of values in decision making means that managers must invest themselves in a long-term perspective in order to achieve the delicate balance between opposing values. More autonomy today may call for greater emphasis on interdependence tomorrow, and vice versa. It takes time for restraint to complement and balance freedom. The unity that becomes possible in a diverse population is an intangible quality that evolves slowly. Accepting the need to balance numerous values necessarily lengthens one's time frame and heightens one's appreciation for the interdependence among parts of a system. Third, recognition of the importance of values leads decision makers to test and validate their assumptions. No one can make valid and reliable assumptions about the importance of specific values to interested parties; only the interested persons themselves can tell us about this directly. The need to clarify and specify the values of those who are or will be affected by a policy naturally broadens participation in the process of policy development.

Framing the problem, lengthening the time horizon, and generating or broadening participation are three recommendations for improving decision making. Together, these qualities embody what is needed to give policy the capacity to lead to the well-being of individual, organization, and society.

INTERESTS AS PERSONAL AND SOCIAL IDENTITIES

Only people have interests. And many interests are immediate and tangible. The dominant language of economics and politics builds on these facts; generally, in the United States, the phrase *personal interests* connotes that which is immediate and tangible. But this language can keep us from recognizing that individuals also have a stake in the vitality of their communities. In earlier chapters I have discussed ways in which individual interests often include the well-being of the community or group. Unfortunately, our language tends to sharpen awareness of the distinction, rather than the interdependence, between individual and community and to reinforce the narrow meaning of the notion of personal interests.

The word *identity* gives a better idea of the close relationship between people and the communities in which they live and work. Realizing that we have several identities, some narrow and some broad, helps to reduce the misconception that "individual" pertains directly to personal matters while "society" involves other people and is distant and removed from the self. On the contrary, the important role of social ideals in people's lives suggests that the origins of many deeply felt values are, in fact, social. The language of "interests" does not encourage us to see the importance of social factors in people's lives nearly so well as does the concept of "identities."

The language of interests distorts understanding of the interdependency of economic factors and social factors. By leading us to think of the immediate and tangible, the concept of interests draws attention to what people possess rather than the forms and processes of cooperation and reciprocity by which possessions are made possible. The valid and important concern over government regulation of economic activities turns our attention to the importance of private property, and an orientation toward property draws attention away from the equally important contributions of social institutions to individual opportunities for learning, growth, and health. The well-established language of interests in the discipline of economics may also take for granted or underestimate individuals' contributions to one another's well-being.

Language that interprets behavior in terms of personal identities may allow us the greater flexibility to recognize that people's social roles are as important in their lives as their economic roles. Heightening awareness of people's identities rather than their interests emphasizes the importance of communities to individuals as well as the importance of what individuals contribute to communities. *Identity*, a social term, reverses the typical assumptions about autonomy and possession implied by the term *interest*, while in no way diminishing the notion of individuality. Thinking in terms of identities rather than interests can break down the artificial distinctions between individual and community and between economic motives and social motives.

The concept of identities accommodates the observation that a person's loyalties exist simultaneously at different levels. At one level a successful player in the prisoner's dilemma exercise is aware of his or her desire to obtain the largest number of points possible, an immediate and direct identity. At another level each is aware that his or her success depends on the success of the other party; the successful player also identifies with the relationship. One's identity as a separate person accumulating points and one's identity as a party to an interdependent relationship can coexist comfortably.

Similarly, a firm may have an identity as an economic competitor and an identity as a participant in a trade association or a business-government-labor forum for encouraging the adoption of innovation. People often identify themselves with specific groups and maintain an identity with the nation as a whole. The notion of having several identities does not deny the validity of the self-interest perspective; it simply suggests that broad self-interest is an equally valid view of reality. Managers need to be able to move quickly and comfortably between narrow and more encompassing views of interests. Many of the dilemmas and paradoxes of organizations require us to work through the tensions between differing identities and loyalties.

I have not been entirely neutral in these chapters on the matter of narrow and broad identities. Americans' dominant impulse is to look to autonomy and independence both to improve organizations and to solve social problems. Yet for many organizations, the process of development requires managers to emphasize cooperation in addition to individuality and to consider the interdependence of people's actions as well as their personal ambitions and desires. Because organizations are typically structured in terms of specialized jobs and hierarchical controls that tend to narrow employees' perspectives, this will even more strongly require leaders of organizations to draw upon members' abilities for broad identification.

BROAD INTERESTS AND IDENTIFICATIONS AS A BASIS OF PERSONAL FREEDOM

Nations have occasionally tried to severely restrict the economic freedom upon which social progress depends. Experiments in authoritarian control have shown, however, that suppressing personal freedom in order to restrict economic motivation saps the vitality and energy of the members of any society. Coercion affirms neither social values nor individual values. Mandating restrictions on personal freedom has failed as a principle of social organization.

One important aspect of individual freedom is the protection of each person from arbitrary invasion by the government. Freedom from infringement by the state, guaranteed in the Bill of Rights, is an essential and vital aspect of a free society. The value of individualism, however, may not be only a matter of freedom from external interference. Constitutional liberty implies no social obligation or responsibility to others; personal rights can be interpreted as freedom to do solely as one pleases. Constitutional freedoms do not convey the reciprocity necessary to maintain the community on which individuals depend. The precious qualities of reciprocity and cooperation that support constitutional freedom lie in the attitudes and values of the people. In this book I have sought to emphasize these values as being essential to freedom without diminishing the constitutional framework of freedom.

We have seen that the U.S. Constitution can be interpreted from the opposing vantage points of economic rights and social rights. Constitutionalizing the rights claims of one set of advocates necessarily occurs at a cost to the claims of the other set of advocates. Thus consistent recourse to the Constitution, recourse to freedom from restraint, does not encourage the positive-sum relationships that society as a whole needs to ensure individual choice.

I have advocated a complementary notion of freedom in this book. Freedom originates in the consciousness of social interdependence and the conversion of that consciousness into personal action. Alexis de Tocqueville calls this attitude "enlightened self-interest"; George Herbert Mead calls it "rational self-consciousness." Rational self-consciousness incorporates a perception of the self as a participant in a community, reducing the chasm in our thinking between economic motives and social motives. From this perspective, we gain freedom through an attitude or approach, rather than through the superiority of a constitutional claim.

The concept of an encompassing definition of self as a source of freedom is not new. John Dewey, for example, advocated this meaning of freedom:

> To foresee future objective alternatives and to be able by deliberation to choose one of them and thereby weight its chances in the struggle for future existence, measures our freedom. . . . We do not use the present to control the future. We use the foresight of the future to refine and expand present activity. In this use of desire, deliberation and choice, freedom is actualized.[1]

Dewey's approach supplements the constitutional basis of liberty; he does not slight the importance and significance of this country's legal framework of individual rights. Individualism based only on freedom from constraints leaves the business creed incomplete. A market economy depends on freedom generated within a context of cooperation. The kind of individualism that recognizes interdependence and reciprocity creates the social foundation needed to support constitutional individualism.

Dewey's approach to freedom allows all players to be successful in a prisoner's dilemma relationship. Freedom as social reciprocity supports the development of institutions and nations so as to achieve unity within diversity. Awareness of the interdependence of economic values and social values breaks the frequent stalemate between political ideologies. The notion of positive responsibility for the future encourages citizens to participate in the political process. The ability to modify present actions in order to reach future objectives has the potential to integrate technology and society. In short, freedom that refines and expands present activity strengthens our ability to fulfill both individual and community needs.

CONCLUSION

This book departs from many other approaches to understanding the business environment. First, I have disputed the assumption that business values and the formation of corporate policy can be discussed independently of the issues facing the rest of American society. I have assumed that the conflicts and opportunities confronting business in the United States are an integral part of American society as a whole. Because the future of business is intimately tied to the destiny of American society, a true understanding of the tasks of management requires that we study the potentials, tensions, and requirements of this nation's other institutions.

This means that managers can usefully learn from a larger set of ideas and experiences than those generally represented in the body of formal management knowledge. Understanding Tocqueville's concerns about isolation and conformity in an individualistic society helps us interpret the requirements for effective relationships in organizations. Seeing the challenge of integrating technology with the society at large contributes to the management of technology inside the firm. Reflecting on the dysfunctions of cultural and ideological polarization in society at large may strengthen managers' will to lengthen their time horizons. Because managers ultimately deal with human behavior, many of the challenges of business administration are universal problems, about which there is much useful discussion outside the specific and immediate concerns of managers.

Advocating the paradigm of individual and community relationships is a second way in which I have departed from conventional approaches to understanding the business environment. I have asserted not only that managers learn from studying wider social values, but that certain generic issues span public and private decision making. Thus tensions between freedom and control, between individual and community, and between social motives and economic motives apply to all social organizations. Managers will be better able to deal with the corporate manifestations of these issues as they come to understand the problems in general societal terms.

Third, this book may be more prescriptive than many other works dealing with business values and the relationship of business and society. My point of view is not neutral; it says that finding effective processes and structures for combining apparent opposites—autonomy and interdependence, freedom and restraint, individual and community—is a pressing task. To the extent that the value of individualism is interpreted narrowly as an unfettered, exclusive, impatient expression of the self, the core American value of individualism will fail to serve people, organizations, and society. Individualism broadly realized expands both personal freedom and social well-being.

My point of view asks much of students and practitioners of management. It asks managers to look beyond codified knowledge and management techniques to identify experiences and insights from other sources that they can apply to management. It appeals to managers to look beyond their allegiance to organization and profession in order to explore the underlying structure of social and political issues. This point of view also asks readers to evaluate whether the familiar social and political polarities in our thinking are not actually unproductive and to consider new criteria for managerial decision making. I ask students of management to put aside the natural instinct to go immediately to a solution and instead to test their experiences against a fresh understanding of each problem. Although I am asking a great deal, I believe that the returns to managers, as individuals, as leaders of organizations, and as citizens, will be comparably great.

[1]John Dewey, *Human Nature and Conduct* (New York: Modern Library, 1922), pp. 311, 313.

Index